Clipper Studies in the Theatre
ISSN 0748-237X
Number Two

POPULAR AMUSEMENTS
IN HORSE & BUGGY AMERICA

*An Anthology
of
Contemporaneous Essays*

edited by

William L. Slout

R. REGINALD
The Borgo Press
San Bernardino, California — MCMXCV

THE BORGO PRESS
Twentieth Anniversary, 1975-1995
Post Office Box 2845
San Bernardino, CA 92406
United States of America

* * * * * * * *

Copyright © 1995 by William L. Slout

All rights reserved.
No part of this book may be reproduced in any
form without the expressed written consent of the publisher. Printed in the United States of America by Van
Volumes, Ltd. Cover design by Highpoint Type & Graphics.

Library of Congress Cataloging-in-Publication Data

Popular amusements in horse and buggy America : an anthology of contemporaneous essays / edited by William L. Slout.
  p. cm. — (Clipper studies in the theatre, ISSN 0748-237X ; no. 2)
Includes index.
ISBN 0-89370-361-3 (cloth). — ISBN 0-89370-461-X (pbk.)
  1. Amusements—United States—History—19th century—Addresses, essays, lectures. 2. Leisure—Social aspects—United States—Addresses, essays, lectures. I. Slout, William L. (William Lawrence) II. Series.
GV53.P67 1995   84-12310
790'.0973—dc19   CIP

FIRST EDITION

CONTENTS

Preface 5

PART I. THOUGHTS ABOUT AMUSEMENTS

1. First Impressions of America, *anonymous* 9
2. Amusements for the Poor, *anonymous* 16
3. Americans at Play, *Edward Eggleston* 21
4. Christianity and Popular Amusements, *Washington Gladden* 24

PART II: SUMMER RESORTS AND WATERING PLACES

5. Domestic Tourism, *anonymous* 34
6. Watering-Place Worries, *anonymous* 39
7. Life at Long Branch, *Olive Logan* 49
8. The New Narragansett Pier, *Brander Matthews* 61

PART III: THE AGRICULTURAL FAIR

9. Cattle-Fair Day in New England, *anonymous* 68
10. The Alabama State Fair, *anonymous* 76
11. The County Fair, *Nelson Lloyd* 78
12. The Spectator (at the Fair), *anonymous* 89

PART IV: WORLD'S EXPOSITIONS

13. The Great Exhibition and Its Visitors, *anonymous* 94
14. A Sennight of the Centennial, *W. D. Howells* 99
15. In and Out of the New Orleans Exposition, *Eugene V. Smalley* 106
16. At the Fair, *M. G. Van Rensselaer* 112

PART V: AMUSEMENT PARKS

17. Niblo's Seen by a Child, *anonymous* 118
18. Sunday in Jones's Wood, *anonymous* 123
19. The Trolley-Park, *Day Allen Willey* 126
20. New York's New Summer Playground, *Theodore Waters* 129
21. The Amusement Park, *anonymous* 133

PART VI: THE TRAVELING CIRCUS

22. Circus, *anonymous* 146
23. Living in the Country, *anonymous* 155
24. Circus Day, *Eugene Wood* 157
25. On the Road with the "Big Show," *Charles Theodore Murray* 171

PART VII: VAUDEVILLE

26. Sketches of the People Who Oppose Our Sunday Laws, *anonymous* 178
27. The Roof-Gardens of New York, *Vance Thompson* 185
28. The Vaudeville Theatre, *Edwin Milton Royle* 191
29. The Life of a Vaudeville Artiste, *Norman Hapgood* 197

Index 201
About William L. Slout 208

WILLIAM L. SLOUT

PREFACE

If you have ever carried water for the elephants, or seen a horse-pulling contest from the grandstand at a county fair, or sweltered on a folding chair in a Chautauqua tent while listening to Swiss bell ringers, or laughed at a Dutch comedian, or sheepishly paid your dime to watch the gyrations of a "Little Egypt," you will find this anthology pleasant with nostalgia. If you are too young to have undergone such "horse and buggy" delights, you will, I hope, at least experience vicariously the popular amusements of days gone by. The material here deals primarily with the nineteenth century, throughout which our amusement forms were so firmly shaped; but what passed as fun for our grandparents and great grandparents is fun still. It is only that the buggy seat has been replaced by the bucket seat. The old amusements have not disappeared; they are merely altered by advancing technology, increasing operating costs, and fluctuating social attitudes and fashions. Disneyland has all the elements of the earlier amusement parks. The circus continues to thrill "children of all ages." Municipalities lay out huge sums for the temporary facilities of a great World's Fair. Yes, the use of leisure changes sparingly. The need for pleasure has not lost vigor.

Early settlement of America by people of diverse religious and national backgrounds in locations of marked geographical differences, and free immigration by people of varied ethnic origins, created a patchwork of cultural interests which was reflected in the expression of leisure. Americans amused themselves through innumerable kinds of play and sport. Social gatherings and celebrations were manifold in character and purpose. Early American amusement was as variegated as early American social patterns. Consequently, it would take several volumes to adequately cover this full experience. Since space is a tyrant in its demands, this book has been purposely limited.

Articles selected for inclusion in this volume focus on activities of a public nature which require people to leave home and mingle with others as spectators or participants in pleasure. The six specific areas chosen—summer resorts and watering places, agricultural fairs, World's Fairs, the circus, vaudeville, and amusement parks—commonly engendered a mass public interest and appealed to all divisions of society. The articles were selected from popular periodicals of the nineteenth and early twentieth centuries with the intention of forming, not an historical narrative, but a cultural expression, an expression developed by those who were there, who experienced, and who responded in the color and attitude of the moment.

The editor has done a small amount of tampering with the original texts of which the reader should be aware. Old methods of spelling and punctuation remain in most cases to preserve the patina; however, occasionally, modern adjustments have been made for the sake of clarity. In addition, again bowing to the demands of space, some articles have been condensed, and the author's footnotes dropped. Where this occurs it is indicated by the conventional ellipsis.

—William L. Slout
San Bernardino, California
May, 1994

DEDICATION

*This adventure is dedicated to Ray Browne,
Russel Nye, and all who are playing
the calliopes for Popular Culture*

POPULAR AMUSEMENTS

IN

HORSE AND BUGGY

AMERICA

THE CIRCUS COMES TO TOWN!

I.
THOUGHTS ABOUT AMUSEMENT

Americans have always considered leisure an important element of life, along with work, education, and spiritual satisfaction. However, their views have differed in how leisure should be spent. The forging of a new civilization out of virgin land led early settlers to devote long hours to strenuous toil. To them, leisure connoted rest which allowed further toiling. Frivolity was firmly rejected. But as they became more firmly entrenched, as nationalization became more secure, as communities enlarged and the individual developed more selective freedom, as industrialization created a distinct class of wage earners, people viewed leisure increasingly as a means for amusement. They allocated more time for sport and play, following the urge for pleasure inherent in us all, and emulated their more affluent fellows in choice of fun.

An increasing receptiveness to organized pleasure encouraged a commensurate growth of commercial amusements. Theatres, concert halls, and opera houses became fixtures in even the smallest of cities, appearing as rapidly as new territory was settled. Resorts sprang up at the places of natural beauty and facility. Parks, gardens, sporting fields and enclosures, and temples of all manner of entertainment materialized as fast as public necessity for them allowed; until, two hundred years after America's beginning, public amusement has grown into a multi-million dollar colossus.

1. FIRST IMPRESSIONS OF AMERICA

LEISURE HOUR, SEPTEMBER 30, 1871

The public parks in New York, Brooklyn, Philadelphia, and other great cities, while they are admirable specimens of landscape gardening, are still more interesting as showing advance in aesthetic culture and in provision for the health and enjoyment of the people. The civic rulers and authorities are displaying public spirit and good sense in this direction. When I was in Philadelphia, the Board of Direction of the Public Park heard that Mr. Robinson, author of the work on French Gardens, and a high authority in landscape gardening, was in the States, and they made a very handsome offer of securing his professional aid for improving their fine demesne. In Prospect Park, Brooklyn, and the Central Park, New York, no expense is spared to improve the ground. In the latter park, Mr. Waterhouse Hawkins is at present employed in setting up some of his wonderful restorations of ancient animals, on the plan so skilfully exhibited in our Crystal Palace at Sydenham. The example of these public places will exert good influence throughout the Union, and will help to diffuse a love for landscape gardening, and the improvement of popular taste in horticulture, in its ornamental as well as useful departments....

...Returning to the parks, one might expect to see there, if anywhere, American equestrianism. But riding does not seem a national enjoyment. On any fine morning in June there may be seen a finer display of well-mounted equestrians, especially of the fair sex, than can be witnessed in all the American parks through the whole of the season. The New England people do not seem to take kindly to the saddle. The Northern papers admitted during the late war that this fact gave to the Southern cavalry so decided a superiority, and will always leave the army deficient in this branch of the service. The establishment of racing parks may give an impulse to equestrianism in some aspects, but these are not of a kind promotive of the best features of the national character. There are now four racing grounds within reach of New York, Jerome, Prospect, Monmouth Parks, and the track at Saratoga. Great crowds resort to these meetings, but few native Americans have any special love for the races apart from their being the occasion of an outing and holiday. So much the better for the national taste and for public morality. It would be baleful influence for them, if this branch of sport extended as it has in the old country.

If they do not excel in riding, the Americans are "thunder at driving." The popular taste in this art has run into wild extravagance. Four-in-hands, and even six-in-hands, with showy harness and gay liveries, are the pride of the vulgar rich. In the parks and on the roads it is amusing to behold the variety of equipages, and pleasant also to see the number of plebeian, square-framed "buggies" mingling in the course. But the greatest specialty of the American driving is the fast-trotting horse, with its spider-like iron bicycle. Portraits of famous trotters and pictures of trotting matches are common in the smoking rooms and drinking saloons, such as the celebrated match between "Hero" and "Flora Temple," when three two-mile heats were run, each heat within five minutes! Wonderful trotting horses may be seen in the morning on the roads, or in the Central Park of New York. A few well-appointed English drags, and other imported carriages of various build, may be seen; but the great mass of the vehicles are old-fashioned native buggy, and carts with light wooden and leather framework for shade and shelter. Even in the rural districts the American farmer rarely walks or rides, but "hitches up" his buggy for any little distance.

The American field sports do not much differ from our own, so far as "the rod and the gun" are concerned. Of the Game Laws in the State of New York I have already spoken, and these afford a glimpse into the public opinion on the subject in the older parts of the Union. In the Far West there is ample scope for sport of a more adventurous kind, and many Englishman every year go to share in these adventures. The fashionable battles and matches of English amateur sportsmen are, as might be expected, held in great contempt by the Americans. A leading article in one of their leading papers on the pigeon matches of some of the English aristocratic gun clubs thus concluded: "The primitive and the true idea of the chase is a direct conflict between man and certain savage elements in the world which must be overcome and disappear before civilisation. Bear, deer, or buffalo shooting seem not unmanly work, nor unsuited to a certain degree of culture and enlightenment. There is at least fatigue to be endured and danger to be incurred. The idea, however, of unlimited members of parliament, hatted and gloved *à la mode*, driving out to the enclosure at Hurlingham, to butcher some dozen caged frightened pigeons, while their lady friends look on exultant, is to us indescribably absurd. But when we consider that out of this occupation this remarkable people hopefully assert their expectation of deriving strength for their legislative duties and religious enlightenment, our wonder can find no words. We can only look on in silence and perplexity."

On one of my first mornings in New York I saw, among the bustling crowd in the Metropolitan Hotel Hall, a group of athletic young fellows in light flannel dress. At first I thought they were cricketers, but the bats and the balls were not those of our game. I was told it was a "Base Ball Club." These clubs I afterwards found wherever I went, Base Ball being recognized as "the national game" of America. Throughout August and September matches were going on, and the newspapers had a column, and often several columns, headed the "The National Game," and filled with reports of the play. City against city, county against county, amateurs against professionals, all sorts of matches were going on, like cricket matches among ourselves in the season. At Chicago, at the time of my visit, there was great excitement on account of the victory of the "White-Stockings" of that city over the "Red-Stockings" of Cincinnati. The "conquering heroes" were met at the railway depot by an enormous procession, with music and banners, and paraded in carriages through the town. The "White-Stockings" also beat another crack club, the "Eagles" of Louisville, and for the time were the champion players, though they had yet to meet the "Atlantics," "Athletics," and one or two other famous clubs.

After hearing and reading so much about the National game, I was surprised to find it only a development of our own homely game of "rounders." There are nine on each side—centre field, left field, right field, first base, second base, third base, catcher, short stop, and pitcher. There is room for considerable skill in pitching, batting, catching, and fielding, but on the whole the game appeared to me a hobbledehoy affair compared with cricket. It is immensely popular, however, among all classes and ages, from lads at school up to "old boys" of business. I saw the report of one match between two corporations in the West, including several "alderman!" Like too many sports, the game has got into the hands of betting and gambling fraternities, and the most celebrated clubs are now the property of stockholders" whose speculations and arrangements are made for gain more than honour.

The grand jury of Baltimore actually reported Base Ball as "one of the gradations of crime," alluding to the temptations to gambling which it has introduced. This is the abuse of the thing, however; the love of the game is creditable to "Young America," and affords a healthy athletic out-of-door sport. Except at Baltimore and Philadelphia I heard nothing about cricket. There is said to be a good club at Germantown, but I suspect the game is comparatively unknown in the States.

Of indoor amusements and pastimes I saw little and therefore can say little. Public amusements whether dramatic or musical, seem much the same as our own, with balls, concerts, and even masquerades, as in Europe. The masquerades are only recognized by professed lovers of such scenes, and are mainly got up by theatrical managers and hotel proprietors. In the list of costumes in the great masquerade of last season at Saratoga, I noticed, among various notorious characters from New York and other cities, the names of at least seven of a well-known hotel-keeping family, at one of whose houses the affair came off.

The amusements of "fashionable life" are very much alike in all countries, and are not worth mentioning among special features of national character or usage. The world of fashion—the world which dresses, dances, sings, plays, bets, and lives only to assume itself—is not greatly different in New York and Paris, Newport and Scarborough, Philadelphia and Milan, Saratoga and Baden. These people count little in the estimate of what makes a nation, and in America the proportion of the idle pleasure-seekers is less than in any other country I have visited.

At the same time, it is to be feared that this annual resort to great watering-places will come to affect perceptibly the national life and manners. It is a new social feature, and on a scale of vastness unknown in the old country. Before the end of the season last summer, I saw an estimate in the papers that there had been above 100,000 visitors at Saratoga, 150,000 at Cape May, 150,000 at Atlantic City, 100,000 at Newport, and 200,000 at Long Branch. Now these visitors come from all parts of the country. They meet people from New York, who are far more likely to influence them for evil than to be influenced by them for good. It is not as in our great English watering-places, where the home life and home customs of the visitors whether grave or gay, for health or recreation, can be maintained at choice. The monster-hotel system of America compels all classes to intermingle. The whole life of the place is public, and not of the best sort of publicity. Of course there are quiet boarding-houses and homes, even in the most crowded summer places, but the general tone of life is a tone of relaxation—not relaxation in the good sense of relaxation from hard work, but relaxation of good habits and homely ways, and relaxation of good morals too often. The rich American paterfamilias takes wife and daughters into scenes from which an English gentleman with his family would shrink. "Life at Saratoga" will not improve the national character any more than "Life in Paris," which many Americans regard as the acme of felicity. In fact, the word has become proverbial that such Americans expect to go when they die to Champs Élysées! There is too much of the Parisian influence apparent at Saratoga, not improved by filtering through New York. At the marine watering-places there is less a stagey-looking life, but there is also there too much publicity for those who wish to see the best features of the national character retained. Last season at Newport it was the fashion rather to affect "cottage" life instead of the hotels, though not with less gaiety of public amusements. I remained at Boston, finding more to see there than I could overtake, when some friends ran down to have a look at Newport. They came back open-mouthed about the gaiety of the place, and especially at the beauty of the women. It was sad to read a few weeks after of the death of the ackowledged belle of the Ocean House. She died of a low but rapid fever—a scourge which will make itself terribly felt in these watering-places, with their huge caravanerais and crowded population. The difficulty is already felt with us in England, some of our watering-places being nests of fever during summer, and yet drainage sparingly used for fear of polluting the sea for bathing. The practical conclusion of all which is, that it would be better both for health and morals to diminish the rush to huge watering-places, and occupy more numerous summer stations, whether inland or on the coast. As with hospitals for the sick, so with resorts for health, the detached system has many advantages over the crowding into great hospitals or hotels.

The Americans have various rural sports and amusements handed down from generation to generation among the rustic folk. The reader will be pleased with the following extract from a genial book on "American Society" by Mr. G. M. Towle, of Boston, formerly U.S. Consul at Nantes, and at Bradford.

"In the autumn, at harvest time, there are numerous merry gatherings, in which useful tasks are joined with hearty amusement. When the Indian corn is gathered, it is the custom to have, at many of the farmhouses, what is called a 'husking.' The object is to get the corn husked: the neighbours are invited to assemble on a certain afternoon at the barn of the farmer whose corn is to be husked. Here are great piles of the just gathered ears. The guests sit about the barn floor and the haymows, and proceed to strip the husks and silk from the corn, and deposit it clean and bare at one side. Meanwhile there is plenty of talking and laughing; the farmer's home-brewed cider and ale are passed frequently about, and doughnuts, pies, and cakes of all sorts are plentifully provided. After the husking is suspended, the barn floor is cleared of the rubbish, one of the boys mounts the haymow and strikes up a lively tune on his fiddle, and the barn fairly shakes with the rollicking dance or the lusty game which ensues. Whatever young man finds in his pile a *red* ear of corn, is entitled to kiss any girl he chooses; if a lass finds one, she must submit to be kissed, and must choose the lad whom she prefers to perform the operation. Another autumn custom is called an 'apple-bee.' Several barrels of apples are collected in the farmhouse, the neighbours are invited in, and all set to work paring them. After the outer skin is taken off, the apples are divided into small sections, the core taken out, and the pieces are hung on a string. These are afterwards put in the sun to dry, and are then laid away with which to make 'apple sauce' or dried apple pies in the ensuing winter.

"The people reciprocate with each other in doing these tasks. When a farm dame needs an additional quilt for one of her beds, she calls in her neighbours and they set to work making one, patching it together with odd pieces of cloth; this is a party at first confined to the women; tea-drinking and gossip comprise the pleasures which relieve the task; in the evening the 'men folks' drop in.

"A famous time in some of the Northern States is that when the maple-trees are tapped, and the delicious maple sugar made. The sugar maple-trees are very profitable, and, often add materially to the income of the farmer. Early in the spring these are tapped; the sweet juice is collected in tubs; great fires are built; huge iron kettles are hung over syrup. It is of a rich brown colour, and nothing can be nicer, especially if eaten on hot cakes or waffles. In the evening, when the syrup has grown quite thick and and ready for 'sugaring off,' the lasses and lads gather at the 'camps,' in the wood, to partake of it. A favourite method is to dip snowballs into the yet warm syrup, and, thus coated, to eat them; these are very delicious. The froth, or 'wat,' of the syrup is also very palatable. The festivities end with dances, games, and ditties.

"In the fall, almost every town has its 'Agricultural Fair,' which is, to the rustic population, one of the great events of the year. It is held not seldom in the spacious airy town-hall; the farmers for miles round have been preparing for it the summer long; the farmer who takes a prize for the heaviest pig or the biggest pears is like the politician who has won an election, like an author whose book was a 'success,' like a lawyer who has gained a famous case, like a parson made a bishop. These Agricultural Fairs are truly interesting and curious shows. Within the hall long tables have been set against the walls and in the middle of the floor; the walls have been decorated by the young women with all varieties of evergreen festoons, fantastic flower designs and pictures, and deftly-fashioned embroidery or worsted work. The tables display every kind of fruit and vegetable, all of the largest, ripest, and most luscious, with little cards on the plates, informing the uninitiated of the particular species, and the name of its contributors. Pyramids of pears, peaches, and apples are followed by monster pumpkins and cabbages, mammoth beets, melons, and turnips, great tempting clusters of grapes, wonderful potatoes, beans, and tomatoes. Farther on you will see specimens of the women's handiwork—wax flowers, pictures made of hair, embroidery, crochet work, odd examples of aptitude with the needle, pen, or penknife. On other tables appear specimens of domestic pickles, hams, and pies. Outside the building are rows of pens where are kept the oxen, cows, sheep, pigs, chickens, goats—the dumb competitors for the prizes; placards announcing the various kinds are tacked to the pens, and groups of farmers are gathered about them, discussing the merits of this hog or that big-headed bull.

"On the open spaces round about are all sorts of small shows and pedlars' wagons drawn up in the eligible places. Tents, covered with large gaudy pictures of giantesses and bearded women, wonderful dwarfs and living skeletons, are thickly set on the sward; and the showmen at the tent openings are talking themselves hoarse, jingling their money boxes for awhile, and describing with oratorical flourishes the wonders to be seen for a penny within. The pedlars are driving brisk bargains with their astonishingly cheap pen-knives, their patent knife-sharpeners and axe-grinders, their little bottle balms for every human ill, their marvelous writing apparatus making half-a-dozen simultaneous copies, their soaps, confectionery, and imposing silver ware. A perambulating photographer had drawn up his portable saloon in a convenient corner, and offers to produce perfect likenesses of loving couples and rough old farmers for trifling prices. The country people are there in multitudes, dressed primly, and deeply interested in all that is going on; the city people, too, have driven out, and mingle in the concourse which is grouped about the tables and on the green. The fair usually lasts two days; the second day is the best attended. In one of the upper rooms a bountiful collation is spread; on the platform at the farther end is a table, at which sit the dignitaries—the president of the agricultural society, the orator of the day, and any notable visitors who are present. Just below them is a table for the reporters, who have come out from the city to take notes for the 'evening edition.' A fee of fifty cents or a dollar is demanded of those who wish to partake of the collation; it consists of cold meats, vegetables, pies, and fruits. The repast over, the orator of the day is introduced and, rising behind the platform table, he proceeds to deliver an address on some agricultural subject. Other speeches are made; the prizes are announced by a committee appointed for the purpose; and then the productions on exhibition are taken away by their various owners. Sometimes, in the evening, a dance at the town hotel concludes the affair. Every one competes for the prizes who so chooses, these being offered by the agricultural societies.

"The country people practise many robust out-door games. There are shooting matches and quoit matches, baseball contests and foot races. Nearly every boy has his gun, and early becomes adept in shooting at targets and hunting in the free forests. Every boy, too, learns to swim and to row; for everywhere in rural America there are, near by the farms, lakes, and rivers, where aquatic sports may be enjoyed without fear of molestation. Of course the country boy sits on his horse, without a saddle, as easily as if he had grown there; and when he is very young, is sent to mill with a load of corn or wheat, sometimes several miles distant from home, returning with the flour after it has been ground.

"In the winter time, the farmers having little to do—their fields being thickly covered with layer after layer of crusted snow—they stay much at home, attending to the cattle in the sheds, reading, and leisurely lounging about. Then it is that the sleighs—long processions of them—may be seen gliding over the roads, full of hilarious parties. The young men of the neighbourhood get together, and arrange to give their sweethearts *en masse* the treat of a sleigh ride. The village tavern is doubtless supplied with a bouncing sleigh, a barge-like vehicle on runners, which the landlord is readily induced, for a modest sum, to lend; and there is besides a general muster of all the farm sleighs for miles around. The horses are decked with bells, and after the accidental slippings and fallings-down, screaming and joking, the party starts off echoing some familiar song. The broad landscape is everywhere white and shining; the fences and walls are half concealed beneath the high drifts, the rails and stones peeping out here and there at intervals; the farmhouses seem imbedded in the flaky mounds; the narrow beaten paths from the doors lead through snow walls often five or six feet high; the road is crusted with a coat of snow frozen into ice; the tree boughs bend low beneath their accumulated burden; everywhere the snow-particles glisten and glitter as far as the eye can reach, hill-top and valley, house and tree, are shrouded in the monotonous and long enduring robe of white. The procession of sleighs glides rapidly over the frozen roads; the joyous jingling of hundreds of little bells mingles with the shouts and laughter of the happy-hearted party, who are wrapt and bundled almost out of sight by capacious blankets, quilts, shawls.

"To relieve the desolate monotony of winter, 'sociables' are often formed. Once a fortnight gatherings take place at the houses in turn, which are all the jollier because the people have so few chances to see each other. In many of the villages concerts are given by choral societies, and lectures, either by the parson or schoolmaster, or some neighbouring notability. The boys and girls have as much skating as they please. The lakes and rivers remain frozen for several months, and moonlight skating parties are among the pleasantest of the winter season."

The taste for yachting has grown recently, and the number of yachtsmen on the eastern coast increases every year. Of some of the crack American yachts we have heard much of late years, and the international races across the ocean have become renowned. But, apart from these displays and competitions, the passions for yachting is on the increase. And no wonder, with so splendid a coast, from New York up to New Brunswick, a stretch of several hundred miles, or the length of the British Islands. For those who like quiet water there is Long Island Sound, a lovely sheet of sheltered water, with many pleasant ports of call. Many families spend most of the summer months aboard these Long Island Sound yachts, and the cheery healthful homes they are for men of business. Then there is the run to Portland and Boston, round Cape Cod, the great part open ocean, and with safe harbours and anchorages at various intervals. Except for the Mediterranean, no cruising ground can compare with this, however it may be winter, or in the poetic description by Mrs. Hemans of "the stern and rock-bound coast." There are no better sailors in the world than the pilots and fisherman and yachtsmen of the New England seas. In the love of the ocean, both for work and pleasure, the Americans are "true chips off the old block."

2. AMUSEMENTS FOR THE POOR

OLD AND NEW, AUGUST, 1874

This is a subject too little considered by America; and it was one of the first taken up by the Department of Social Economy, formed last winter in the American Social Science Association. A sub-committee of ladies, being invited to make suggestions in regard to amusements in Boston, reported to the department; and their report was then submitted to a member of the committee in New York, and to another in Indiana, for such comments as the difference in locality and circumstances might call forth from experienced persons in those States. In substance this report, and the comments thereon, were as follows:

I. THE REPORT

The committee who were delivered to report on the subject of "Amusements for the Poor" have so little that is conclusive, or even definite, to state, that they would have excused themselves from making any report, were it not that the statement of the case may elicit suggestions from others. Their first endeavor was to get a definite notion as to who are classified in this case as "the poor." We take them to be those whose daily bread is provided by their daily work, and who have little or nothing laid by. Just above these in the social scale are those who live sparingly that they may lay up even a trifle. In both these classes, illness, causing expense, and at the same time cutting off the supply, lowers families from decent comfort to real poverty. Skilled mechanics and skilled laborers of any kind are hardly to be called *poor*, since their skill stands to them in place of capital, lifting them above the precarious region where the supply of ignorant labor presses hard upon the demand. The French word *prolétaire* perhaps most justly expresses what is meant by "the poor" in this connection.

Now, in Boston and its neighborhood, unskilled labor is almost exclusively performed by the Irish, with a slight intermixture of Germans and perhaps Swedes. We have therefore to provide for people whose temperament and mental organization differ essentially from our own.

The American seamstress or shop-tender goes to lecture and to concerts. The American mechanic is a deacon of his church, and attends the Lowell Lectures: his children are elaborately cared for in Sunday-school festivals and floral processions. What are the amusements of their Irish neighbors? A wake, an occasional procession, and, on Sunday afternoons, the aimless standing outside of their houses, like bees clustering round the entrance to the hive. "To amuse an unamusable king" was the penance of a worldly woman; but these people cannot be called unamusable. They are quick-witted (on their own ground), imaginative, and enthusiastic; and the question for us to consider is, how these good gifts might be employed to vivify and brighten their lives. To inquire what amusements they have had in their own land avails us little, since their position at home was rarely a prosperous one; and such pleasures as they have had may have been chiefly of the fighting and drinking sort. Out of drinking and fighting they have hitherto got the excitement they inevitably crave; and the question is, how to elicit pleasurable sensations to take the place of this coarser stimulus.

The Irish are excellent listeners to each other. We have heard the wild mournful notes of Irish songs rise for hours of a summer's evening, while groups of twenty and thirty of the singers' fellow-laborers sat silent, apparently fully appreciating the charm of the melody. We have all overheard the unending rigmaroles, which seemed to have unfailing interest, of some elderly digger or ditcher. Might not their fanciful but fervent patriotism, and this endurance of long talks, make them listen to speakers who should half read and half recite to them? There are treasures of beautiful legends in what they fondly call their national history; and a skilful lecturer might pass from the home they have left to the home they have found, and give them *pictures* of American history which would stir their hearts. He would not read to them the dreary correspondence with Congress which swamps most of the biographies of our American heroes, but with the daring of Gen. Putnam, the sufferings of Valley Forge, the romantic exploits of Marion, and the dash of Light Horse Harry, kindle their feelings, till they rose to the contemplation of that magnanimous and dauntless man, who out of thirteen States made a nation. These people are to inhabit the land which our fathers won, to fulfil, or to render futile, the hopes for which our fathers fought. Let us try to furnish their memories and imaginations with some of the traditions that are winning and stately and potent in our own. To do this effectually, however, it must be done sympathetically; and, if well done, it may at once amuse the poor, and cause them and us to feel that they are of one blood with ourselves.

Another characteristic of the Irish, as we see them, is their uneducated love of beauty. The little hand-maiden rejoices almost unselfishly in her young lady's beautiful array. The servants smuggle in their friends for a look at the fruit and the flowers laid out, and the glittering appointments of a feast which they are not to share; and they take an essentially aesthetic in the beauty of other people's possessions. Lovers of nature they do not seem to be; but they have an especial taste and faculty for design. In the Great Exhibition of London, in 1862, Irish designs in lace and damask had a conceded superiority. May we not, then, appeal to their eyes for their amusement? Would it be possible, or perhaps only possible in the new Sybaris, to have public exhibitions of pictorial representations, with some recitations or dramatic performance combined with it? Imagine Faneuil Hall, or the Music Hall, bestowed on us by a sympathetic city government the 22nd of February. We will begin with an historic tableau of Washington crossing the Delaware (In every generation there is some man who looks like Washington); then let some high-spirited, sweet-voiced person recite parts of Longfellow's "Building of the Ship;" then a tableau from "Rich and rare were the gems she wore," and some other of Moore's songs; then some humorous Yankee piece, and, for *finale*, extracts from Mr. Lowell's "Commemoration Ode," or "The Color Sergeant." Let all this be given twice (from 12 to 2 and from 2 to 4), and you have at least attempted to furnish people with pleasure that is a help, and not a hindrance.

Pleasures which are habitual in other countries can hardly become such in New England. Out-of-doors concerts three times a week are hardly practicable in a climate which is always doing something violently—freezing, blazing, or blowing. Baseball and cricket are (we believe) very little played by the Irish; and even to them we Americans are apt to add an element of unwholesome excitement.

II. COMMENTS FROM NEW YORK

There is not a doubt that some of the vast evils which result from intemperance could be prevented, if only we could satisfy the natural appetite for pleasure by innocent excitements. It has been an experience of the last decade that the greatest rival of the grog-shop is the park, or the industrial palace, or the popular picture-gallery. Wherever a grand exhibition building has been erected, there the liquor-shops in the neighborhood find a poor run of custom. The throng in the rum-holes and taverns is always most dense in those quarters where there is no garden, or gallery, or public place of amusement. One of the most remarkable efforts to provide amusements for the poor in these latter years has been the opening of the wonderful "Bethnal Green Museum" in one of the worst quarters of London. This is a collection of pictures, pottery, furniture, glass, and numberless objects of curiosity, unequalled in London, and visited by strangers from every quarter of the globe. Yet it has been placed in the midst of this destitute district, and on certain days is open free to the poor. All testimony agrees that the conduct of these people within the building is without fault, and that the influence of this remarkable kind of promoting temperance and good order.

In every New-England village, a certain degree of amusements is provided for the laboring or mechanical classes, by the cheap lectures and concerts in the village lyceum. But this is for a somewhat intelligent class, and does not reach the German or Irish laborers. In New York and in Brooklyn the German poor have no difficulty in amusing themselves. We have fortunately enjoyed in both cities, the ingenious services of two landscape artists, who have made the habits and amusements of the foreign class their study. This art has not been merely to draw a beautiful picture on what would otherwise be a dreary surface, but to study the science of popular amusements. In the Brooklyn Park especially, there are endless contrivances for amusing and gratifying laborers' families; with arbors where they eat their lunches, near cool springs, and look into wild and bosky ravines; houses where they get milk fresh from the cow for their children; paths for forest rambles; beds of bright flowers; towers with wide views and a bank of a lake, where they can sit of a summer evening and listen to the music of a band, or watch the little boats crossing and flying over the water. The Brooklyn Park is the laborers' pleasure-ground, and is greatly frequented in fine weather by the Germans of a poor class. The New York Park is perhaps less enjoyed by the laboring class, on account of its distance from the poor quarters. Yet great crowds of German families of laborers and artisans may be seen in the pleasant season, rambling through its paths, or sprinkled around on the grass, eating their lunches, and taking the Teuton enjoyment in the free air and bright sunshine. We all know the many ingenious and beautiful contrivances in these grounds to amuse and instruct these working classes.

The Irish are, of all races, the most ready for amusement: their temperament is proverbial for its genial quality. They enjoy dance, a good song, a spectacle, fine costumes, and games of skill and strength; but they do not care for nature. Parks and gardens are by no means so necessary for them as for the Germans. I believe that free and respectable saloons, under good supervision, opened in the poor Irish wards, where there could be music, singing, recitation of stirring poems, and an occasional dance, with cheap refreshments, would be great rivals to the whiskey shops, and would tend immensely to check hard drinking, and encourage temperance. Such amusements, free and innocent in their character, would suit the Irish population. The entertainment would have to be somewhat Celtic in its style; but fortunately, Irish poetry, song, oratory, and wit have resources enough to supply amusement and instruction for a great many evenings. If one of these free music saloons were opened by philanthropic persons, it would not be long before others would be provided as a matter of business; and we might have Irish music-halls as common as German dance-halls. Amusement is a necessity; and, if the poor do not have it in one way, they will in another.

III. COMMENTS FROM INDIANA

1. The report is not applicable to this latitude, except, perhaps, to the Irish population, which is small, and confined principally to the larger towns. I fear that, even with these, it will be impractical to bring them under the influence of amusements, refined and rational.

2. We know no *distinctive* class of poor in this State. A very large part of the laboring population earn but a small amount more than is necessary for their subsistence; yet *most* of them are gradually rising in the scale, and many of our leading citizens have risen from this class.

3. The laboring population about the larger towns and cities consist mostly of German and Irish, about whom it is unnecessary to speak, as they abound everywhere, and their characteristics are well known.

4. The farm-laborers are mostly Americans. They have but few amusements; and they are mostly of the most simple character, affecting principally the body: the young men run races, jump, wrestle, etc.; the sexes, when associated, tell stories, play common games, etc.; sometimes a neighborhood singing or spelling school affords them pleasure. There are no organized *public* amusements. If something could be found for this class of persons of a more elevated character, it would be desirable; but the small number who can be gathered together at any one locality renders it difficult.

5. Will there not be a difficulty in carrying out these suggestions in reference to "historic tableaux," etc., from the lack of suitable persons to do it? Would they afford amusement to uncultured minds? Does not the idea of amusement involve the necessity for something which can be done by those who engage in it *themselves*? Would not any thing conducted *wholly* by others soon lose its charm?

6. As the minds of the laboring classes become enlightened by education, and the effect of our system of common schools becomes more fully felt, amusements of a higher and more ennobling character will be sought. Is not this the right place to begin?

IV. ANOTHER BOSTON VIEW

A lady whose occupation and interests take her much among the poor, after reading this report, has added still another suggestion, which is worth quoting here, in conclusion. She says:

"I should, perhaps, dwell with more earnestness upon the necessity of taking amusements into the midst of the classes under consideration. They cannot be called out of their haunts. Whatever is done for them must be taken to them, and be at first offered free of all charge. There should be established, say, in such regions as the North End and South Cove, reading-rooms, or, if the name would be more attractive, club-rooms, cheerful, light, and warm, and furnished not only with reading-matter, but pleasing games. In these rooms there should be weekly entertainments, music, recitations, an occasional debate upon some topic of general interest, etc. Secure, wherever it is possible, such a man as Prof. Morse of Salem, or the late Prof. Agassiz, whose skill with crayon could make, by catching the eye, the dull understanding grasp pleasurably even scientific subjects. By the aid of illustration, the common things of every-day life become illuminated with interest. There is nothing, not even music, that will hold an uneducated crowd like a stereopticon. Under the microscope a drop of water becomes a miniature ocean of life; and so the skin, the hair, the teeth, and the tissues of the body, can all be made themes for the illustration of practical lessons. The marvellous beauty that chemistry reveals, and the wonders of astronomy or of electricity, can be turned to elevate and instruct this class of people. Scientific and hygienic lectures have proved a success among the working-people of England. It is no hopeless task here to provide wholesome and relishing mental food for the now famishing ignorant of our cities.

"We must not be unmindful how much the Old World gave the foreigner who takes up his abode with us, that he is here deprived of—parks, lovely and numerous, everywhere free and open for all to ramble in at will on Sundays and week days; added to these, on the Continent, excellent music, as free to the laborer as to the nobleman; art-galleries and museums also, open and free to all, and thronged usually by the working classes on Sundays, when, also, they have reduced fares on public conveyances leading to the country; so that hundreds of families can spend a day once a week during the summer, away from the crowded city and their stifling tenement-rooms."

3. AMERICANS AT PLAY

by Edward Eggleston
CENTURY MAGAZINE, AUGUST, 1884

If the future social historian of America shall put much trust in the propositions about the character of the American people of today that are current in essays, newspaper leaders, sermons, and elsewhere, he will miss the mark. Some false theories, from frequent repetition, gain an authority equal to that of the Apostles' Creed. Since the first seed of the English race germinated in these shores, several theories about them have been accepted as generally true. The most of these have been false. It was very nearly believed that Americans were shorter-lived than their English progenitors; the falsehood is so vital that even life-insurance experience cannot quite kill it. It was long held, and I suppose it is yet held, that Yankees love money more than any other people; but does an American like a dollar any better than an Englishman or Scotchman like four shillings? Will not the generous-hearted son of Erin haggle for a half-penny in a bargain? Isn't a franc very dear, also, to a Frenchman? In one breath Old World writers dub the people of the United States a nation of "dollar-hunters," and in the next berate them for an excessive liberality that "spoils travel." Most Englishmen hold to the opinion that Americans sit up of nights to corrupt the English language. But the most curious of fallacies about Americans are those which they hold themselves. One of these is that we are an overworked race, incapable of amusing ourselves. Over and over again the leader-writers—the only real *ex cathedrâ* preachers of our age—assure us that we are incapable of merry-making, that our attempts at fun are cumbrous failures, and that, as a people, we are quite incapable of play. The best of the joke is that we all believe this, and feel sorry for ourselves accordingly.

To one of the most refined and fastidious of New England scholars I once remarked that the American writer best known in Europe was Mark Twain. "He ought to be," was the reply. "Anybody who can make our melancholy people laugh deserves the highest honor." The foundation for this belief is that American melancholy, with a college man leading a life of scholarly seclusion, is easy to find. He reads of May-poles in old ballads, but we have none; he sees merry-making from a distance as he travels in Europe, and sees them through the atmosphere of old poetry—all the rudeness and brutality in them fail to reach him. He only knows that our people do not dance on the village green, or kiss their sweethearts under the mistletoe, or carry in a grinning boar's head at Christmas. Our shepherds do not play upon any pipes but those that hold tobacco. Are we not, therefore, a lugubrious people?

But how even a college professor should get the notion that the American people are incapable of amusement, I cannot see. The gymnasium is rather more prominent than the library—in Harvard itself there is a professor whose business it is to teach athletics. What would the venerable founders, who adopted the solemn Latin motto which devotes the college to religious and ecclesiastic uses, have thought to see a member of the Harvard faculty taking the flying trapeze. Twenty years ago every well-informed man knew who were the great professors at the leading universities; now it is much if you can keep the run of the young men who row a stroke in the boat crews, and who, with the base-ball, foot-ball, and lacrosse players, have somewhat eclipsed the renown of the great teachers.

I have been for some months involved in all the toils of building in a place remote from supplies. When the Fourth of July came, my stone-masons, living for weeks in a tent away from their families, and consequently anxious to complete their work, agreed to work all day. But, like true holiday-keeping Americans, they could not stand it; the lake was too tempting; at noon all three "knocked-off" and went-a-fishing, after the ancient example of Simon Peter. The only man left on my hands was a Scotch tender, who would not lose his wages, though he had no masons to tend. The carpenters at work for me are men of about fifty years of age, who do not, it is true, dance on the green or keep house-warmings, like ancient Englishmen, but all of them left me for a week at a stretch to attend the county fair, and the intelligent America "help" in the kitchen went also. My French-Canadian plasterer stood solitary at his post like another Casabianca; but the brick-mason couldn't lay the hearth—his duties as village-fiddler detained him at the fair. I wonder if the social philosophers who are so sure we have no holidays, just because everybody has always said so, ever considered what a great element in our rural life the so-called agricultural fair is, with its pumpkins and bicycle races, its big oxen, trotting-horses, gypsy fortune-tellers, needle-work, female equestrians, firemen's "tournaments," side-shows, dances, and other amusements. We have two of these in our county every autumn. Only last week I rowed five miles against a head wind in a hot September sun, on a pressing errand for my builders, and then found the steam-planing mill as still as death; proprietors and men had shut down and gone off to see the fair, six miles away—except one fellow, who alone chose to amuse himself, in the way supposed to be congenial to our race, by attending a murder trial in the village hard by.

Living as I do on the lake that is preferred to all others in America as a resort, it seems ridiculous to talk of Americans as incapable of enjoyment. For thirty miles north and south, on both shores, Lake George is peopled in summer by many thousands who give themselves up to the pleasure of every healthful sort—rowing, fishing, driving, bathing, mountain-climbing, boat-racing, canoe-racing, steam-boat excursions, moonlight sailing, lawn-tennis, base-ball, mooning on the piazza, and other outdoor recreations, to say nothing of indoor games. Nor are all these rich people; farm-houses and shell cottages are occupied by multitudes of people with little money who love recreation like good Americans, and who take vacations of a length unknown to Europeans in similar circumstances.

But these are not the peasants you say. Alas! we have no peasants to attend feasts given by patronizing lords-of-the-manor. But our country people have their own recreations. Joshua's Rock, within a gunshot of where I write, is now inclosed and forbidden; but it has been a picnicing and chowdering place for the neighborhood probably ever since the land was inhabited by white people, and, from the relics we find, it appears to have been the scene of Indian fish-suppers for centuries before. A chowder was given a few weeks ago at the head of our little bay; there was no end to the carriages, wagons, row-boats, sail-boats, and little steamers that waked the resounding echoes of our usually quiet cliffs. There were perhaps a thousand people in the crowd, and not a city person among them. They were yeomanry from the rugged flanks of French Mountain, and from the fertile grain and grass country to the south and east, with mechanics, clerks, and store-keepers from half-a-dozen villages in a radius of fifteen miles. A horse ran away, and several persons injured. One of them thought to be fatally hurt, but when the wounded had been cared for, the irrepressible American went on with his merry chowder as though nothing had happened. Each comer paid twenty-five cents as his contribution toward the fish chowder, and furnished the rest of his provisions himself. There was no music, no dancing, no beer, no singing, no May-pole, no gracious lady-of-the-manor, but there was unintermitting enjoyment for all that.

In vain will the historian of the future look for any reflection of all this in the novels of society that graze the cuticle of our national life. Our novelists, for the most part, shirk the chowder and the county fair. If you should write of these things frankly, you are sure to be snubbed by the refined critic, who will accuse you of "a latent sympathy with vulgarity." But we shall never have a genuinely American literature so long as we shrink from the life of our common people. Isolation and exclusiveness is not a mark of superior culture, though it passes for something of the sort. There is no vulgarity so vulgar as that which feels itself liable to contamination by contact with people of no pretensions.

In estimating the capacity of Americans for amusements, it should be remembered that if they have fewer troupes of strolling players than other peoples, they compensate themselves with no end of church "entertainments." If we keep few ancient holidays, we take liberal vacations; if we buy few comic papers, we exact that our sober journals shall keep "funny men" as jesters to King Demos. The predominant quality in two-thirds of our most popular men of letters is either wit or humor. Even in the pulpit the most popular men are amusing, either purposely or otherwise, and it is doubtful if any other nation ever had so many humorists among its legislators as we have had.

We are accused of grimness and lack of joyousness in our merry-making is serious business when the observer is out of sympathy with it. One delicious late afternoon, in a town on the banks of the Lago Maggiore, six or seven years ago, I saw the pole of an acrobat set up in the street. The fellow performed some commonplace feats of agility, such as you may see on a summer's day at Rockaway when our city people, rich and poor, are airing themselves along the shore. But the Italian was jauntily dressed in colors, and aided by the clown; his two children, mere infants, were forced to perform with him, and his wife, bedizened with tinsel, showing off her meager ugliness in tights, solicited contributions by passing round a tambourine. The oldest little boy, of five years, after performing several dangerous feats, grew nervous, missed his hold, and fell heavily on his back. The father cuffed him, and he ran, hurt and sobbing, to his mother. A charming gentleman and lady from Weimar, who had crossed the Simplon in the coupé of the diligence with me, stood by. I shall never forget the indignant emphasis of this gentleman's exclamation when the poor boy fell: "*C'est abominable!*" But the crowd of people took no notice; the tumbling and contortions of the actor, and the capers of the clown, continued to excite applause. The poor mother, in her ridiculous tights and furbelows, alternately fondled her frightened children and jingled her tambourine, praying the bystanders to contribute. I do not believe that our amusements are any more grim or disagreeable than this one which gave the common people of Stresa so much delight. Even the fun of dancing on a hay-barge towed slowly through the Kill von Kull on a moonlight night—which is so common a recreation with Manhattaners of a certain class—can hardly seem drearier to the observer than the Italian street circus did to three foreigners.

4. CHRISTIANITY AND POPULAR AMUSEMENTS

by Washington Gladden
CENTURY MAGAZINE, JANUARY, 1885

The historical relation of Christianity to popular amusements is one of antagonism. The philosophy of the church respecting the whole subject may be summed up in the cynical counsel of Douglas Jerrold to persons about to marry, "Don't!" There have been contrary voices, and not a little practical dissent has found expression; but the tenor of the ecclesiastical utterances respecting amusements has been prohibitory, not to say objurgatory. In some of the sects a less stringent doctrine has been taught; but it is not very long since the average Protestant church-member took no diversion without some compunctions or questionings of conscience. John Bunyan's experience at the time of his conversion for the awful wickedness of his youth—which awful wickedness consisted in ringing the bells in the church-tower, in dancing with the girls on the village green, and in playing the nefarious game of tip-cat—shows in what light all worldly amusements have been held by great numbers of Christians in the reformed churches. "In the middle of a game of tip-cat," says Macaulay, "he paused and stood staring wildly upward, with his stick in his hand. He had heard a voice asking him whether he would leave his sins and go to heaven, or keep his sins and go to hell; and he had seen an awful countenance frowning on his from the sky." When we reflect that this game of tip-cat was regarded by Bunyan as one of his darling sins, continuance in which would land him in perdition, and remember that it is none other than that innocuous diversion still played by small boys in the streets of our cities under the various titles of "cat" or "kitty" or "shiny," we discover how conventional the treatment of this subject has been, and what grievous burdens of ascetic self-denial have been bound upon men's consciences.

Doubtless this inveterate hostility to amusements of all sorts is partly traditional, a survival of that wholesome horror and righteous enmity with which the first Christians resisted the amusements in vogue throughout the Roman Empire. The frightful debaucheries and cruelties which constituted the sports of the Romans merited the holy indignation with which the disciples of the early days denounced them. The conflict of Christianity with heathenism began in this very arena. One of the broad lines of distinction which the Christians drew between themselves and their pagan neighbors was their refusal to attend the Roman games. When we know that the best actor was the one who could behave the most obscenely; that the chariot races at the circus, where there were seats for three hundred and eighty-five thousand spectators, were deemed most successful when horses and men were killed in the contest; that the spectacles at the amphitheatre derived all their relish from the butchery of gladiators by scores and hundreds in their battles with wild beasts and with one another; that the public executions also offered a delectable entertainment for the populace, the condemned sometimes appearing "in garments interwoven with threads of gold, and with crowns on their heads, when suddenly flames burst from their clothing and consumed them," all for the amusement of the people—we are not disposed to find fault with the protest of the early Christians against the popular diversions. "Bread and games!" was the cry of the Roman populace. "Work and prayer!" was the watch-word of the Christians. Against the indolence and savage frivolity of the people about them, they lifted up their standard of industry and soberness. It was a great conflict on which they thus entered; and there was small opportunity for compromise or discrimination. The sentiments and maxims which had their origin in this early warfare have been perpetuated in the Church, and the judgements of the early Christians upon popular amusements have been repeated in modern times against sports altogether different from those of Rome in the first century.

At the time of the Reformation in England, the hostility of the Puritans to popular amusements was even more bitter than that of the early Christians to the Roman games, though the reasons for this hostility were much less cogent. Doubtless there was good cause to protest against the roystering sports of that period. The desecration of the Lord's Day by noisy and and wanton pastimes was common everywhere, and this called forth their loudest protest. But when they entered upon their crusade against the diversions of the people, they became so extravagant in their judgements, including in their denunciations so many harmless things and failing so utterly to preserve any moral perspective in their teachings, that they never could have carried with them the consciences of intelligent persons. Those who were trained in their own households and who were subjected to the strenuous pressure of their public opinion could be brought to adopt their theories. By an educational process as careful and insistent as that, for example, to which John Stuart Mill was subjected, a child can be made to believe or to disbelieve almost anything. Bunyan was not a fool, yet he honestly thought that he was in danger of being sent to hell for playing tip-cat. By such rigid training the Puritans did create in the minds that were brought under their influence the strong belief that every species of amusement was sinful; and this theory they enforced with all the fervor of religious enthusiasm, and, when they were able, by all the power of the State. But it was only from those who had been subjected from childhood to the pressure of this intense philosophy that any steady conformity to its rules could be expected. Nature and reason were against it. The utter disproportion of its judgements must soon become evident. The moralist to whom the dancing of the boys and girls around the May-pole on the village green is a "horrible vice;" who cries out, with Old Stubbes. "Give over your occupations, you pipers, you fiddlers, you musicians, you tabretters, and you fluters, and all other of that wicked brood," holding that "sweet music at the first delighteth the ears, but afterward corrupteth and depraveth the mind;" who damns the simplest and most wholesome sports quite as roundly as the worst debaucheries—will soon find himself speaking to a limited audience. If it be true, as Knight tells us, that "drinking, dicing, bear-baiting, cock-fighting"—the coarsest temptations to profligacy—are not such abominations in the eyes of the Puritans as "stage plays, interludes, and comedies," then the Puritans ought to have lost their influence with the English people.

Macaulay's remark that the Puritans opposed bear-baiting less because it gave pain to the bear than because it gave pleasure to the spectators, has often been quoted as an example of his vicious fondness for antithesis; but it is by no means clear that the cynicism lacks justice. Many a Puritan did think merriment a worse sin than cruelty to animals....

That this overstrained asceticism of the Puritans was excusable, in the view of the excesses against which they testified, may be freely admitted; albeit the revealing Cavaliers might doubtless claim some similar mitigation of their condemnation, in view of the rigors of the Roundheads. Each party was driven into worse extremes by the extravagances of the other. The philosophy of life which underlay the Puritan regimen has given way slowly. Down to the present generation it has been the received doctrine in most of the reformed churches, that all the "worldly pleasures" ought to be eschewed. If personal testimony may be offered, the writer remembers very well that, when a boy of twelve, he mentally debated the question of conversion, under the impression that the change involved the sacrifice of base-ball, and base-ball was then an innocent game. This impression was gained in the religious services upon which he was a constant attendant. It is true that at that time, and long before, members of churches did engage to some extent in sport and merriment, but generally under some protest of conscience, and with the feeling that the indulgence was a charge against their piety. The ideal Christian of the reformed churches was a man who had no use for any kind of diversion, and whose neighbors would have been shocked if they had seen him unbending in a merry game....

Out of this traditional estimate of the nature of religion, and its relaxation to what is known as the secular life, came the maxims which the Church for many years applied to amusement. It is needless to say that these maxims are obsolete. In this case, at any rate, prohibition has not prohibited. The parson, with the pitchfork of excommunication, has not prevailed over nature. The rigorous rule of the Puritan, long enforced by the most tremendous motives, is utterly broken, and will not in our day be restored.

Failing to prohibit, the Church has now for some time undertaken to regulate amusements by drawing the line between the clean and the unclean. Certain diversions have been allowed, and certain others forbidden. Much casuistry of a dubious sort has been expended on this discussion; the questions whether dancing is sinful, and whether billiards are worse than croquet, and whether cards are always an abomination, and whether church-members ought to be disciplined for attending the theatre or the opera, have been widely and hotly debated; most of us have had a hand in the threshing of this chaff. Whether these controversies have aided greatly in the formation of a sound public opinion on this subject may well be doubted; the grounds on which the permission of some amusements and the prohibition of others have been rested are often inconsistent and irrational; and the Church would be far wiser to give over these questions of casuistry, and insist upon a few general principles, such as these:

1. Amusement is not an end, but a means—a means of refreshing the mind and replenishing the strength of the body; when it begins to be the principal thing for which one lives, or when, in pursuing it, the mental powers are enfeebled and the bodily health impaired, it falls under just condemnation.

2. Amusements that consume the hours which ought to be sacred to sleep are, therefore, censurable.

3. Amusements that call us away from work which we are bound to do are pernicious, just to the extent to which they cause us to be neglectful or unfaithful.

4. Amusements that rouse or stimulate morbid appetites or unlawful passions, or that cause us to be restless or discontented, are always to be avoided.

5. Any indulgence in amusement which has a tendency to weaken our respect for the great interests of character, or to loosen our hold on the eternal verities of the spiritual realm, is, so far forth, a damage to us.

These principles will apply to all kinds of amusements, but the application must be made by individuals. Parents must reduce these principles to rules for the guidance of their children, for the power to comprehend and use principles is only gradually gained; children do not always possess it; authority rather than reason must often be their guide. But the Church must use reason rather than authority; and the pulpit can do better than faithfully to enforce some such general maxims as I have suggested. Whatever the Church can do in the regulation of amusements, can best be done by this method.

But is this all the Church has to do with the amusements of the people? Is its function fulfilled in this important realm of human conduct, by repressing or regulating the diversions of the people—by preventing excess and abuse? Has the Church no positive duties to perform in providing popular amusement?

Let me say at the outset that the churches are doing already all that they ought to do in a way of furnishing amusements of various kinds in connection with their own organizations and in their own houses of worship. The church sociable has become a recognized institution; and, in spite of certain scandalous reports, its influence, on the whole, has been salutary. It is certain, however, that the churches have gone fully as far in this direction as it is safe for them to go. It is not the business of the Church to organize dramatic troupes or minstrel companies for the amusement of the people in its own edifice. The proper function of the Church is that of teaching and moral influence; and when it goes extensively into the show business, it is apt to lose its hold upon the more serious interests with which it is charged. The duty of the Church, with respect to the provision and direction of popular amusements, will be discharged, if at all, as its duty to the unfortunates of the community is discharged—by inspiring and forming outside agencies to do this very thing. The hospitals and asylums are the work of the Church; it is neither economical nor desirable that each church should undertake to provide in connection with its own edifice, and under the care of its own officers, a hospital, an asylum for the insane, and a home for the friendless. When it is said that the Church ought to provide wholesome diversions for the people, it is meant, therefore, that the Church ought to stir up the intelligent and benevolent men and women under its influence to attend to this matter, and ought to make them feel that this is one of the duties resting on them as Christians. And the question now before us is whether any such obligation as this is now rested on the Church; whether this is a field which Christian philanthropy can and should enter and cultivate. In answering this question several considerations must be borne in mind.

1. Popular amusement is a great fact. A large share of the people are seeking amusement of one sort or another continually. In every city or considerable town the opera-houses, the concert-halls, the rinks, the museums, the beer-gardens, as well as many lower and less reputable places of diversion, are always open and generally well patronized. It is probable that more persons attend places of amusement than attend church; or, rather, that there is a larger number of persons in almost any large town or city who seldom or never visit any place of worship, than of those who seldom or never visit any place of amusement. The places of amusement are generally open six or seven days in the week, while most churches are open only two or three days. Even the poorest, those who obtain but a meager subsistence by their labor, and who often appeal to their neighbors for charity, spend a good part of their scanty earnings for amusements. A family, known to the writer, that sold the last feather pillows in the house for money to go to the circus, is a type of a large class. Church-going is a luxury too expensive for multitudes who spend three times as much as a seat in church would cost on the theatre and the variety show.

2. The business of amusement constitutes a great financial interest. An army of men and women get their living by providing diversion for the people. Millions of dollars are invested in buildings, furniture, instruments, equipage, scenery, animals, vehicles, and appliances of all sorts, devoted to this purpose. Busy brains are all the while contriving new forms of diversion that shall prove attractive to the people and remunerative to their projectors. Large fortunes are made by successful managers; indeed, the capital of a millionaire is required for the han-

dling of some of our great popular amusements. This liberal outlay and this enterprising provision involve a general and large expenditure of money on the part of the people. In one inland city of sixty thousand inhabitants there are two opera-houses. In each of these there is an average of five performances a week during the season, which lasts about forty weeks. Four hundred performances a year, with average receipts of two hundred and fifty dollars, give us one hundred thousand dollars expended for amusements every year in these two houses—more than is paid for the support of all the Protestant churches in the city. A base-ball club in the same city received during the last season, for gate money that was paid for diversions of various sorts at the other halls, and the rinks, and the public gardens of the city; all that was taken by several circuses and other outdoor shows; all that was devoted to billiards, and to dances, and to horse-races, and to a multitude of other amusements, more or less refined—and it can be easily seen that the amusement bill of a city of this size must reach a formidable figure. Not counting the cost of drink and debauchery, which is not properly reckoned against amusements—counting only the expense of what may be fairly classed among the diversions of the people—we see that a large share of their earnings is devoted to this purpose. Complaint is sometimes made of the cost of education and of religious privileges; but it is safe to say that the people of this country spend every year for amusements more than they pay for their schools, and three times as much as they pay for their churches.

3. Amusement is not only a great fact and a great business interest, it is also a great factor in the development of the national character. If a wise philanthropist could choose between making the laws of any people and furnishing their amusements, it would not take him long to decide. The robust virtues are nurtured under the discipline of work; if the diversions can be kept healthful, a sound national life will be developed. The ideals of the people are shaped, and their sentiments formed, to a large extent, by popular amusements. It is claimed that the drama renders important service to public morality in this direction; but the claim can hardly be allowed. A careful collection and analysis, by a well-known clergymen, of the plays produced at the leading theatres of Chicago during a given period, clearly indicated that the actual drama is far from being a great teacher of morality. Doubtless many plays are produced whose moral lesson is helpful and stimulating; but it cannot be claimed that the preponderance of the influence of the drama is on the side of virtue. It is conceivable that the drama might be a great friend of morality; it is possible that it will be one day; it is undeniable that there are a few noble men and women now upon the stage who are doing what they can to lift up standards; it is not necessary to indulge in any sweeping censures when we speak of it; but it is quite clear that this form of popular amusement, as at present administered, tends to the degradation rather than the elevation of the people. It is not only nor chiefly by the questionable morality of many of the plays that this injury is done; it is by their flippancy, their silliness, their sensationalism, their unreality. Their effect upon the intellect is like that produced by the reading of the most trashy novels, only more debilitating. So far as the drama is concerned, therefore, I fear that it must be said that the net result of its influence upon the national character is injurious rather than beneficial. And the same thing must be said of popular amusements in general, as at present organized and conducted. Although the people receive much wholesome refreshment and innocent pleasure from the diversions now provided for them, yet the effect of these amusements, as a whole, upon their minds and their morals and their physical health, is not salutary. I am not inclined to pessimism on this or any other subject, and I am able to look without horror on many diversions commonly regarded as wholly pernicious: yet careful observation of the effect of the popular amusements upon the people at large leads me to believe that

the balance of their influence is on the side of injury. They are a great factor in the life of the people, but their product, on the whole, is evil; they do much good, but more harm.

4. Seeing that amusement is so large an element in the life of the people, seeing that it lays so heavy a tax on their resources and affects their character so powerfully, the questions naturally arise: How is it managed? By whom is it furnished? How much of intelligence and of philanthropic purpose enters into the plans of those who provide the amusements of the people?

Concerning the class of persons who devote their lives to the business of amusing the people, it is best not to make any unqualified statements. Among them are many who are exemplary in their conduct, and who would never engage in any enterprise the tendency of which would be immoral or degrading. But if what has been said is true, that the preponderance of the influence of the popular amusements is on the side of evil, then it is reasonable to conclude that the majority of those who furnish them are not persons of exalted character. As a matter of fact, the business of diverting the people is largely in the hands of men and women whose moral standards are low, whose habits are vicious, and whose influence upon those with whom they come in contact must be evil. It is to people chiefly of this class that this most important interest of life is intrusted.

When we ask on what basis the business of amusement is conducted, the answer is that it rests almost wholly on a pecuniary interest. The principle that regulates it is the principle of supply and demand; and this principle is interpreted, as we have seen, by persons who would not be likely to discover a demand for diversions of an elevating nature, if there were such a demand.

The question now arises whether this great interest of human life ought to be left to settle itself in this manner, by the law of supply and demand. It may be wise to allow the material interests of men who adjust themselves according to this law. But amusement is not one of the material interests of men. Man's need of amusement is one of the needs of his higher nature—his spirit, as well as of his body; his use of amusement affects his mind and his character directly and powerfully. And whatever may be said about the introduction of the principle of good-will into the business of producing and distributing commodities, there can be no question, when you enter the realm where those forces are at work by which character is to be produced, that the principle of good-will must come in, and must be allowed to rule. If this is true, the business of providing amusement for the people ought not to merely or mainly a mercenary business; the intelligence, the conscience, and the benevolence of the community ought to recognize this realm of amusement as belonging to them, and ought to enter in and take possession.

Does the Church leave the religious wants of the community to be provided for under the law of supply and demand? Is it supposed that this matter will properly regulate itself; that the people will call for what they need and get it; that no care is to be exercised and no effort made to provide wise and safe religious teaching for them? By no means. It is assumed to be the function of the Church to provide Christian institutions and Christian instruction for the people; to spread the gospel feast before them and send forth the invitations to them; not to wait and see what they would like, and give them what they may ask for; not to leave this matter to be attended to by those who seek to make gain of godliness.

How is it with the intellectual wants of the community? Does the State leave these to be supplied under the economical law? Is it imagined that the people will get all the education that they need if they are left to provide it for themselves, irregularly and spasmodically, according to their own notions of what they want? Not at all. The intelligence and philanthropy of the best citizens, expressing themselves in the laws of the state, provide education for the people, build school-houses, organize systems of education, employ teachers, offering thus to the public a large and wise and constant supply of one of their deepest needs. It may be said that the provision is only a response to the popular demand, but this is not true. The great motive power of education is not the cry of ignorance; it is the offer of intelligence. How is it in our homes? Is the education of our children the result of their call for learning, or of our constant and insistent proffer of learning to them? Here and there is a child that hungers for useful knowledge; but the great majority need to have this hunger created in them, and need to have it stimulated continually by a wise and patient presentation to them of the knowledge which we wish them to acquire. Thus all popular education proceeds, and has always proceeded, from an altruistic motive. The demand has been created by furnishing the supply; it is intelligence, the conscience, the patriotism, the philanthropy of the best citizens—that have taken this business of education in hand and managed it for the benefit of the whole people. A large part of the work of education—the work of school-boards, and trustees, and visitors—is done gratuitously. Philanthropy is not the sole motive in the work of education; the self-regarding motives have large scope among teachers as well as pupils; but the philanthropic element is an integral element in all our best educational work. Benevolence is one of the forces that keep the machinery in motion. Education deserves always to rank as one of the great missionary enterprises. The best reward of the faithful teacher is not his salary, but the consciousness that he is rendering a valuable service to those whom he instructs and the state. When a prominent educator announced, not long ago, his purpose of abandoning his profession that he might devote himself to the getting of money, a murmur of indignant comment was heard from the noble fraternity of teachers. Among them are thousands who fully appreciate and adopt the saying of Professor Agassiz, that he had no time for money-making. If there are millions in the land to whom such a statement is incredible, and the man who makes it a hypocrite, this only indicates how deeply we have sunk into that abyss of mercantilism, wherein, as true prophets are warning us, the best elements of our national life are fast disappearing. A sorry day it will be for this land when the work of education is wholly or mainly done for mercenary reasons.

Now, amusement, like education and religion, is a real need for human beings—not so deep or vital a need as education or religion, but a real and constant need of the higher nature as well as of the lower; an interest that closely concerns their characters; and it is almost as great a mistake to leave it to take care of itself, and to be furnished mainly by those who wish to make money out of it, and who have no higher motive, as it would be to leave education or religion to be cared for in that way.

It is time that we begin to comprehend the idea that this is one of the great interests of human life which Christianity must claim and control—one of the kingdoms of the world which, according to the prophecy, are to "become the kingdoms of our Lord and of the Christ." When these words are quoted, the thoughts of the disciples are apt to fly off to Burmah and Siam and Timbuctoo; these are the kingdoms of this world that are to be Christianized. Doubtless they are; but the text ought to mean more than this. It should signify that all the wide realms of human thought and action are to be brought under the sway of the King of righteousness; that the kingdom of industry, and the kingdom of traffic, and the kingdom of politics, and the kingdom of amusement are all to be made subject to His law; that all these great interests of men are to be brought under the empire of Christian ideas and Christian forces; that instead of standing aloof from them and reproving and upbraiding them, Christianity is to enter into them and pervade them and transform them by its own vital energy. The duty of the Church with respect to popular amusements is not done when it has lifted up its warning against the abuses that grow out of them, and laid down its laws of temperance and moderation in their use. It has a positive function to fulfill in furnishing diversions that shall be attractive, and, at the same time, pure and wholesome. This cannot be done, as we have seen, by the churches as churches, but it can be done by men and women into whom they breathe their spirit, and whom they fill with their intelligence and good-will....

TAKING IN THE SIGHTS

II.

SUMMER RESORTS AND WATERING PLACES

The majority of early Americans, living remote from urban centers, were surrounded by resources for summer pleasures. Unspoiled lakes and rivers were abundant with fish and provided an inviting beauty for boating, picnicking, and mere solitude. Hill and vale, forest and glade, mountain and prairie, as a continuing environment, were natural places of resort for those rare occasions when leisure was practical.

Early city dwellers were not so fortunate. There was little natural landscaping. Streets were narrow. Sewage disposal was primitive. Structures were erected with poor ventilation and no provision for cooling. Heat, stench, fear of disease, and a desire to enjoy the beauties of nature, influenced a pattern of summer migration for those limited residents who had adequate means and leisure. During the hottest months, they left for attractive environs where ocean breezes and elm-shaded streets provided greater comfort, and where no bustle of commerce intruded upon their quiet. Lakes, ocean fronts, and mineral springs were logical tracts for expensive summer homes and large pleasure hotels. Such resorts and watering places began a growth of novelty and magnificence that extended throughout the nineteenth century, until luxury steamboats made European travel more attractive, and railroad and automobile transportation made all of America more accessible.

5. DOMESTIC TOURISM

Southern Literary Messenger, June, 1851

For years past, annually on the increase with the improved facilities of locomotion, setting in about the middle of the leafy month of June and reaching its flood in the dog-days, there has flowed northward a continuous stream of travel from the sunny region of the cotton-plant and the sugar-cane. This stream is swollen, at various points, as are the natural rivers of the country, by tributary rills and accidental accessions, though it sometimes reverses the order of nature in this—that it goes up to the mountains, while the torrents of the *Pluvii Hyades* descend always to the sea. Planters, with their families, flying from the malaria of their lowland estates to the breezy hillsides of a cooler latitude—professional men snatching a brief respite from their toilsome duties—merchants in quest of their regular supplies from the great cities—college boys larking in vacation—such are the classes, yet all wearing a generic resemblance as Southerners, which form the bulk of this tide of travel. The fairer portion of the throng—those dark-eyed daughters of a generous clime whom we used to see for a moment, *in transitu*, as they passed onward to Saratoga of the White Hills of New Hampshire—we may well represent as the gleaming sparkles that dance upon the crest of the wave.

Time was when this yearly migration, so far as it was connected with the seekers of pleasure at the watering places, was done, for the most part, in private vehicles. We can recollect the day, perfectly well, when the proprietor of Congress Hall strained his eyes wistfully at evening down the long vista of the Albany Road for the four-in-hand turn-out of the Carolina gentlemen, and when the rumbling of the wheels of one of those equipages created a sensation through every corridor of the building. The whistle of the locomotive had not yet been heard amid those quiet woods, nor had the cockneys monopolized the trout of Saratoga Lake. No internecine struggles for supremacy in Japonica-down, between the Browns and Smiths and Joneses, had ever interrupted the gaieties of the season. Fashion had not then erected her booths, along the quiet street of the village, nor imposed her laws upon the internal economy of the hotel. At that time, the Southern gentleman might take with him his dark body-servant Sam, without fear of having him stolen by the philanthropists of the North, and Caesar, the carriage-driver, might handle his ribbons unassailed by any pious attempts to dethrone him from his exalted station. The conservative, looking back to this happy period and contrasting it with the present condition of affairs, will perhaps say, in the true spirit of the *laudator temporis acti*, that the old time was decidedly the better.

But *nous avons changé tout cela*. We manage these things, in some respects, much more sensibly than our fathers. The private traveling carriage, at least beyond the line of Mason and Dixon, has had its day. The very expression of "slow coach" has become aphoristic, and we now whirl along after a steam engine which puffs its smoke into the most sacred haunts of muse and dryad, having for our fellow passengers five hundred people "of all ages, sexes and conditions." With the introduction of the rail into the non-slaveholding States, have also been brought forward more enlarged views of the rights of man, by reason of which the old family servants of the South are invariably stolen, should the Southern gentleman be imprudent enough to take them along, so that they must be left at home if a Northern watering-places is the point of destination. This little drawback upon the comfort of the Southern families traveling in the Northern States, together with the chance of getting a seat in the car, for your wife or your daughter, next to a runaway negro and the certainty of insult from abolition agitators has, in a great measure, checked the Southern travel in that direction, and turned the attention of our people to the long-neglected charms of their own upland section, the music of its waterfalls, the wild magnificence of its sierras, and the unequalled virtues of its perennial springs. There seems to be a growing determination to encourage domestic scenery and to bestow patronage upon home mountain atmospheres....

And here let us ask for what purpose it is that the more sensible portion of our summer ramblers leave their homes, when the mercury mounts up to ninety degrees in the thermometer! The answer is ready—for health and relaxation, that relaxation which is afforded by social intercourse with well-informed and well-behaved people, by pleasant variety of new sights and scenes, by communion with nature and entire freedom from the restraints of cities and the fashionable world. If we can show that these objects are most certainly attained in the mountain region of the Southern States, we shall establish our position that it is better to go there than to regions farther removed.

No one who is at all familiar with the daily routine of life at Newport or Saratoga can have failed to recognize the fact that it is but a dreary repetition of the dissipations of winter on the metropolis—with this difference to its disadvantage—that there one sees all the petty coteries of "society" brought together upon a theatre disagreeably narrow, each striving to outshine the other in dress and display. The languishing young gentlemen who creep out along the colonnade of the Ocean House, at eleven in the morning, belong to the same regiment of invincibles that has done such execution upon female hearts the previous season, in the glittering circles "above Bleecker"—are habited in the same coats and wear the same monotonous expression of weariness. The "fine looking women" are the same exquisite creachaws that held undisputed sway in "our set," and practise the same arts to catch moneyed husbands—showing off the steps of Saracco in the schottische but with a freedom of their own, and talking "an infinite deal of nothing" which is, if possible, more insipid than the small gossip of the dead parties of the winter gone by. The matchmaking mammas are brought into a contract that exhibits to great effect their bickerings and their diplomacy, and if a young foreigner with moustache and title should by chance be passing a few days at the hotel, their plots and counterplots to entrap him are infinitely amusing. If Madame Greatdasher of Fourteenth Street has gotten up a picnic at the Lake, and has found its appropriate column in the New York *Herald*, Mrs. Grand Splurge of Union Park must give a *fête champêtre* to cause the laurels of Greatdasher to wither and perish. Over these symposia, as indeed over all the arrangements of the place, fashion sits supreme and with her iron rule makes the whole season extremely uncomfortable....

The fact is these people go not to their watering-places for enjoyment or health, they go to make a sensation—and accordingly are careful to have their movements chronicled, in the daily papers, which obligingly inform us where the A--'s have gone, and what a magnificent figure the B--'s are cutting at such a place, and how much Miss C--'s ankle is admired somewhere else, with other items of intelligence, equally important, of the remaining one and twenty letters of the alphabet. And when a fancy ball is given, happy fellow, indeed the reporter! upon whom fall the sweetest smiles of two hundred young ladies, each anxious to secure the modicum of incense which is due to her charms, in the Springs' Correspondence of the next day's paper.

Some of our readers may suppose that our remarks bear with undue severity upon Northern watering-place society. In the absence of authority of this subject derived from books, we might make our appeal to the individual experience of every Southern gentleman who has been a summer lounger at either of the more fashionable places of resort for the *beau monde* of the Northern cities. For ourselves, we must say that whenever we have attended church service at Newport or Saratoga, during our loiterings there, we have felt (perhaps wickedly) inclined to throw an unusual emphasis into that supplication of the Liturgy—"From pride, vainglory, and hypocrisy; from envy, hatred and malice, and from all uncharitableness, good Lord deliver us."....

...Happily in the South it is different. At our summer retreats, we have neither the ostentation nor the toadyism, the jewels nor the jealousies, the vice nor the velvet, that deform and bespangle and set off the characters and the persons of the Northern notabilities. It is not our purpose to inquire into the causes of this difference; it may be, and most probably is owing to the institution of slavery, but the process of making this apparent is roundabout, and we care not now to pursue it. We thank Heaven that the fact is so. We rejoice that it has never been our ill fortune, in going to the White Sulphur, to fall in with any Lady Kicklebury such as Thackeray has drawn for us on the Rhine. Above all, we are thankful exceedingly that public sentiment among us does not sanction that prurient taste for newspaper celebrity which causes a young girl satisfaction in having her charms paragraphed as are the good points of a favorite race-horse. Our people do not care to inform the world how they eat and sleep and drive, and their daughters shrink yet from daily bulletins of their changes of toilette, with remarks of the comparative advantage of varying styles in displaying a fine bust or arm. Their amusements are, perhaps, primitive and the New Yorker, who has accidently wandered so far out of his orbit as to find himself in the mountain region of Virginia, declares the springs very stupid, laments the ignorance of the company in the last dances which he has seen at the *Salle Valentino* in Paris, and goes back wondering, by what evil destiny, he had come among a people in whose horrid society the Reporter of the *Herald* could no longer take cognizance of his movements....

...The White Sulphur Springs, though not so subjected to the tyranny of fashion as any of the haunts of the Northern circles, has been nevertheless, for many years, the gathering point of the most refined and cultivated people of our section of the Union. The very difficulties of getting there have had the happy effect of rendering the society more exclusive, and though the "pomps and vanities" do often manifest their influence over its *habitués*, yet mere pretension finds itself woefully out of place on Virginia or Alabama Row. The mode of living in cottages which obtains there, adds vastly to the comfort of visitors, and is far better than herding people together by the hundred under one roof. To the family circle it is like carrying their own vine and fig tree with them. They may be as secluded, or as much in the daily whirl of amusement as they please. And there are no more agreeable receptions any where than those impromptu little assemblages at nightfall, on the cottage porticoes, particularly when the moon lights up the whole lawn, and half reveals through the trees the white buildings that surround it. The ball room is not near enough to annoy with its din such as are not attracted by its fascinations, and the evening air of this healthful locality brings no poison on its wings. From the first of July until the frost-rime whitens the neighboring hill-tops, the observer will here see enough of character to engage him, if he is fond of the study, for character here, like the waters, is capable of analysis, while on every side, he has at ready command sources of recreation the most salutary and exhilarating. In the inviting umbrage of the trees around the spring, a spot which seems designed, in the fitness of things, for the consumption of cigars, he may puff the morning away in friendly chit-chat with judges, divines, M.C.'s, and other eminent individuals, and for the afternoon there are drives about the vicinage where he may dash with his curricle, or practise quadrupedal hexameters on horseback. Parties, too, are frequently made up for a deer-hunt, and those who engage in the sport have the advantage of witnessing the novel phenomena of day-break and sun-rise under the most favorable circumstances. The East seems streaked in that highland section with rosier dyes, as if aurora wished to reward such as are not accustomed to look upon her advent, with an exhibition of peculiar splendor. We like deer-hunts. Not that we are anything of a shot, for whenever we have engaged them, we have killed nothing but time, but there is a certain degree of luxury in being able to button up a warm shooting-jacket over your person in August, which, added to the auricular delight of the chorus of dogs, and the quiet self-assurance of your ability to have dropped the buck in his tracks, if he had only passed by your stand, make such expeditions in the highest degree pleasurable. We will not deny that we enjoy, too, the venison at dinner, for it is seldom that a party come back venisonless....

...We do not know how the fagged and faded inhabitant of Baltimore, Richmond or Petersburg can obtain as sudden a transition from a hot to cool atmosphere, as by taking the steamboat in June or July for Old Point. A few hours time will place him upon the beach where he may catch at evening the invigorating breeze that comes in from the Atlantic, and feel like a new man. There is indeed nothing to see at Old Point, apart from the extensive fortifications, but the waste of waters as it stretches out between Capes Charles and Henry, yet that "rapture by the lonely shore," which Lord Byron has sung in his immortal Spenserian verse, is a delight that does not pall. Often have we strolled for miles along the beach, playing with the advancing surge in very childishness, and drinking in the "music of its roar." And as the ships went by, or appeared as white specks upon the distant outline of the sea, we have loved to speculate upon their probable missions—how this one might have come from the Far East and laden with all precious merchandise, or that might be destined to plough the sunny main of the Marquesas, and what perils of the deep the one had safely passed through and the other was fated to encounter. Such idle fantasies as these are are best suited to the solitary walk, but for the social promenade with a fair companion, what *trottoir* at all comparable to the ramparts of the Fortress? Here you may walk a mile and a half in making the circuit, and for the greater part of the distance the ocean is before you. If the single gentleman should try this by moonlight, while the Military Band plays its inspiring airs within the Fort, and if he should chance to have as fascinating a partner as we have had there, he must be very little of an enthusiast if he does not "bless his stars and call it luxury."

But if it be worthwhile to look upon the sea, at the quiet hour of the gloaming, alone, or when, with a pretty woman for companion, you catch the shimmer of the moonbeam upon its placid surface, how much better to see it lashed in fury by the storm! Softly, good reader; we are not going to try our hand at a description of this phenomenon; we wish merely to say that perhaps there is not a place upon the Atlantic coast where the exciting play of wind and tempest may be seen to such advantage as at Old Point. The long, frantic procession of billows dashes into the Chesapeake with a fury that is indescribable. During the last summer we happened to witness, from this spot, the full energy of a violent Northeaster (the same which drove the bark Elizabeth upon Fire Island) and it was a sight to remember! The scuds of rain that you could see approaching with a rapidity beyond the flight of swiftest bird, the flakes of foam upon the beach, the sudden darkness that occasionally came athwart the sky, the Titanic violence of the waves, combined to form a scene at once of beauty and of terror. At such time it is not desirable to go out in a sail-boat. Indeed, we passed across Hampton Roads in a small steamer, during the fiercest of this gale, and though we had a capital opportunity to observe the wild magnificence of the angry element, we were very much of opinion with the Englishman who got wet at Niagara, that "certainly it was very well in its way, but that, on the whole he preferred looking at an hengraving of it in the 'ouse."

The Hotel building at Old Point is elegant and commodious, and has been recently transferred to new proprietors who have made, we learn, every arrangement for the comfort of guests during the current season....

WILLIAM L. SLOUT

6. WATERING-PLACE WORRIES

PUTNAM'S MAGAZINE, NOVEMBER, 1854

After withstanding, for these five years, the annual urgency of my wife and daughters for a peep at the seaward border of our great metropolis, during the season when all the world flies about "like thin clouds before a Biscay gale," I promised, in some desperate or happy moment, that the summer of 1854 should not pass away until I had given them a taste of the home ocean breezes, to say nothing of salt water and roasted clams, the proper dainties of such excursions. To tell the truth, I was myself not a little inspired by the animating images called up by the talk of my girls; and I fancied them walking on the beach, with good thick shoes, their fair hair blown back and tendrilling around their sun-bonnets, and their cheeks rosy with health, early hours, and exercise; or sporting in the surf, taking the wave with shouts of innocent laughter, and emerging round-headed and shining, like seals or porpoises, only to plunge again for fresh exhilaration. Who does not love to see his darlings enjoying themselves in the sports proper to their age, that "bring no afterthought of pain," but stores of health and gladness, and the power of cheering others? I consented with a good grace (my wife said, for once), and was as impatient for the day to come as the youngest of the party.

What pleased me, especially, and silenced the last doubt, was the reiterated assurance of wife and daughters, that nobody dressed at Rocky Branch. Not that an altogether Paradisiac state was intimated, but the expression was offered as a type of the utter indifference to outward adornment in which ladies visiting the sea-shore habitually indulge. "Why *should* they dress," my wife would emphatically ask. "Why should we dress just to run about the sand, or drive in a country wagon, or go fishing in a muddy boat?" Why, indeed! It was my own sentiment exactly. So we were all of one mind, and the third day of July was fixed upon as that of happy escape from the heat and noise of the city, the day commemorative of our national independence being unhappily now-a-days chosen by the "better classes" (!) to signalize their contempt for the rude pleasures of "the masses." *Quere*, whether this does not appear, to eyes looking upward, something like "kicking-down the ladder?"

But we had no time to philosophize. The business of the moment was to enjoy. The day being decided on, and the plan laid, I went to my office with renewed spirits, visions of rural repose and quiet throwing a golden haze over musty books and o'er-labored pen and ink.

It occasioned some slight shock to the fair fabric that had sprung up in my imagination, to find that the very next morning after the grand decision saw three dress-makers installed in our sewing-room; but as I had not been so silly as to take literally my wife's assertion that no dress was needed for a jaunt to the sea-shore, I made no remark, though I inwardly ejaculated a hope that the sojourn of these Parcae might be short, since much experience has taught me to class mantua-makers (*qu.* man-tormentors?) among the absorbents, in no commendatory sense. A day or two after, coming home to dinner exhausted, and perhaps a little cross, not a lady of the family was to be found, and it was ten minutes past five when Mrs. Q. and the

39

girls came in, like the Miss Flamboroughs, "all blowzed and red with walking," but rather silent (for awhile), and, to speak within bounds, in not much better humor than myself. This had the effect of what is called at the West a back-fire, which they kindle about the homestead to prevent that which approaches from the forest from becoming too destructive. My ill-humor was chastised and kept under by the evidence of disappointment and displeasure on the faces of my dear ones. I said nothing about having waited dinner, but only asked (mildly, I assure you) what had happened to disturb the newly-arrived.

This brought down a shower of words. All spoke at once, and it was not immediately that I could discover the source of unhappiness. But it resulted in this—Madame F. (celebrated for making loves of caps and darlings of bonnets) "says she cannot possibly get our hats done by the third, because all the Bloomingfords had already bespoken theirs; and the Gossins and the Tarnes theirs, a week ago. That's always the way with us! We leave everything till the last minute, and that's the reason we never can have anything like other people!"

This glanced rather sharply upon me, as my habitual reluctance to undertake expeditions of this nature—a reluctance, let me say, founded on much experience—had been the cause of delay in the present case. But I kept my temper, and took the blame meekly, simply observing that I had supposed in a case where no dress was needed, two weeks would afford ample time for preparation to pass three. This proved an unlikely venture, for my wife's feelings were deeply hurt at what she felt to be an imputation upon her well-known economy. Did I suppose she would buy a single thing for so short a sojourn that would not be useful—nay, necessary—afterwards? And my daughters—were there any girls in town that dressed so plainly, and with so little expense? Had not Caroline had her blue silk turned and made over and new-trimmed, at a cost of barely ten dollars, and Alida worn her mantilla ever since April? There was certainly no pleasure in going anywhere, unless we could look like other people!

Truths like these are never disputed by prudent husbands and papas, and from that time forward till the day of our migration, I never opened my lips on the subject of dress or dresses, nor my ears when bonnets, bracelets, cashmeres or cameos were in question.

My good wife on these occasions is less intent on deceiving me than herself. She desires in her heart to do the thing with little cost, and imagination draws a flattering picture of success which reality fails to fill out, making the forgotten accessories come to ten times as much money as the carefully counted must-have. What right have I to play the master, and try to substitute my wants and wishes for hers? We look at the matter from different points of view, and only the petty domestic tyrant forgets this. Thus I lectured myself, and resolved that no frowns of mine should embitter the taste of rural pleasure we had all promised ourselves.

All I stipulated for was that we should have no cumbrous loads of baggage, cramming our little lodging-rooms, and tormenting waiters and stage-drivers. O! certainly not, a few summer articles could not take much room; we would take a moderate trunk a piece. (I have generally found those single trunks to possess a good many branches.) Bathing-dresses were of course in request; and these it was proposed to make up in various economical ways, out of old materials; but afterwards my good wife, with her usual foresight, came to the conclusion that when one is getting a thing, it is by far the best economy to have it good; and so she purchased various brilliant stuffs and resplendent borderings for herself and the daughters, and a scarlet and orange outfit for myself; so that when, on the night before our departure, we tried on this "simple" gear, we looked fitter for a dance of witches or a bandit pantomime, than for sober bathers, who desire no spectators with better eyes than porpoises. But as I was told that "everybody" had such, I had not a word to say. Let me always do as "everybody" does!

The days of preparation completed, we found ourselves in a condition to set out—comfortably, my wife said—and the carriage came punctually, and New York waved her fiery sword behind us to chase us away. Two men, perspiring profusely, brought down a trunk about the size and shape of a two-story house, and as they rested it on the door-step, I could not but congratulate myself that my dear Sally, knowing my aversion to the care of a complication of movables, had put the family luggage into such a compact form; for, although bulky and heavy, it was but once, and all was over. The poor fellows could wipe their beaded brows, and go their ways. Alas! this House of Pride was but the advanced guard of an army of baggage—a trunk apiece and one extra—as good tea-makers put in a spoonful for each of the company and one for the pot. O for the days of trunk hose, when a man could carry in his pockets wearables and eatables (if Hudibras is to be trusted), enough for a tolerable campaign! Mrs. Parkington didn't wonder that there were "trunk railways," nor do I. Our army of trunks was attended by a whole park of flying artillery in the shape of band-boxes. I demurred a little at this; but as each particular piece that I proposed to leave behind, held, as I was assured, something essential to the comfort and respectability of the trip, I was fain to make the best of it, especially as my daughters declared, with one breath, that the array was absolutely nothing compared with what Mrs.-- and her two daughters took with them for a single week at Rocky Branch.

After all—I philosophized to myself, as usual—though we make so much selfish outcry at the trouble occasioned by female paraphernalia, should we be the gainers if they took us at our word, and left behind and out of use all those delicate and characteristic superfluities that contribute to make more obvious the distinction between man and woman? Should we enjoy travelling and visiting with ladies who carried only a spare suit apiece? Do we covet the companionship of strong-minded women, who delight in broadcloth and leather, or fast women, who go out to tea in riding-habits, and carry switches instead of fans? If there should be a ball at Rocky Branch, and my daughters had to stay home for want of evening dresses, would the remembrance that we had travelled without band-boxes console me for their loss of pleasure?

Thus I reasoned after my fashion, and soon found that the seemingly great difficulties were not able to destroy my pleasure, and determined they should not, by my means, interfere with that of others.

I need hardly say that, to a man like myself, tied, from year's end to year's end, to the dull routine of business life, a journey of even twenty miles is no small pleasure. The very crossing of the ferry, to which my ordinary affairs never call me, was a delight. When I gazed upon our lovely bay and its islands, and felt the fresh breeze that had "been out upon the deep at play," I was ready to wonder that anybody should ever wish to go further for health or pleasure. My heart swelled and my eyes overflowed, as I contemplated the splendid aspect of my native town, the evidences of her prosperity, the promise of her future pre-eminence. Even London herself, queen of the world's commerce and intelligence, scarcely reposes her river-shores with more magnificent effect, though London is the work of two thousand years as New York is of two hundred. No city on earth possesses such unlimited natural advantages as ours, such as no amount of misgovernment and desperate shameless corruption can—

Here my wife whispered to me that she hoped I saw the Z-- family on board, with new travelling dresses that threw ours completely into the shade; a fact which I was fain to receive on authority, for the most dutiful scrutiny on my part failed to discover the superiority of our neighbors' outfit. I believe Mrs. Z-- had one more bow on her bonnet than my wife, and the Misses Z-- higher heels to their little, ugly, brown boots than my daughters to their ditto, but further I could not penetrate. There must have been something, however, for it considerably dampened the spirits of our party for some time.

Once seated in the rail-car, after our *impedimenta* had been safely stowed and ticketed, I had leisure to observe the various individuals and groups that were, like ourselves, setting out for the country—many of them well-dressed merchants and lawyers, to whom a peculiar air of domesticity and kindliness was imparted by the various baskets, parcels, and flasks of which many of them were the bearers, as they returned to their expectant families after the labors of the day. My imagination followed them to their rural homes, more or less elegant, and pictured gentle, loving wives and fair daughters, awaiting their return in vine-shaded porches, while the setting sun covered the landscape with a tender glow, like the flush of a sweet welcome. I rejoiced that so many of our men of business provide these pleasant homes for their families, far from the city's noise and dust, and at least somewhat removed from the city's hardening influences. The weariness of some of the faces about served to enhance the expression of the scene, for it suggested most forcibly the sweetness of repose, and the value and happiness of these country homes. One by one, and group by group, we dropped the home-goers, and at length my pleasant reveries were broken by the sight of a long row of uncouth vehicles drawn up at the side of the platform, and labelled in every variety of lettering and illustration that the taste and means of the painters allowed. I was quite amused with these anomalous carriages and the throng that hurried towards them, but my wife put to flight my quiet thoughts, by an exclamation that we were losing all the best places, and might even find ourselves without any places at all, if we did not make a rush and take care of our rights. So on we dashed, a pell-mell, elbowing and elbowed, crowding into seats and being turned out again by somebody's assertion of a prior claim; until, at last, I thought we were finally, if not fairly, squeezed into some very uncomfortable nooks and corners, when it was suggested that all the trunks and band-boxes were still standing on the platform, and that I had very much failed in escort duty, in not having seen them properly bestowed outside before I buried myself in the interior. I tried to do the necessary shouting from a window, but the lady who occupied it remained, as it seemed, totally unconscious of my desire, and I was, after all, obliged to drag myself and my boots through the flounces of two or three others until I reached the scene of the *melée*, when I found the last piece of luggage had just been hoisted to the top. Once more I had to pass the frowning ordeal, amid the crush of skirts and the artillery of indignant eyes, before I could subside into the welcome obscurity of the corner, and take up the thread of my thoughts, woefully frayed by the last rub. Yet I could not help being amused at the impudence that provided and stowed such carriages, and the simplicity that endured them; and after I had sagely asked myself if this was what is called "Pleasure," I more wisely answered the question in the affirmative, since the occupation of my own thoughts with those trifles, had already served, I was conscious, to smooth some of the ruts of care, and rub out a few of the wrinkles of application. Counter-irritation is an important agent of medication—of the old school, yet homeopathic—and I acknowledged its good effects. Not so Mrs. Q. and the girls. Jam is not good for ladies' *crinolines*, and the crowded state of the coach certainly threatened the fashionable orbicular contour of skirts too severely not to have some effect upon the brows of the wearers. It was plain that the balm of the rural quiet had not yet begun to make itself felt among us. The coach was like the branch of a tree on which bees are swarmed, and the heat and the buzz were worse than Wall Street. Green plains, dotted with trees, lay everywhere around us, a perpetual soothing platitude, like some companionships. Here and there would be seen an old-fashioned farm-house, with its grass-plot and honeysuckles, and, perhaps, a maid with a milk-pail; but the landscape had no points more salient than these. The fields grew sandier and more thinly covered as we neared the ocean; the sea-breeze met us with a flurrying welcome and with it came a cloud that we were not at all disposed to welcome—composed of myriads of mosquitoes that had evidently come a long journey, by the keenness of their appetites. In vain the ladies veiled their faces, and the gentlemen plied their handkerchiefs. Piquant were the attentions of the newcomers, and rather impatient the gestures with which we attempted to repel them, while it was provokingly suggested by an old stager that if we had only rubbed our faces and hands with camphorated spirits just before we started, we should have been of far less danger of blotches. This might not be true; but it annoyed us to think it might. One of the greatest comforts under misfortunes is to think it inevitable; and I have always dreaded those good people who feel it their duty to show you, when it is too late, how easily what ruffles you might have been avoided. Instruction is valuable, but it should be well-timed; one does not care much about the future while suffering from the mosquito-bites of life.

The last expanse of bare sand having been passed, we drew up before a piazza long enough for St. Peter's, the roar of ocean in our ears, and its wind stimulating every nerve. I sprang out of my troglodytish nook with a feeling of delightful relief, and Mrs. Q. and the girls forgot their annoyances, and inhaled the new life with evident pleasure. The breeze was now quite too much for the mosquitoes, who lack the parasitic power to "pursue the triumph, and partake the gale." They disappeared, and we felt with delight that we had only to find our rooms and bestow our movables, and then return to enjoy the evening among the motley company that thronged the piazza, which, to our tired eyes, wore the appearance, at the moment, of a disjointed rainbow, swaying and fluttering in the breeze.

Here, it will be perceived, an important item had been momentarily forgotten—the evening meal, rendered a matter of consequence by the journey and the sea-air, to say nothing of the depletory labors of the mosquitoes. But of that anon.

We found rooms considerably larger than those recesses in which refractory nuns used to be immured, and most carefully excluded from every sight and sound of the ocean, though not from the odors and din of the kitchen and stables. To the narrowness of our lot we submitted, as we best might, but to the total absence of what we had most particularly come to enjoy, we demurred a little; our remonstrates, however, were at once silenced by the intelligence that we must have these rooms or none, as all the seaward ones were already engaged by "permanent boarders," or for their friends. Indeed, before we got fairly settled, we began to feel quite like intruders. Everything was pre-engaged by the "permanent boarders."

Our rooms were entirely destitute of wardrobes and bureaux, as the "permanent boarders" had required all that had been provided for us. Even our washing apparatus, woefully scanty at best, had been sifted by the lady on the opposite side of the entry, who had come with seven children and three nurses, for the summer, so that we were fain to borrow and lend sundry articles usually thought indispensable. We rang and rang in vain to have these deficiencies remedied, for as far as we could discover, the "permanent boarders" required all the servants as well as all the furniture of the house.

This was quite a new aspect of hotel life for my experience. I had always considered an inn or boarding-house a place of equal rights—where each inmate, paying his way, had as good a right to whatever his habits required as his neighbor. But my wife and daughters decided that this was always the way at such places, and that to expect anything else only betrayed our want of fashionable habitudes. The only way, she said, to secure any comfort at Rocky Branch was to take the best apartments for the entire season.

Before we were half settled in our closets, the gong howled, and we hurried down to tea, not, however, quickly enough to find anything but bread and butter upon the table. There had been fruit, as we saw by the plates of our neighbors, but when we desired a share, we were politely told that it was all gone. The lady with seven children had, I should judge, concluded that her first duty was to provide for her family, and, accordingly, divided everything within reach among them. At least I could not help noticing, at the close of the meal, that the little dears had not been able to devour half she had endowed them with. For myself, I wanted specially seafare, so I asked for some roasted clams, which I saw much relished by several gentleman who seemed as hungry as I felt; but alas! I only touched the old string. All the roasted clams had been absorbed by the "permanent boarders," and I was obliged to content myself with a slice of cold ham.

But the fine air that we were to enjoy on the piazza till bed-time soothed our irritation, and made us forget for the time all meaner wants. We promenaded till we were tired, among the ladies whose ornamentation reminded me of that of ships of the line on gala days, and gentlemen flaming all over with gilt buttons, diamond brooches, and cigars, and then found a corner to sit down, thinking no sight so fine as the rising moon, no music so delightful as the roar of ocean.

We were scarcely seated when a piteous shriek reached my ears, and I jumped, thinking some unfortunate cat or dog had been trodden upon in the parlor. I found, however, that it was only the beginning of a favorite Italian song, with which a young lady was favoring a circle of her fashionable friends. I looked in at the window for a moment; but the poor girl appeared in such distress that I could not bear to see her contortions of face and person, though I was assured she was only singing in opera style. I thought within myself—"*Hic labor, hoc opus est*"— but I said no such word, believe me; I felt more like knocking down some coarse young men, who were quizzing her unmercifully, as they walked up and down the piazza, looking in at the windows.

By the way, and let me say it here, as I dare say it nowhere else, by what strange perversion of nature and taste is it that music, meant by Almighty Providence for the soothing and sweetening of poor human nature, has become, in our time, a laborious thing—a thing of exhibition and emulation? There is, indeed, a class who must make music a labor—those who practise it as a profession; but why do our young ladies feel it necessary to imitate these people? It seems to me rather humiliating that a few imported opera singers and pianists have the power to effect a domestic revolution in this respect, so that the present object of singing and playing is no longer the pleasure of husbands and fathers, and little brothers and sisters, and the home circle generally; but the imitation of Signora So-and-so and Herr This-or-that, who may have the public by the ears. I have felt sometimes that I should enjoy playing St. Dunstan to some of these sublime gentry, whom I regard with about as much affection as the saint felt for this infernal adversary.

I do not complain that the girls sing Italian songs, or play elegantly, but only that their inducement is a mean and not a generous one; the excessive labor required by the new standard absorbs much of the interest and attention due to other things, and that it is difficult for them to condescend to please the vast majority of their hearers, who desire something simpler and more easily comprehended. If one succeeds in obtaining a ballad or a sweet English song, it is so bedeviled with incongruous graces, that it is, after all, no more than a very insipid hybrid, lacking both the homesweetness we covet and the scientific perfection that the Italian music is so prized for.

I do not pretend to be a connoisseur in music, but I will yield to no man in my appreciation of what makes home happy; and I know, to an absolute certainty, that to sing like a dog whose tail has been trodden on, or even like an indignant or melancholy cat, is not the music of the home circle, though it may obtain white-gloved applause in company, or the envious commendations of those whose organs are less docile. To me, the cold, staring circle that gathers round the fashionable performer looks like a committee employed to test the pretensions of a fire annihilator, or a crowd watching the progress of a dog-fight in the street, with not the least personal interest in the result. Is there not a sad blunder somewhere—in the heart or head?

...The next morning saw us on the alert for breakfast, determined to be ready at the first sound of the gong, before the "permanent boarders" had had time to make a locust progress over the eatables. But we missed it again; for there was a fixed determination on the part of the waiters not to bring on anything but the commonest fare until the favored class saw fit to descend from their rooms. In vain I asked for oysters and chickens; the first seemed to be in the vasty deep, and the others would not come when I did call for them; so we breakfasted humbly on ham and eggs, with bread by no means sweet, and butter that would have been too much for its parent cow. But we did not mind it much, for we were going to bathe.

Here was a fine day for the surf; the sky a little veiled, but the breeze full of balm, and the numerous guests that dropped by in twos and threes till they filled the tables, promising a gay time. We retired from the field just as the broiled chickens came in, and walked the piazza a while, waiting for the hour at which it was fashionable to go to the beach. Here were polychromatic morning dresses in abundance, and innumerable puppies and children, whose gambols occupied pretty much the whole space. I observed that most of the permanents soon disappeared, but thought little of the matter until, on inquiring for places in the vehicle provided for those who wished to go to the beach, I found it had already started, being primarily at command of the favored class, with their *bonnes* and children, dogs and baskets.

"It will soon be back," said my informant, consolingly; "it does not take them more than an hour," but as this included the top of the tide, we felt a little put out, especially as we ascertained that the huge old lumbering vehicle had not been quite filled, the permanent ladies not liking to admit strangers.

We got down after a while, however, just as most of the dripping and frolicking was over for the day, and with rather tamed enthusiasm, sought bathing houses in which we might prepare for the water. But not only were most of the bathing-houses "private," but unhappily those who had bathed were now dressing, and we were obliged to walk up and down in the deep sand, under a broiling sun, while one and another of the *habitués* arrayed himself or herself with (as it seemed to us) uncommon deliberation, after which we enjoyed the privilege of bathing alone, with the tide half out and the surf quite subsided.

"What shall we do with our bathing dresses, Papa?" my little Dora called from her sentry-box, the door of which was off its hinges, and had to be lifted bodily every time the occupant of the sentry-box wished to pass.

Here again I was at fault. The knowing ones had packed their wet garments in the wagon which had now gone up for the last time, and I was fain to confide ours to an old sea-dog in red flannel, who professed to assist bathers, though he was reputed always to make for the shore when there was the least alarm. (The next morning when we came down to the beach we had the pleasure of finding all our various and partycolored gowns and trousers made spread eagles of, on the broadside of a shed under which the ladies and gentlemen were in the habit of reposing and cracking jokes at odd hours.)

But, not to get before my story, at dinner, after our first bath, I observed with no little uneasiness that my wife and daughters, who had professed themselves hungry enough to eat even the poor leavings (on the dishes), of the "permanents," touched scarcely anything, and after a few whispers among themselves, sat silent and relatively unhappy. When the dessert came on, I made desperate dives after spoonfuls of various puddings that were passing towards the head of the table, and once came nearly to blows with the waiter, who snatched from my hand a tolerable tart that I had in my secret mind appropriated to my family's wants. But though the war thus resolutely carried on was not without its trophies, in the shape of sundry little spots of sweet things on our plates, no relaxation of the gloom on each side of me was discernible. I inquired in anxious whispers, but the thing was evidently not of a nature to bear talking about. I secured three almonds a piece, and some of the loose raisins that remained in the fruit-dishes after all the bunches had been snatched to load the plates of a row of children, with large bows on their shoulders and their hair excessively bandolined; and very soon after, obeyed my wife's signal of withdrawal, longing to know what unhappy contretemps could have occurred beyond and besides all the petty vexations I had already become cognizant of, only a part of which I have attempted to describe here.

In a remote corner of the great dining room, out of hearing of the "permanents," who already occupied, either in person or by proxy, every window that faced out to the sea which we had all come to look at, the sad truth came out. It had been discovered that all the stylish people—all who went from home often enough to know what other people did—wore *masks* while bathing, so that we, ig-nora-muses convict, protected by nothing better than huge *flats* that we would blow about—had burned our faces red, while the knowing ones were fair and calm as a summer morning, quite at leisure to stare at our tell-tale rudiness, and to conjecture that we had emerged from the submarine regions of East Broadway or Henry Street, into which, the doings of the New York great world are longer in penetrating, than the original rumors from Paris take in crossing the Atlantic to the happier imitators in Fifth Avenue.

Here was a horror. The thing was done; there was no help for it. No application of oiled silk, or Indian rubber, or even a *papier maché*, would now avail. Nothing could touch us further! Our three weeks would not clean us of the stain. The red would turn brown after a day or two, and the skin must either peel off, like bad stucco, or wait in leathern pertinacity for the slow process of natural wear and tear. My bright Alida, who is always a little brown, declared she should not be fit to be seen all the winter; and when I hinted that I did not think a shade more or less would be noticed in her complexion, she did not seem at all comforted. Caroline, who had light hair and blue eyes, felt that she was a peculiar sufferer, because if a *blond* is not lily fair, she is nothing. Dora did not mind the matter so much, for she is a lively little gipsy, and can get fun out of anything; but Mrs. Q. was so seriously hurt, that I could not, as a good husband, do less than let her lay all the blame on my shoulders, where, indeed, it generally alights by hook or crook. In truth, I consider this a covert accomplishment, both to my good nature and to my importance in the family; and the habit of blaming me in private has the advantage of enabling my wife always to be perfectly amiable in company.

All I could propose was, that since the misfortune had happened, we must only make the best of it; and to this end I suggested that the next best thing to being fair was being good-humored and lively, laughing off what is inevitable, and turning our attention to the rural enjoyments, for which we had expressly come. I thought the girls had better dash out and behave as the other young ladies did, *i.e.*, as if there were nobody in the world but themselves.

"Nonsense!" my wife said. The girls were not fast girls, nor couldn't be. It wasn't their style; and besides, they hadn't brought even their riding-habits, or whips or dogs. Caroline had a guitar at home, to be sure, but even if she had it here, she could not muster courage to play unasked, among so many strangers. Elinor had a Fanny-Kemble suit, that she had had for the woods a year or two since, when she went to Uncle John's, in the wilds of Albany County; but what could she do with it on the beach, where the winds were always blowing in that violent, unmeasured sort of way? Dora was naturally a romp; but where was the use, where we didn't know any young men? We never went anywhere—never did as other people did—were really unfitted for good society, &c., &c., &c.

Upon this, the ladies all betook themselves to their rooms, while I, full of regret at their various disappointments, lighted my invariable after-dinner cigar, and walked up and down the piazza for an hour or two, jostled on every hand, but pondering the whole subject of these summer sojourns, and marvelling within myself whether these things must be so, now and for ever.

Can there be no rural retreats for us o'erlabored citizens, driven from our homes by heat and dust, and natural desire of variety—wherein may be found comfort, repose, amusements, and wholesome air and food, instead of the poor, ill-managed, partial, scrambling (I had almost said swindling), uncomfortable, and ruinously-expensive abiding-places, which are now denominated fashionable? I know there are farm-houses, so-called, where one can find quiet, but nothing else; neither amusement, nor comfort, nor even country-fare, since every atom of first-rate provisions is sent to the great cities. But these are not what we need. They too often swindle on a small scale, as the greater humbugs do on a large one; that is to say, they take your money without rendering or seeking to render a just and equal return, or planning for anything but the filling of their own pockets, trusting to your patience, and the natural reluctance to "make a fuss," by returning to town before the specified time of endurance has elapsed. The grander take-ins not only give you poor living and uncomfortable lodging, and allow all the comforts and advantages there might still be found to be usurped by certain people, who seem never to reflect that their grasping selfishness amounts to absolute dishonesty; but they are kept in such a way as to encourage a rude and loose, if not vicious tone, especially among the young men who frequent them, till the whole air seems, to the sensitive apprehension of the father of a family, unfit for the breathing of wives and daughters.

If it be said that the proprietors and heads of these large establishments cannot be answerable for the manners of their guests, I reply that if the favor of arrogant and overbearing people were not especially courted, the whole state of things would be very different, and quiet and respectable families could enjoy the sea-side without being starved or insulted for the sake of those less scrupulous than themselves. We all know very well that ladies are rather unmanageable—(none better than I!)—but no one should be allowed to usurp the rights of others, and the evil is by no means solely ascribable to the female portion of these partial and ill-conducted households. That this is winked at, if not planned, at many of our so-called fashionable places of summer resort, is past all denial, and hundreds grumble at it every year without thinking of a remedy.

But the question recurs—where are we to go for seaside recreation?

After much cogitation, as I promenaded the piazza with a hundred others, yet alone, for my dear ones were still pouting upstairs, I thought I would try my unpractised pen on a little sketch of a corner of our vexations, and send it to *Put-*

nam, as we put an advertisement to the newspaper, trusting that the operation of the well understood law of demand and supply, might, before next summer, induce some of our enterprising citizens to get up a real family hotel, at once elegant and comfortable, where all who pay alike shall be treated alike, and whence every shadow of partiality and exclusiveness shall be carefully excluded. I put my name down first on the list, for a suite of rooms looking on the ocean.

Perhaps I am only wanting a chance to try my own grasping powers!

7. LIFE AT LONG BRANCH

by Olive Logan
HARPER'S MAGAZINE, SEPTEMBER, 1876

Long Branch is like the lady's foot of *Punch's* shoe-maker—remarkably long and narrow. The fashionable watering-place reaches from Financier Jay Gould's cottage on the north to President Grant's cottage on the south, a distance of two or three miles, and somewhat suggests a carpenter's set scene at the theatre; it is painted on a straight piece of canvas: what is behind it, the audience neither knows nor cares. Those who have taken the trouble to look behind the scenes at Long Branch—a proportion of the great public which bears about the same relation to the mass that the actors, scene-shifters, and other employees of the theatre do to the public in the auditorium—are aware that there is a little New Jersey village back there, with some pretty farms and parks, a race-track, and a few such trifles. But the crowds which come and go in the season, on pleasure bent, do not for the most part take cognizance of anything but the gay scene along the shore, with its straggling hotels and abundance of piazza looking ever out to sea. The popular drive is along the beach road called Ocean Avenue, which is the main artery, the Broadway, the Boulevard, of the "summer capital." It has been a newspaper fashion to call Long Branch the American Brighton, but a Brighton it certainly is not, and will never be until the barn-like frame buildings which serve it as hotels are pulled down and others erected of a material more solid, substantial, and imposing. It is these sprawling wooden structures which give to Long Branch that cheap and tawdry air, that gingerbread appearance, at which solid old Newport and substantial Saratoga sniff with scorn. If there is any lover of Long Branch who does not accept the theatrical scene-painter illustration as befitting, he has the alternative of confessing that the place is very suggestive of a circus. When the dinner train arrives from town—the last of the day—just at that delicious hazy hour of mid-summer eve when the sun is gone but the dusk not fairly come, and Ocean Avenue is lively with fast-flying horses, driven by men in livery—sometimes as gaudy as those of the equine dramatic tent—conveying loads of human freight to places of residence, cottage, hotel, or boarding-house; when numberless flags in brightest red, white, and blue flutter from liberty-poles on lawns and hotel-tops; when brass-bands blare on the grassy lawns, and here and there side-show-like tents for the sale of pop and gingerbread, or practice with air-guns at striped targets, flap their canvas sides in the breeze from the swashing sea—indeed, the whole thing is irresistibly suggestive of sawdust and a ring, and one looks about instinctively for the red-lipped clown, and listens for the merry "Houp la!" of the riders. The bands and the flags and the fast-flying horses are no doubt intended by the inn-keepers, who principally plan and shape the manners and customs here, to awaken a mad feeling of hilarity in the bosom of the arriving guest; but they are destructive to the sentiment of quiet and elegant repose which should no doubt inspire the existence of an altogether high-toned summer resort.

Long Branch is *sui generis*; and it is perhaps better in accord with the spirit of American institutions than any other of our watering-places. It is more republican than either Newport or Coney Island, because within its bounds extremes of our life meet more freely. It is not so aristocratic as Newport, yet the President of the United States lives there, and so do many other prominent examples of our political, literary, artistic, commercial, and social life. It is not so democratic as Coney Island, yet the poorer and more ignorant classes are largely represented throughout the season. On hot Sundays there come to Long Branch great throngs of cheap excursionists, small tradesmen and artisans with their families, with a sprinkling of roughs and sharpers—just such throngs as also go to Coney Island on the same day. Long Branch has equal attractions for rich and poor. It is quite astonishing with what ease the millionaire can get rid of dollars there, and it is almost equally astonishing what cheap and comfortable quarters are at the command of the humblest purses. The same magnificent sea view which is put so heavily in the bill of the lodger on the first floor of the big hotels can be enjoyed by the poorer lodger near the roof of the cheaper houses at a comparatively insignificance cost. If there are great taverns where one pays four or five dollars a day, with huge extras for special rooms and luxuries, there are also cheap hotels and even German Gasthausen where poorer folk can live. If there are elegant cottages for Presidents and merchant princes and railway kings, there are also abundant boarding-houses for people who count their pennies carefully before spending them. Some of the most crushing dandies who loaf in the parlor door at the fashionable hotels when the Saturday night "hop" is on, faultless in attire and killingly eyeglassed and mustached, might be traced to humble abodes in the back region behind the theatrical scene when they saunter homeward in the hour approaching midnight. They sometimes condescend to join the dancers on the floor, and they bathe at the fashionable hour with great assiduity, but where they eat and sleep can only be conjectured. They are just as well-bred, well-mannered, and well-appearing gentlemen as any at Long Branch, and are just as well received by what is there called society.

Long Branch further illustrates a side of American character in the fact that it is a direct result of business energy, enterprise, shrewdness, and "push." It did not grow up slowly, year by year, an outcome of the natural fitness of things, as Brighton did, and as Dieppe and Trouville did—nay, as Newport and Saratoga did. As things go in this country, Newport and Saratoga are old. They figured in the Revolutionary period, and were even known as watering-places as far back as 1800—further, perhaps. But Long Branch is as striking an example of rapid growth in its way as Chicago itself is. Twenty years ago it had no fashionable existence, which is only saying it had no existence at all. There was nothing there but a lonely stretch of sandy shore, against which the surf beat unhonored and unsung. If the slow-going villager back under the trees there, a mile from the beach, had been told that Long Branch was the future great marine suburb of the great metropolis, he would no doubt have smiled incredulous. And even now one seeks in vain for the reason why this particular spot was chosen for this purpose, until his seeking brings him to the simple truth that certain speculators willed it so, and set about making their scheme a reality by those methods which are so well known to the builders of paper cities in this country. They willed that the tide of New York's summer-resort seekers should pass by the charming Highlands of the Navesink, which now blink dully at the long whizzing trains flitting past them five or six times a day, loaded down with merry throngs all the summer through. Along the road from Sandy Hook to Long Branch lie beautiful little villages which have their yearly throng of summer patrons, but they are not "the Branch," and their strongest recommendation as watering-places is that they are within easy driving distance of the summer capital. The glory and gain of transforming Long Branch from a deserted stretch of New Jersey coast into *the* sea-side city of to-day, and of familiarizing its name to the popular ear to such an extent that Chicago itself is not more celebrated, undoubtedly rest with a few capitalists, who bought farms in Monmouth County for thirty or forty dollars an acre, and set about turning their corn fields into villa plots. Easy enough to do this much on paper, but to make the public buy the plots was something calling for ability and energy of the first order. A scheme of advertising was adopted, brave, expensive, and perilous, by which the place was persistently brought before the public attention summer after summer. The ubiquitous correspondent of the daily press was sent down to report. It was not a very fascinating spot in those early days, but the reporter who can not write an attractive letter merely because there is nothing attractive to write about has mistaken his vocation. A vivid imagination, a touch of Thackeray's wit and Dicken's inventive genius, are much more valuable in a watering-place correspondent than the mere photographic faculty of reproducing facts. To "call a spade a spade" is fatal to the charms of letters from the sea-side, especially if the place be dull and uninteresting. There were as many charming letters from Long Branch when it was dull and uninviting as now when it is animated and attractive in the season. By one device and another, legitimate and illegitimate, by building a new railroad, by improvements of various sorts, and diverse plans for attracting public attention to their pet and pride, the capitalists forced the growth of the place in public appreciation, and achieved a veritable *coup d'ètat* when they induced President Grant to go and live there in the summer. Long Branch became the summer capital, and its fortune was made. The villa plots sold like the proverbial hot-cakes. The hotels built huge additions to themselves, and all the world rushed to sleep in them. Those who had money in their pockets found it burning most uncomfortably there until they had bought a villa plot, or a corner of a farm, or an old house that could be turned into a summer-seat. Many outsiders made large sums by buying this week to sell the next at an enormous advance. Lots that one summer sold for $500 were held the following summer at $5000. Every body was elated, excited; there was Champagne in the air; and life was gay and fascinating to residents as to the going and coming crowd. The summer capital was a success.

There have been unfavorable comments made upon the President's course in accepting his handsome cottage by the sea, and for living in it a portion of his time in summer; but the American public must always have something it can scold Presidents for, and I do not suppose General Grant slept less soundly, lulled by the murmur of the waves upon the beach, because of his critics. Probably Presidents get used to being scolded. From Washington's time to the present, they have all had a goodly share of the thing. The city of Washington is not the healthiest or pleasantest of abodes during the fierce heats of July and August, and others than our present Chief Magistrate have avoided it as much as duty would allow. Thomas Jefferson spent some months of each year at his remote home of Monticello, on top of a woody Virginian hill, while he was occupying the Presidential office; and Monticello in his day was further from Washington than Long Branch is in this Centennial year. The rumbling old gig in which Jefferson trundled to and fro between Washington and Charlottesville did not accomplish its journey of a hundred and odd miles in as little time as the palace-car now takes to pass over the two hundred and odd miles between Washington and Long Branch. And although axe-grinders no doubt followed even Jefferson to his sky-perched retreat, it need hardly be said that he was, while there, far less capable of attending to the business of the government than Grant is in his sea-side home. It is a lovely home; and when the President sits on his back piazza of a summer evening to smoke his after-dinner cigar, with his gentle and amiable wife and his comely children about him, it is a sight which no lover of his country need feel uneasy at seeing. At such time, doors and windows all wide open, and the interior furnishing glimpses of a comfortable but not a showy home, with pictures and books about and lamps burning, perhaps a group of carriages will come rolling down the road from the hotel region, and a crowd of friends and fellow-citizens, with a band of music, will invade the lawn. Then the dulcet strains of a serenade will rise on the evening air, and the family group will sit listening, to break into a little ripple of applause now and then, and Mrs. Grant, leaning over the piazza railing, will chat familiarly with whomsoever chances to be standing near and press her visitors to come in. "Do come in," I once heard her say on such an occasion; "we can give you a cracker at least in our little cot." Simple, unpretentious, and kindly, a scene like this is worthy to live in the records of our republican land, a type of its best spirit.

In the vicinity of President Grant's home are the cottages of a number of people more or less known to fame. Conspicuous among these are several members of the theatrical profession—a class of people usually clannish, and avoiding familiarity with the world outside its own ranks. The time has gone by when the members of this profession were classed with the Ishmaelites and Bohemians of society, and those who have been so fortunate as to penetrate to the friendly acquaintanceship of the actors in their homes at Long Branch have found the domestic altar as charmingly surrounded as in any homes in the land. The cottages and hotels at Long Branch are built very much alike in essential details—that is to say, as much like "all out-doors" as possible—with abundance of piazza stretching on every side, and often on every story; with large windows, wide halls, and airy rooms. The cottages occupied by the dramatic fraternity present no features differing from others, unless it be a superiority in the matter of interior adornment. Their luxury in this respect is, indeed, in several cases very striking, the reason for it being partly, perhaps, that the players have no town homes, as a rule, their winters being mostly passed in traveling, and dwelling in hotels. So their summer homes, to which they hie for rest as soon as their "season" of active labor is over, become in a peculiar sense dear to them. One of the most conspicuous examples of the luxury of these homes is furnished in the cottage owned and occupied by Maggie Mitchell, "The Cricket." She owns a number of cottages and farms at Long Branch; the one in which she dwells was built by Edwin Booth, and in its large parlor he was married. It is profusely ornamented within with paintings, statuary, *objets d'art*, rare and costly volumes, and especially with quaint and beautiful articles of Japanese manufacture. Among her books is one of the three copies of Boydell's 1793 edition of Shakespeare—a huge volume containing a hundred steel plates, and valued at several hundred dollars. A striking picture of an English village, with a crowded mass of picturesque houses, an ivy-hung church, an antique bridge, and a crumbling castle, is Knaresborough, in Yorkshire, where the actress's mother was born. All the evidences of an affectionate domestic spirit are abundant in this little artist's abode; and the same is true of the other homes of the player folk at Long Branch. Children make merry in their roomy halls; gray-haired parents sit at the hospitable board; the house-dog barks and the chickens cluck and the cattle low about these homes as about the homes of other good and gentle people. For the most part they are somewhat remote from the gay scene which looks on the sea, where Pleasure holds her court in hotel parlors, on the lawns where the brass-bands blare, and up and down the drive. The players rather favor a quieter mode of life in summer than that which is popular with the majority of visitors to Long Branch. They like to be near it, but they are seldom of it. Their time is passed in home hospitalities, in the entertainment of their friends, in reading the long summer hours away in their piazzas or lolling in tree-swung hammocks, and in driving about the country in cozy family carriages, rather than in the feverish atmosphere of fashionable ball-rooms, the daily gambol in the surf, or the exciting delights of the gaming table.

A flavor of Baden-Baden, as it was in the days before gambling was prohibited, is furnished at Long Branch by Chamberlin's club-house, an elegant "cottage"—for every building is a cottage here, unless it is a hotel—situated within a stone's-throw of the West End Hotel, and within sight of the President's home. (The "West End" at Long Branch, it may be explained in passing, is, in fact, the south end, and the "East End" is the north end, so complacently does fashion ignore points of the compass in its nomenclature.) In the club-house there are tables for roulette, *rouge et noir*, and other games of chance, and I am told the scene late at night, when the place is thronged with Wall Street men and other skillful skirmishers with the goddess of luck, is a very brilliant one; but unlike the gaming *salons* of Baden-Baden, the gentler sex do not mingle in the scene at Chamberlin's. Those ladies who wish to indulge their passion for winning and losing at hazard can do so on stated days at Monmouth Park—a racing ground a short drive back in the country, where the "Jersey Derby" holds its "meetings." These races are really under the same management as the gaming tables on the shore, and there is here also a "club-house," to which only members of the Jersey Jockey Club are admitted, with their friends. Fashion is a queer moralist; and the same people who would be horrified at the thought of joining the throng in Chamberlin's club-house to toy with its tiger, go without a qualm to the races at Monmouth Park, and bet their money on the running of horses instead of on the turning of the card. It is true that a large proportion of those who go to the races go as lovers of horseflesh, and never gamble there; but is equally true that betting is freely and openly indulged in by many ladies as well as gentlemen, who have been taught to look upon gambling as a terrible vice. Nor do they confine themselves to betting such trifles as gloves and *bonbons*, but boldly join in the ticket buying of the "pools," to win or lose hundreds of dollars. The system of "mutual" pools, invented by the sporting men of Paris in connection with the races at Longchamps and Chantilly, has been introduced at the Long Branch race-track within a year or two, and by it the number of bettors has been increased a hundredfold; for this system permits one to stake as small a sum as five dollars on a race, with a chance of winning something handsome. Generally, when they win, they win but a trifle—a dollar or two or three—and generally they lose; but occasionally it has happened, when a horse that almost nobody trusted in has miraculously won the race, that the investor of a five-dollar bill in the "mutual" pool has won two or three hundred dollars. It is easy to see what temptation these possible prizes offer, and how enormously this system must increase the number of bettors.

As a spectacle of our democratic Americans tricks and manners, a visit to Monmouth Park on a race-day is, no doubt, instructive to the foreigner who visits Long Branch. It is not so gay a scene, either on the road or at the track, as that which one views who goes to the English Derby at Epsom, where the road is thronged with thousands and thousands of equipages of every conceivable variety, and the grounds are crowded with people, among whom negro minstrels bang their tambourines, and jugglers juggle, and gymnasts tumble, and fortune-tellers and thimble-riggers drive their trade. But it must be a novelty to an Englishman to see elegantly dressed ladies complacently trundling to the races in a common hotel omnibus—fare, twenty-five cents. There are many fine turnouts on the road, to be sure, but a man worth a million is capable, at Long Branch, of bundling his wife and daughters into the omnibus at his hotel door, in case of no other conveyance conveniently offering, and it is not considered a matter for special remark. It is noticeable, too, that the American generally goes to the races in a grave and sedate manner—he might be going to a Methodist camp-meeting so far as hilarity indicates his destination. There is none of that wild chaffing and outlandish prankishness which make the road to Epsom Derby one continuous raree-show. On the ground he walks about decorously with his hands in his pockets; he buys at the pools with the serious air of a man investing his money in grain or real estate. There are on the grounds no sports, shows, or incidental diversions; no loud talking, no quarreling; very little tipsiness; and there are long years, eternities, of inane dullness between the "heats," in which one is nearly consumed with *ennui*. All this is characteristically American.

The season of Long Branch is supposed to open about the 15th of June, and to close about the 15th of September—at least this is the period fixed by the hotel-keepers, who would, however, willingly extend it. But the fact is, the weather regulates the matter, and it has happened that Long Branch has been less full in the middle of July than it was at a far earlier period in the summer. A cold wind may come blowing out of the sea in the midst of a "heated term," and send the crowd of pleasure-seekers scurrying away to their homes inland like so many flies, while those who remain huddle together in their bedrooms, or sit about in the least airy corners of parlor and hall, wrapped in warm shawls. The long cool piazzas which furnish such a delightful lounge when Sol smites saucily at noonday, or on a warm moon-lit night, are then deserted. In the ocean gale the frame hotels quiver and rattle and shed clapboards in the most surprising way, and whispers of doubt and fear pass from lip to lip as to the likelihood of a roof being sent flying inland or of windows tumbling into the room. A sudden storm came up one day last summer which played queer pranks in the parlor of the Ocean House. This parlor is used for dancing, and its carpet is covered over with a linen cloth; the furniture is of a willow; and though the servants made all haste to close the windows and fasten the blinds, the wind swept in under the dancing cloth and blew it up like a huge bladder, upon which tables and chairs rode high in air, like little ships upon a rolling sea. Children were in ecstasies of delight at this phenomenon, and went wading out upon this airy sea, which tumbled them about shrieking with laughter and excitement.

Stormy weather by the sea-side is not without its charms to the thoughtful mind, however. A grand storm at Long Branch, if one is not too timid to relish the novelty, is a glorious experience; for thus one may enjoy one of the most thrilling sensations of an ocean voyage without the unpleasant accompaniment of seasickness or the possibility of shipwreck. The first week of August, 1875, was characterized by a prolonged series of storms, which vied in intensity with those of winter. The great waves roared and plunged upon the beach, a gigantic wall of foam, noisy as Niagara, and the sea was white with rage as far out as the eye could see. Bathing was put a stop to completely for several days, and the huts on the sands were so drenched with water that they were hardly dry again that season, but set one to sneezing whenever they were ventured into for disrobing purposes. Many of them were washed away; and after the storm was over, the shore was strewn for many miles with strange objects, *débris* of shipwrecked craft, great piles of the slimy vegetation of the sea, dead fish and animals. What wild tragedies were enacted out upon the bosom of the broad ocean, amidst the warring of the elements, with thunder and lightning more terrific than that which took place on the blasted heath where Macbeth met the witches, who could tell? But it set us thinking to walk on the beach that Sunday morning after the long storm, and view the snapped masts, broken spars, baskets, boxes, and other *disjecta membra* of foundered craft—among them a defunct camel, water-swollen and hideous.

The stormy weather furnished grand sea sights for those who stayed at the Branch; but it was as bad as an epidemic for the hotel-keepers. The "season" took a disheartening nap right in its natural noon-day, and Ocean Avenue became more deserted than Wall Street after three in the afternoon.

The bathing arrangements and customs at Long Branch could hardly be worse, in some respects, than they are. In this regard particularly we need to go to school to the English and the French to learn some valuable lessons from each nation. Both as concerns the comfort—not to say luxury—of the bathers, and as regards the safety of their lives, the beach at Long Branch needs thorough reformation. I do not mean to say that life is often lost there, for it seldom is; but it sometimes is, and it is a wild absurdity that this should ever be. When we commit ourselves to an ocean steamer or to a railroad train, we know that there is a certain definite danger in so doing, and we deliberately accept the risk and peril, because they are to a certain extent unavoidable. Those who go down to the sea in ships do so in spite of the fact that innumerable lives have been lost at sea, and put their trust in Providence; but those who go down to the sea to bathe, in the heart of a populous community whose very existence is based on the idea that people shall bathe in the sea, ought not to feel that there is one iota more danger in the surf than in a bath-tub under a roof. Yet not a summer passes but a life or two is lost at Long Branch, which need not have been lost if the precautions used at European watering-places were practiced here.

At the opening of the summer season the shore in front of each hotel at Long Branch is taken possession of by certain men of semi-seafaring appearance, who proceed to set up on the sands, just under the bluff, rows of bathing huts of an architecture so contemptible that even Uncle Tom and Topsy would have turned up their noses at them—shanties, of course, weather-browned boards, unpainted and often even unplaned, rudely nailed together, sides and roof of the same material, as incapable of keeping out wind and rain as so many paper boxes. The same men also set up a shanty of a larger sort, with a roof that is water-tight, which they occupy in company with piles of faded woolen garments which they facetiously denominate "bathing dresses," and which they still more facetiously let to ladies and gentlemen throughout the summer at the rate of half a dollar for each bath. I suppose these men do not really look upon this transaction in the light of being the huge joke it is, but it certainly would not surprise me to learn that the beginner at the business was tortured with mad longings to rush behind the shanty and relieve his pent-up risibles in writhings of laughter after each successive letting of a damp woolen shirt and trowsers tied with a string as a "bathing dress" to gentlemen in the ordinary attire of civilization. Those who pass any considerable time at the Branch, and bathe with regularity, of course provide themselves with bathing suits of their own; but transient visitors do not find it convenient to do this; and how greatly in demand the garments of the bath-keepers are, is shown by the fact that they are often furnished damp and clammy to the new-comer, having had no time to dry since their last tenant paid for their occupancy. If the Witch of Endor had presided at the construction of these miraculous bathing suits, they could scarcely be more ugly and fantastic than they are. That so many Americans are to be found who are willing to put them on, and walk unflinchingly across the stretch of sand between disrobing hut and surf, under the fire of hundreds of glances from the ladies and gentlemen present, is proof that the bravery of the nation should not be lightly impugned. True, they have their reward when the kind ocean covers them with her modest mantle of cool waves. There is no heroism without some guerdon.

Bathing dresses less shabby, and which are scrupulously dried between lettings, to be leased for a sum less absurdly close to their net value, are one item of the reform which is imperatively demanded at Long Branch. If the semi-seafaring Jerseymen who "farm out" these garments can not make a large enough profit—or think they can not—without continuing the existing reproach, the hotel-keepers should take the matter in their own hands. It would certainly be found a wise policy to make the surf bathing a more attractive feature of life at Long Branch than it now is. More people would bathe, and as a consequence—for surf bathing is a passion which grows with indulgence—more people would stay at the hotels, instead of hurrying away, bored, amused, half disgusted, by the wretched customs of the beach. The very scene would be more attractive to those people—always in considerable force at Long Branch—who do not care to bathe, but like to see the bathers at their frolics. It is a mistake to think that the spectators derive any considerable amusement from the shabby and wretched aspect presented by a bather in an ugly suit. But a group of bathers, such as may sometimes be seen at a French watering-place, where the suits are varied in color and pattern, and fit neatly, is a sight so picturesque that one does not tire of it. There is no good reason why gentlemen who are well dressed in the city should look like scrubbed chimney-sweeps on the bath-ground; nor why ladies should not display coquetry in bath dresses as well as in ball dresses. The idea that a handsome bathing suit "attracts attention" is absurd; nothing attracts so much attention, nor attracts it so unpleasantly, as an ugly and unbecoming bath dress. French ladies realize this, and dress accordingly, selecting their bathing outfit as carefully, with respect to becomingness in color and cut, freshness and fit, as any dress they wear. It is a delicate rose flannel, with pleatings of white; hat trimmed in accordance; pink hose and straw shoes; or it is a navy blue serge, with stripes of yellow, or of white, or of brown merino, or some other tasteful combination. At Long Branch it is almost a coarse dark flannel, much too large, and crowned with a rough straw hat more fit for a gutter than for a lady's wear. And as for the gentlemen! Ye heathen deities! what scarecrows they usually are! Description could do them no justice. Yet once in a while a handsome or picturesque costume may be observed among them—a tight-fitting blue *gilet de laine*, with a white star on the breast, or a loose sailor's shirt and trowsers handsomely braided. There was one tall athlete seen on the sands for a few days last summer who wore while bathing the veritable "togs" of a professional gymnast—hauberk and foot-pieces, tights and trunks. He was really a trapeze performer at a variety show somewhere back in the village, I was told, and so was no true part of the fashionable throng; but he helped to make it picturesque, and his departure left a sombre void.

Another imperative need of the bathers at Long Branch is the hot-water foot-bath, to equalize the circulation after the surf bath is over. This, also, is a feature of French watering-places which we might occupy to advantage. So is the provision of better bath-houses. But this, perhaps, is too much to expect; and, after all, it is a minor matter. Not so, however, the matter of safety for the bathers while in the water.

The semi-seafaring Jerseymen who lease the bathing dresses are the only guardians of the beach. Sometimes they are two in number; at the larger hotels, three; but they ought to be a dozen. They loiter on the sands—when not otherwise occupied with their tenancy work—and keep a good-natured eye upon the bathers, ready to go in and help should there be a cry for help. But it is easy to see that when their presence is most needed, when the bathers are most numerous, why, precisely then their garment-letting trade is liveliest, and absorbs all their attention. There should be men to guard the beach, like watchmen, at all hours, with no other duty than to dissuade persons from bathing at unsafe conditions of the tide, and watching those who do bathe, assiduously and unceasingly. Life-boats should be constantly plying. This is done in France, and it can be done here. The only protection our bathers have is a rope fastened to stakes on shore and in the water—a great convenience certainly, but puerile indeed when viewed as a measure of safety. When the surf is strong, the rope becomes useless to women and children, whose hands are torn violently from it by the power of the waves.

The Centennial visitor to Long Branch, if he be the brave reformer we hope he is, should insist on clean and dry bath dresses, hot foot-baths, and protection from the dangers of drowning. The futility of having lived a hundred years, if we can not yet compete with the effete despotisms of Europe in such a matter as this, is apparent.

The bathing-machines of Brighton are an institution which it would be agreeable, to the softer sex at least, to have at Long Branch. The long walk across the sands from the disrobing huts to the water's edge is a painful ordeal to many ladies, especially those who do not bathe often. Use breeds ease, and ladies who have dwelt summer after summer at Long Branch, bathing regularly throughout the season, find the walk down to the surf no more trying than another. Certainly, in the matter of modesty, there is no special offense to be taken herein, for the simple reason that custom rules in this as in all things. The innocent Irish maiden who shows her bare legs to the knee is certainly as modest as the society lady who bares her shoulders in the glare of a gas-lit parlor. In fact, neither is immodest, for she is merely doing what custom ordains in her sphere of life. So the lady who would not show her boot-top in a ball-room (though she would freely accept the close embrace of the waltz) will walk on the sands in a Bloomer costume with knee-reaching Turkish trowsers, and propriety is not offended, for custom rules. Probably the English bathing-machines are not altogether feasible on our softer sand and in our rougher surf.

The bathing hour at Long Branch is generally in the earlier half of the day, but occasionally it falls in the afternoon. It is regulated, of course, by the tide; when the tide is lowest, bathing is safest. The signal to hotel and cottage people is a white flag, which is seen flying from a short staff at the head of the wooden staircase that leads from the grassy summit of the bluff down to the sands. Each of the great hotels includes in its grounds a strip of beach, as do those cottages which look on Ocean Avenue. There is nothing exclusive about any of the hotel bathing grounds, they are actually open to any one who chooses to avail himself of their limited conveniences. When the white flag is seen flying, there begins a hegira of men, women, and children, who go streaming down to the beach in crowds, some to bathe, some to look on. The scene when the day is fair and the bathing good, the water mild in temperature and the surf rolling gently in with a long shallow stretch, is a very animated one. From a central point, like that of the Ocean Hotel grounds, one may look up and down the beach at frequent intervals throughout the entire distance. Some days one may see two or three thousand bathers in the water at once, making the air vocal with shouts and laughter, the nervous shrieks of the timid and the boisterous merriment of the brave. The sexes mingle freely in the pastime, and it is no uncommon experience for the belles and beaux of the ballroom to make appointments between the figures in the Lancers for the next day's bath.

The morning being usually devoted to the bath, the afternoon is set apart for excursions and drives. The drives we have always with us; the occasions for excursions are afforded from time to time variously. In general terms they may be specified in three divisions: first, excursions to Pleasure Bay; second, excursions to Monmouth Park; third, excursions to Ocean Grove. Those to Pleasure Bay may be subdivided into the ordinary and extraordinary, the ordinary being that which is available on any pleasant day throughout the season, the extraordinary that which is warranted by the announcement of special festivity at Pleasure Bay, such as a clambake or a regatta. You are liable to meet the most important people at the Branch at these festivities. The President himself, who never goes to the races, has at times deigned to attend a clam-bake. Pleasure Bay is a charming drive, from the centre of gayety at the Branch, just a mile and a half, through a lovely open country, to an old-fashioned original New Jersey tavern, in the midst of a green grove on the bank of a placid sheet of water. There is a flavor of combined Bohemianism and rustic simplicity about the place which contrasts delightfully with the ostentation and luxury of the sea-side hotel where you are staying; and it is but a carping critic who would discuss, while enjoying the cheap delights of the Old Pleasure Bay House, whether the landlord maintains its primitive simplicity out of sentimental, poetic love of nature, or merely because (as some assert) he is too stingy to spend any of his profits in modern improvements. Be this as it may, it is pleasant to sit at the weather-beaten tables under the green trees and eat his crabs, and then go and catch some. It makes you think of Squeers and his class in "bottiney;" first they spell it, and then they go and do it. A fairy-like yacht with spreading sail receives you at the water's edge, and you are blown over to the opposite shore, where, with a chunk of fish at the end of a string, and a net at the end of the pole, you find that catching crabs is as easy as eating them. The sail gives you a glorious appetite, and if there is a clam-bake when you return, you will proceed to eat ravenously of a conglomeration of green corn, clams, crabs, potatoes, and yellow-legged chickens that would make Delmonico's head cook turn green with horror merely to smell of it; taste such a savage mess I am sure he would never do—no, not if thumb-screws and red-hot plowshares were the alternative.

The excursions to Monmouth Park are afforded by the races; of them I have spoken. The excursions to Ocean Grove, like those to Pleasure Bay, are both for special and general reasons, the special being the camp-meetings which are held there at intervals during the summer. Ocean Grove is a summer city of Methodists, an hour's brisk carriage drive from Long Branch, through a somewhat monotonous country. It is on the sea-shore, and its bathing habits are precisely as those of Long Branch; in most other respects there is a complete dissimilarity. No balls, no billiards, no bars, no late hours, no dissipations of any sort of a poor man's paradise, though there are rich people there; but even the rich dwell in modest cottages, while those who must practice a close economy live in tents or in cheaply constructed cabins in the woods. The place is curious and interesting in many respects, and visitors to Long Branch do not feel that they have seen all the "lions" until they have driven down to Ocean Grove. The gates of the community are closed at an early hour in the evening and on Sundays; but as one side of the Grove is not fenced in, but looks on a pretty sheet of water, visitors to the Sunday camp-meeting quit their carriages on the shore of the little lake, and are smuggled over—not very surreptitiously—in row-boats for a one-cent fare. The meetings are sometimes held on the sea-shore, right down where the surf makes music in harmony with the human chorus, and sometimes under the trees in the grove.

The amusements of the evening at Long Branch are varied: not to speak of such favorite diversions as lovers' strolls in moonlight or starlight on the beach, there are dancing parties every evening in the parlors of all the large hotels, with occasional concerts, dramatic entertainments, etc., usually given by amateurs and for some charitable object. Occasionally, too, a circus comes along and pitches its tent on the vacant lot near the Ocean Hotel, and, strange as it may seem to those who know not the ways of the fashionable world, the circus is packed full, not with the Jerseymen from the back village merely, but with the leaders of the *monde* at

Long Branch. The favorite night for dancing is Saturday; custom has made this the most brilliant night in the week in the parlors of the hotels; more people arrive on Saturday than on any other day, and in the height of the season on a Saturday night the piazzas will be so thronged that it is almost impossible to move about, thousands of men and women in gala attire sitting by the open windows to listen to the music and see the dancers. They have the best of it too, for dancing in midsummer ballrooms is hot work, and the sterner sex invariably maintain that they thus make martyrs of themselves only to please the fair. Dancing is always concluded at half past ten, except on Saturday nights, when it is sometimes prolonged till the stroke of twelve. On Sunday nights, at some of the hotels, an instrumental concert—called "sacred" by courtesy—is given on the balcony, the piano being wheeled out there for the occasion. On other nights, after the dance is over, parties will sometimes be made up to go and serenade the President, or some other person of consequence, or lady of social popularity. Groups go strolling on the grassy bluff, or gather in some favorite nook to sing hilarious songs, with wine and wit and spirits bent on driving dull care away.

Beyond all question, the most delightful time of the year at Long Branch, but not the most fashionable, is the autumn, when there comes upon the shining face of the sea a soft haze, which is most agreeable to the eye, and the air is full of balmy odors. To many people the sight of the sea with the sunlight beating on it in the bright days of summer is painful and wearisome. "Oh, I can't bear that sea!" cried a poet of my acquaintance, one day, as we stood on the bluff; "It puts my eyes out." On some hot days the great waters will lie almost rippleless, save for a little surfy dog-day frothing at the mouth, all the long hours from morn till dewy eve, glittering like a burnished shield, and flashing in the eyes of the beholder until he is fain to fly. But in the mellow days of autumn this is not so. Though the ocean then grows smoother than even in the hottest of the dog-days—though it will sometimes lie for days together like a mirror, it is not a mirror which flashes back dazzling sunbeams, but absorbs them, and the eye is rested. Then the lapping waves woo the shore so gently and playfully that bathing therein is an Oriental luxury not to be resisted. The atmosphere is so sweet and pure you can almost taste it, and the waters, warmed by the long heats of summer, are as balmy as the air. When the tide is low, there lie exposed such long reaches of shallow bathing ground as the bathers of the midsummer would hardly believe possible. On the same spot of shore where, in July, the surf buffeted strong men in its giant arms as pigmies, and tossed them, panting with exhaustion, on the hot sands, now, in September, they might wade out half a mile from shore before they would meet surf sufficiently strong to knock them off their feet. But in September, when the surf-bathing was like this, there would be no more than three or four lonely bathers in the sea at the hour when formerly there was a hundred. The writer remained at Long Branch last season until near October, and does not speak from hearsay. The hotels were utterly deserted; cows pastured on the lawns in front of them; the windows were nailed up with boards; the bathing huts were torn to pieces, and lay piled, mere every-day lumber, in heaps on the grassy bluff; no carriages rolled up and down the Avenue; no lovers strolled upon the sands; yet the days were simply heavenly, and passed by like dreams of fairy-land. Long Branch was at its loveliest, but the crowds were gone. Fashion is the jade who has wrought this grievous wrong upon our fellow-men.

The cottage owners of Long Branch do not obey the orders of Fashion so meekly and with such alacrity as the hotel dwellers. After the latter rush away, the former stay—just as long as they can. The President's family stay till October, some few cottagers even till November; and the bravest are the happiest. But there is something about the aspect of those huge deserted hotels that is awfully depressing as the lonely cottager drives down the Avenue at dusk. So brilliant but a week or two ago, with colored lamps flashing on the lawns, and gayly dressed throngs moving in the glare of the chandeliers, a thousand windows lighted, and streams of music issuing in harmony with the sound of voices and laughter from the crowded parlors; and now, utter desertion, barred windows, silence like that of the dead. And the cottager pulls his hat over his eyes, and whips up his nag, eager to reach his cheerful home circle. This sort of thing wears on the stoutest nerves at last, and the panic takes them one by one, and off they go by the first train they can get. Nature has charms, but to the most of us human nature is the more potent winner. We long for our kind. We love to keep the crowd. Hence great cities, and hence, also, watering-places.

The cloud of financial depression which has cast its shadow over the whole country for two or three years past has not failed to include Long Branch in its gloom. Property has depreciated in value there as elsewhere, and the grand industry of the place—which is hotel-keeping, I take it—has not thriven as of old. It is quite possible that, unless our next President should choose Long Branch as his summer residence also, many years will elapse before the flow of prosperity will lead to the high prices in real estate which formerly prevailed there. Yet the prediction would be childish which should intimate that the best days of Long Branch are over. The probability is rather that this charming resort will grow more and more in favor; and not only this, but it is likely that other localities by the ocean's brink, easily accessible to the great metropolis, with develop their resources in like manner, and blossom into summer resorts for an overheated city populace year upon year.

8. THE NEW NARRAGANSETT PIER

by Brander Matthews
HARPER'S WEEKLY, JULY 7, 1906

The first thing that a newcomer to Narragansett Pier does is to ask for the pier itself; and he is always surprised when he is told that Narragansett has no Pier. Science informs us that there is no soda in soda-water and no lead in lead-pencil, so also, is there no pier at Narragansett Pier. It is true that there has long been a coal-wharf in a cove sheltered behind a rocky promontory; and this was the only safe landing between Point Judith and Conanicut. It is true, also, that a few years ago an iron pier was run out from the bathing-beach to accommodate excursion-steamers on their voyage from Providence to Block Island. But neither of these landing-places plays an important part in the summer life of the most individual of water-side resorts; and there is no denying that the verdict would go against Narragansett if it had to be tried by its Piers.

It is the beach which is the centre of life at Narragansett, its reason for existence, its title to supremacy—the splendid beach, a mile long, with its firm sand, with its freedom from seaweed, its gently shelving slope, and with its surf, rolling in superbly from the ocean, yet mitigated by the thrusting out of Point Judith, which breaks the full force of the waves that may have swept riotously across the broad Atlantic. It is the beach, first of all, which has given Narragansett its fame throughout the United States, and which has irresistibly attracted, year after year, the families from all parts of the Union who have built the summer city of cottages that extends along the shore for half a dozen miles, stretching away almost to Point Judith itself. It is at the beach, at noon, that Narragansett holds its parade of pretty girls, plunging into the surf and swimming out to the raft, before they adorn themselves again in all the glory of their sumptuous sailor suits to lunch at the new Casino, which now nestles just at the edge of the rocky shore. It is on the beach at the bathing hour that the transient guests of the hotels have their chance to mingle with the cottagers who have been coming summer after summer, unable to keep away, and who are swift to insist that there is nowhere else a seaside village worthy of comparison with Narragansett.

Down past the Casino, across the street from the post-office, there is a one-sided lane, a single row of the usual little shops that offer needless little luxuries to the host of summer idlers; and this lane leads to a series of wooden bath-houses, each with its broad veranda stretching out over the sand and splashed by the waves at high tide. These covered verandas touch one another, and they afford a thoroughfare for the throngs that wish to bathe and to see the bathing. At the edge, near the water, sheltered from the glare of the summer sun, there are seats for those who do not care to adventure themselves in the water or who have come merely to observe the parade and to take part in the midday *conversazione*. In these seats one can always find a group of young mothers, placed advantageously to greet their friends, while able to keep a watchful eye also on the youngsters who are digging in the sand in front of them.

At the far end of this tier of old-fashioned bathing-houses there is a new-fangled bathing pavilion, with all the modern improvements, absolutely up to date in every respect. And nothing could be more characteristic of the conservatism of Narragansett than the fact that this new establishment, offering every latter-day convenience. has never tempted the cottagers away from the shabby old houses where they had long been in the habit of making ready for their daily dip. They looked it over and declared it excellent—and then they left it severely alone, returning to the less-commodious places they were accustomed to frequent, and abandoning the spacious pavilion to the unknowing newcomers and to the transient visitors who had just alighted at the hotels. The cottagers are not avid of novelty, rather they are staunch respecters of established custom. Therefore, it is that the most of them can be found every noon at one in particular of these unimproved bath-houses, primitive enough, and yet satisfactory for all these many reasons. They are loyal to this house, perhaps because it is the oldest of all—even if it has been rebuilt more than once; and perhaps because it is carefully conducted by the son of the man who opened the earliest hotel at the Pier, now some two score years ago.

During the bathing season, which stretches from the first week in July to the last week in August, the verandas begin to fill up a little after eleven; and the throng does not thin out until half past one. Anchored a hundred feet out from the shore is a raft, with a spring-board for the more venturesome divers; and during the bathing hour two watchful oarsmen in a staunch rowboat keep patrolling to and fro just outside the main body of the bathers, ready to render prompt assistance to any exhausted swimmer. There are no life-lines; and there is no need of any such spoil-sport devices here, however necessary they may be on the coast of New Jersey and on the shore on Long Island. At Narragansett the surf is rarely dangerously fierce—never, unless there has been a three-days' storm. Generally the waves, however high they may curve, are gentle enough—gentle, yet invigorating; and there is far less undertow than at most of the other beaches on the Atlantic coast.

Just as the visitor to Narragansett is disappointed on his arrival to discover that there is no Pier, so he is surprised on his first visit to the beach at the bathing-hour to find that there are on exhibition none of those eccentric and fantastic bathing costumes which the comic papers may have led him to expect. The same decorum is visible here as may be seen at any other watering-place made fashionable by two generations of self-respecting American families. Simple black is the color most popular with pretty girls who come here to splash in the inviting breakers; and yet there are not a few coquettish bathing-suits to be observed, simple black though they may be, set off with fetching little caps, often of a more salient color. Now and again a girl can be found topped with an unobtrusive hat to protect a timid complexion from the full glare of the midday sun.

Not only is there many a Venus to be seen rising from the waves and diving into the billows, but there are also young men ready to bear them company in their aquatic gambols and to guard them from the buffeting of the breakers. Whatever the reason, whether it is the attraction of the Casino and of the Country Club, whether it is the temptation of the beach itself or the allurement of the Pier's richly deserved reputation as the haven of a host of pretty girls, gathered from all parts of the Union—whatever the reason, the fact is undeniable that Narragansett has a fuller proportion of available men than falls to the lot of most American summer resorts. Not here is the Scripture fulfilled which prophesied a time when seven women shall lay hold of one man. Men there are, and of all ages, some mature in years but made young again by the stiff stimulus of the surf, and some still youthful enough to sport with pride on the breast of their swimming suits the class number or the more glorious initial of the college itself. These lusty young fellows go into the water early and go back again frequently, after running races with one another along the dampened shore, or after taking sun baths in the sand at the feet of some girl who does not care to take a dip every day.

No one who chanced to be a spectator of a pretty scene visible here a few years ago is likely to forget it; and although it might have happened anywhere, it seemed to be characteristic of Narragansett. There was one of the most famous Southern belles at the Pier that season, and she went into the water almost every morning, although she did not know how to swim, and although she did not like to get her hair wet—her beautiful, luxuriant hair, most effectively arranged. One day she bemoaned the fact that she had never been out to the raft, and that she never could achieve that feat. Then her bodyguard of young men consulted together and devised a method of convoying her in safety. Finally she was persuaded to adventure herself in their devoted care. She was towed out by two brawny college athletes, one of her little hands on the shoulder of each of them, the men swimming high, so that the delicate structure of her hair should not be endangered. A third volunteer swam in front as a pilot, cleaving a triumphal passage for her; and a half dozen spare men brought up the rear, available reserves in case of any unexpected mishap. Arrived at the goal, she lifted herself up on the raft and rested a little while, and then she lowered herself once more in the waves, and her manly escort bore her back to shallow water, with her hair unsplashed.

Yachts drop anchor just in front of the bathing beach, a spot most convenient to the landing-stage of the Casino; and sometimes there are half a dozen pleasure-craft lying there lazily and swinging languidly as the waves roll under them. Their launches can come close in almost to the mass of the bathers, and on occasion a few stalwart swimmers make the watery circuit of the anchored vessels. Often these yachts have run across from Newport merely for the day, to enable the owners and their fellow passengers to avail themselves of the advantages of the beach. Sometimes the bathers in the water can catch sight of a torpedo-boat shooting past stealthily, a little beyond the cluster of peaceful yachts. Sometimes, again, there is the grimmer spectacle of the cruisers and battle-ships of the North Atlantic Squadron, powerful and silent, steaming slowly out of Narragansett Bay on their way out to deep-sea maneuvers.

A little after one o'clock the beach begins slowly to empty itself of bathers, and a few minutes later the throng on the sheltering verandas of the bathing-houses commences to thin out. A procession starts up the one-sided lane, with its single edge of little shops, streaming casually toward the inviting portals of the new Casino. This low-lying Casino building, with its abundance of white columns and prim balustrades, stands on a point of land thrust out beyond the end of the beach. The new Casino is a simple affair, far more unpretending than the old Casino, due to the skill and the taste of the same architects. The new Casino is of wood; and the old Casino, built in 1885 and burnt down in 1900, was of stone for the most part. The stone skeleton of its springing archway, which still spans the broad Ocean Road, is majestic even in its empty uselessness. And so long as it is allowed to stand there, lonely and desolate, Newport is not the only watering-place that can boast of a ruin. The arch of the old Casino at Narragansett is quite as picturesque as the old mill at Newport, even though it cannot claim to be a mysterious relic of the enterprising Norsemen.

The new Casino has a charm of its own, even if it lacks the spacious solidity of its predecessor, which was widely recognized as one of the most beautiful examples of our later American rural architecture. It is exactly what it pretends to be, no more and no less; it is a restaurant, with a ballroom attached. The restaurant has broad windows facing the ocean, and opening upon a terrace set out with little tables, sheltered by gaily striped umbrellas. At the edge of the terrace there is a bandstand, and below and beyond there is an Italian garden, extending out to the solid stone wall which protects this exposed point from the assaults of the sea. If the spectacle to be seen on the beach between twelve and one is characteristically American, the spectacle to be seen in the grounds of the Casino an hour or two later is strangely foreign. There is a kaleidoscopic variety of costuming to be observed among the little parties sitting under the gaudy umbrellas on the terrace. There is color, and there is music, and there is incessant movement and vivacity. There is an atmosphere of enjoyment unexpected enough in the sober community that was founded by Roger Williams.

The new Casino is not a hotel; it is hardly even a club; it is, in fact, as has already been stated, a restaurant with a ballroom attached. The restaurant is the centre of attraction after the noonday hour on the beach and once again as the twilight settles down. The ballroom has its turn on hop nights, and more particularly on the Saturday evenings of August, when the season is at its full. While the restaurant is only a single story in height, the roof of the ballroom rises aloft high enough for a shallow gallery to encircle the dancing floor, so that the matrons and the old fogies of the other sex, whose dancing days are over, may have a chance to look on without obtruding on the precious space available for those who take part. The ballroom is decorated with chaste simplicity, in keeping with its rural surroundings; it is admirably ventilated, and it opens on a veranda on one side, while on the other it touches the restaurant, through which the young men and maidens descend into the Italian gardens, going down to the edge of the water and profiting by the cool breeze that is ever blowing across the broad bay.

From the Casino the wide Ocean Road curves for nearly a mile to the old coal-wharf, the original pier, just where The Rocks begin that extend five miles further to Point Judith. This imposing Ocean Road is protected by a massive sea wall, the building of which was due to the forethought and to the tactful perseverance of one of the most public-spirited of the summer residents. On this stretch of road, facing full on the ocean and looking across to Newport, are strung out more than half of the hotels of Narragansett, interspersed with perhaps a dozen cottages. Here, as at most other summer resorts, the cottager is slowly ousting the hotel guest. As an American family comes to perceive all the manifold advantages of a long vacation in the country in a home of its own, even if this shelter is only rented for the season, it gets out of the hotel habit, so to speak.

More than forty years ago one of the leaders of Newport society, as it was then constituted, was overheard to declare dogmatically that "the cottager had the inside track;" and it is quite forty years ago since the hotels of Newport began to disappear, one by one, some of them being sawed into sections and moved away to serve other purposes. And the same process has been going on at Narragansett, although it began later and has been slower in its operation. The scattered farmhouses along the shore, and not too far from the beach, into which the original discoverers of Narragansett had to beg admission two generations ago, were soon expanded into boarding-houses and were then rebuilt as hotels. Then the original discoverers began to buy lots here and there and to put up cottages of their own. Their friends followed their example, and summer homes multiplied along the Kingston Road; and there came in time to be a cluster of them between the Casino and the railroad station, while braver spirits built houses of more stately dimensions on The Rocks, half-way down to Point Judith. So it is that the more prosperous hotels have been enlarged and rebuilt, while the less-successful have been abandoned and torn down. In the past fifteen or twenty years the number of cottages must have doubled at least, and perhaps trebled, while the number of hotels has actually diminished.

In the more thickly settled part of the village, from the Ocean Road and the Kingston Road back to the neat railroad station, with its finely kept surroundings, land is held at fancy prices, and few of the places contain more than an acre of two. And here the houses are truly cottages; but out on The Rocks, on the way to Point Judith, the places are far more spacious, and the houses are, many of them, not fairly to be termed cottages, even if none of them are sumptuous enough to vie with the marble palaces of Newport. The most noteworthy are Hazard Castle, a stalwart stone structure, with its tall tower rising high above the thick growth of trees by which it is sheltered, and Dunmere, with its lovely little lake and its graceful gardens overhanging the sea.

Just as the Cliff Walk at Newport is open to all comers, so there is at Narragansett a right of way along The Rocks, due to the solicitude with which the State of Rhode Island has reserved free access to the shore at all times. And at Narragansett the custom has been established to profit by this privilege and to stroll along the shore on Sunday afternoons, traversing the outer edge of the private grounds. Indeed, this walk along The Rocks is not only the favorite promenade; it is, in fact, almost the only walking available, for the Pier, like most other American wateringplaces, is deficient in those pleasant rambles which are abundant in most European summer resorts. Seemingly the American does not greatly care to walk, he prefers to drive, and of late he delights in automobiling. And here the Pier need confess no deficiency; if its paths are few, its roads are many and excellent. Broad and properly macadamized and well kept, these roads extend in every direction—to Point Judith, to Kingston, to Saunderstown, where the ferry plies to Conanicut and so across to Newport. At the height of the season the four-in-hands of Newport are frequent on the roads of Narragansett; and now that the automobile is forcing itself into general use as a superior substitute for the horse and wagon, the trip across the bay can be made in a scant hour and a half. Often of late a swift automobile brings over a gay party for a plunge in the surf, with a luncheon at the Casino, and for a game of tennis, with afternoon tea under the trees of the Country Club, getting them back to Newport in the fading twilight in time to dress for dinner.

The Point Judith Country Club is established on an old farm, a couple of miles from the centre of the village, high up on a broad ridge, overlooking the ocean on the east, and on the west the long Salt Pond that empties itself into the harbor of refuge which Uncle Sam has been building just beyond Point Judith. For a country club no better site could have been found anywhere; and what nature provided has been bettered by art. The old farm-house has been extended not a little, and it has been tastefully transformed to suit the needs of the club members. There are lounging-rooms and dressing-rooms and dining-rooms; there are sheltered verandas, and there are also tables sprinkled abroad under the trees of the old orchard. There is a golf-course of eighteen holes, and there are a dozen tennis-courts scattered here and there on the level sward. Best of all, there is a polo-field, spacious and splendidly green, with its springy turf. Here for ten days, early in August, the best teams in America contend every afternoon. Here, also, a little later in the month, is held a horse show, which is the final function of the Narragansett season.

As the bathing-beach is the centre of attraction at noon, so is the Country Club the meeting-place of the cottage colony in the afternoon. There are men toiling joyfully over the golf-course that encompasses the whole estate. There are mixed doubles engaged in sharp tussles at the tennis-nets. There are less-energetic sportswomen walking through a more stately game of croquet. There are lively groups about the little tables under the trees. There is a constant coming and going of carriages and of automobiles and even of bicycles. And those who gather here at the Country Club are chiefly the cottagers with their house parties, and with only a few of the more prominent visitors at the hotels. This marks the distinction between the more or less permanent cottage colony and the transients who may alight at a hotel for a few days only. The Casino opens its doors widely, welcoming any presentable person who can pay the modest admission fee, whereas the Country Club elects those whom it desires for its members. Although the club is hospitable to newcomers with social credentials, it is unhesitating in its intention of excluding all those whom it may deem undesirable. Any one is allowed to buy tickets to witness the polo games and to see the horse show; but even on these days, when the broad field is thronged with spectators, the privileges of the club-house are reserved for the members of the club and for the friends whom they may have vouched for.

After the full glory of the polo fortnight, when every hotel is packed, and when late comers are glad to have permission to sleep on the billiard-tables, and after the subdued splendor of the horse-show week, when the ways to the Point Judith Club are still cluttered with vehicles of all sorts—after these two final functions, the season often wanes abruptly. As soon as these spectacles are over and the sports are at an end, the casual guests of the hotels make ready to depart, and the hotels make ready to put up their shutters once more for the long winter's emptiness. Even by the first week in September the beach begins to be less crowded at noon, and there is no longer any difficulty in finding a vacant table at the Casino. A little later and the music ceases; then the Casino itself closes, and in the eyes of the world the season is over.

There is truth in the assertion that Narragansett's chief charm is not to be sought in any merely physical combination of land and water and air, but rather in certain of its social aspects. To many, the abiding attraction of Narragansett is not the gift of Nature, but the work of Man—extending here to Man, for once, the privilege of embracing Woman. They insist that the real reason for its persistent popularity is to be found not in the place so much as in the people who have made it what it is, and who shaped its social character.

If these students of social conditions are pushed to the wall and forced to declare with precision exactly what they may mean by this assertion, they will point out that society at Narragansett Pier is like the melancholy of Jaques, "compounded of many simples," and that there has been from the beginning a commingling here of families from all parts of the Union. A few New-Englanders there are and a few New-Yorkers also, with a fair sprinkling of Philadelphians; and no doubt these all contribute their special attributes to the total flavor. But the irresistible individuality of the social life to be observed at the Pier, summer after summer, is due rather to another element, with a savor of its own which combines most successfully. This other element comes from the South, and more particularly from Washington and Baltimore, from Richmond and Louisville.

In this explanation there is a large proportion of truth. It is not so much that Virginia and Kentucky are wont to send their Southern belles to conquer Northern hearts, although much of the brilliancy of the season at Narragansett must always be ascribed to this delightful custom; it is that the tone of the summer's colony at the Pier is rather Southern than Northern, with the warmth and the heartiness of the one and without any of the frigidity and affectation which only too often chills social intercourse in the other.

III.

THE AGRICULTURAL FAIR

European pleasure fairs, traceable to the Middle Ages, celebrated the coming together of people for the purpose of buying and selling wares and produce. Interest in these events was augmented by the presentation of entertainments of infinite variety. Booths were set up to form a compound about which cloth, leather, pewter, crafted merchandise, and untold other "stuffs" were peddled. One could purchase anything from popular ballads to gingerbreads to roasted pigs. There were stalls for the selling of domestic livestock and farm products of every kind. There were musicians, jugglers, acrobats, conjurers, rope-dancers, trained animals, and strolling actors. The fair was a seasonal happening that was unexcelled in pleasure and excitement.

Similar collective enterprises were developed in America, the most popular and the most colorful of which is what we call the county fair. Throughout the nineteenth century this country was primarily agrarian in nature; and early fairs were the ceremonial culmination for the seasonal ritual of planting, growing, and harvesting, where produce and livestock were displayed and judged, and where new methods of farming were shared. If unrelenting amusements sometimes over-shadowed the business of agriculture, such frivolities can be excused by noting the arduous and isolated life of the nineteenth-century farm family.

9. CATTLE-FAIR DAY IN NEW ENGLAND

HARPER'S WEEKLY, AUGUST 8, 1857

Every nation has its commercial peculiarities, and each geometrical section of the country, in a degree, possesses in this respect its own local characteristics. Paris boasts its *Bourse*—the leviathan stock-mart of France; Venice its *Rialto*—the famed "high 'Change" of Southern Europe; the market-days of London are as noted as are the November fogs of that huge metropolis; and "Cattle-fair day at Brighton," Massachusetts, has long since, by universal assent, passed into "an institution" in New England.

Once a week throughout the year, in storm or sunshine, a motley multitude gather at this point, and from break of day to sunset on these occasions, the hours at Brighton are passed amidst a continuous murmur of bargaining for every description of live stock—cattle, sheep, swine, or poultry—varied by the not infrequent disposal of ancient horses, decayed wagons, worn-out (or stolen) harnesses, dilapidated butchers'-carts, and the like, at public vendue, or by private negotiation, the purchasers of the numerous "outside" articles of traffic there most commonly coming off decidedly second-best in the trade thus consummated.

For a long series of years these weekly cattle-fairs have been held in this thriving town, which is largely indebted to their establishment and continuance there for its present state of prosperity. The contributions which serve to make up the vast aggregate of livestock which finds its way thither upon every Thursday through each succeeding twelve-month, are driven in from every section of New England, but principally from Maine, New Hampshire, and from along the valley of the Connecticut River. Thousands of cattle, fat and lean—immense flocks of sheep, good and bad—myriads of porkers, large and small—and hundreds of horses, indifferent or miserable—pass here finally, every year, from the hands of those who raise the stock, or who "forestall" the purchase of it in quantities, into possession of the dealers of smaller calibre, who in turn job the animals in pairs or dozens to the retailer, or fit them for the shambles.

The *horses* offered for sale in this mart, are usually in the most wretched condition, physically and mentally—of the thoroughly demented "pelter" description, and are traded in chiefly by the lower grade of tip-cart "jhintilmen," who seldom embarrass their finances by the investment of more than "two-an'-a-quarther" dollars in any single specimen, unless the animal may chance to have been newly shod within three months previously, or the "harlter goes wid the baist"—two provisions which but rarely occur among that fraternity in their horse-trades at Brighton.

The congregation of purchasers in this market weekly is varied and curious. Among the crowd at the earliest hours, and most prominent from his position and large means, may be seen the forestaller from Quincy Market; who, as every frequenter of Brighton knows, is prone to buy largely and briskly, who always comes into town with a plethoric pocket book, whose smile or frown is of material consequence to thew vendors, and who takes precedence in his selections. Near by follows the professional slaughterer, a jolly individual, whose countenance is shiningly clean and very red, with a wallet also well puffed out and excessively greasy; but everybody is aware that his balance in bank is ample too, and he readily takes the "second cut." Then appears the stray "middle-man," who picks up the best bargains he can get at. He is succeeded by the smaller butcher in turn, and so on.

An hour or two later may be observed a well-attired man, of sombre dress and mien, who moves about somewhat mournfully through the mingled throng, nodding merely to one or another, but very chary, watchful, or moody in his demeanor, as he passes slowly around. He is one of the Brighton "humanitarians," and will cheerfully loan any "good" man a small sum of the ready, upon call, at a *reasonable* percentage, although "the fact is, money is very tight," whenever said good man may happen to find himself "short." If you do not want his aid, it is all the same thing to him. There is no compulsion. Happy to accommodate you another time. But money is money.

Here and there the shrewd Hibernian and the sharper Yankee chaffer together glibly over their miniature transactions; the patient cow-boy at the corner unobtrusively awaits a customer for his cosset three-year-old heifer, with her first-born beside her; a loquacious Vermonter beyond him, continuously urges upon the notice of the passer-by the superior excellence of his twain of steer, which he is bound to get rid of before night; the blear-eyed jockey by the road-side informs you for the fiftieth time that if you are in search of a horse as *is* a horse, he is ready to accommodate you with a tip-top trade; the belated drover comes yelling along behind his jaded herd of fat cattle, jostling the crowd and tumbling the orange-women right and left, *en route* to the pre-engaged fold which he failed to reach at an earlier hour; the wiry-voiced auctioneer over the way keeps up his incessant shout of "Going, gentleman; going!" though few in the great multitude seem to care a whit who or what is being thus disposed of, inasmuch as every thing around them appears to be emphatically "going;" the latticed wagons with their broods of unctuous Suffolk piglings, nestled cosily among the clean straw-heaps, are ranged along the way, while from the open pens directly behind them may be heard the mellifluous voices of a score of neglected native grunters, whose bones are barely covered with skin and bristles—the two porcine collections furnishing a striking illustration of substance and shadow; the herdsmen, and shepherds, and swine-drovers, hurry to and fro continually; the shouts of anxious men and noisy boys, the lowing of the uneasy cattle, the bleating of the weary-footed sheep, the squealing of the worried pigs, the yelling of quarrelsome dogs, the thunder of ever-moving vehicles, the cries of the zealous peddlers, the neighing of hungered horses, all conspire to render this scene a continuous "Babel of strange sounds," such as one encounters at no place in this country save at Brighton—upon Cattle-fair day.

One feature of "melancholy interest" invariably attends upon the commerce of these weekly fairs. At a respectable distance from the main squares, occupied by the established folds and pens for cattle, but within sight of the hotel and moving crowd of visitors, may always be found a collection of cheap samples of living horse-*frames*—skeletons of worn-down and ruined animals, blind from old age, knock-kneed and toothless, starved, spavined, crippled, and sore, the veriest wrecks imaginable, huddled together in groups, oftentimes leaning against the fences near by or upon each other for temporary support—and brought hither by their merciless owners (who have previously goaded the very last jot of availability out of them), to be sold for the nominal value of their skins—more or less.

The traffickers in these unfortunate quadrupeds are uniformly proprietors of one-horse city gravel carts or offal wagons, a single team of this character, with harness to correspond, comprising the entire sum-total of the worldly possessions of this enterprising class of individuals. They are usually of foreign extraction by birth, and from their generally brief residence in this country prior to embarking in this peculiar species of commercial undertaking (as prosecuted at the Brighton fairs), they are hardly expected to be conversant with the exact orthography of Webster or Johnson. It is therefore not uncommon to learn that the valuable beasts of which they desire to become dispossessed are "Fur Sale," or "4 sail," or frequently "fore Sail;" the announcement being occasionally varied by the syllable-compound "foresell," as is indicated by the "notis" written upon a patch of card or paper, and fastened to the nearest post, or to the halter that hangs about the lean and haggard necks of their overtasked and wretchedly worthless victims, as they stand waiting for purchasers.

If you chance to be of a curious turn of mind, and venture an inquiry regarding the animal thus advertised, a son of Erin at your elbow instantly responds to your inquisitiveness, and you learn that the forlorn beast in which you have become interested is " a beutiful crathur, inirely—in haarness, or out—an'll worr'k the skin arf his boanes fer yez, wit'out wincin' at it." But, as his owner has "got troo wit' his jarb in the city," he will "paart wit 'im fer three dollars; an' not wan cint less, with'out the harlter."

Three dollars is not a very large sum to pay for a horse, even without a halter, to be sure. But you naturally observe that "he is thin in flesh;" his owner, while admitting this fact, however, quickly assures you (though he has certainly never tried the experiment!) that "it's aisy enuff fattin' 'im, shure." When you discover that he is very old and decidedly lame, your Hibernian friend insists that "divil a bit o' harm is there in that at all." He has "druv 'im day an' night for siven lang months, an' shure his yairs an' his lame fut niver hurt 'im a hap'orth." Still, you do not wish to be "saddled" by this apology for a horse, and you ascertain that he has only one shoe left. His master consoles you with insisting that "it's aisy fixin' that at the smith's fornent ye." And when, as a *dernier* resort, you complain that the *price* is much too high, and move on, your Irish friend simply desires to know "What the divil the man expects to git in a horse at three dollars!"

Before night "the poor remains of beauty once admired" are deposited at the nearest slaughter-house, at a dollar and a half; and the days of the miserable hack are numbered at last.

The thorough-bred Yankee *drover* is part and parcel in the making-up of these weekly congregations at Brighton. His occupation is that of successive days of toil; and the vigorous prosecution of his calling, from its incessantly roving character, brings him largely into contact with all sorts of people. Your drover, therefore, is emphatically "a man of the world," in its everyday sense, and he most naturally sees "human nature" without glasses, as it exists, broadcast. He is a close observer of men and things, and, first of all, is a bold bargainer, by necessity. In his purchases, he is cautious, keen, and prudent, nevertheless—for his average margin of profits throughout the season is, at the best, but trivial; and he makes a little money go as far as possible in buying. In selling, he is fair and manly—for there be those above his grade in the trade, who are able to get nearer the wind than he can sail, ordinarily!—and is content with ready returns and moderate profits. "Quick in, quick out!" is the experienced drover's motto, for live stock must be fed; and after a certain point of stalling, the game is a losing one if the cattle remain on his hands.

In the American acceptation of the term, he is a clever fellow—frank in speech, quick in his perceptions of the right, and inclined to pass by rather than to quarrel over the wrong he may encounter. He is open-hearted and happy among his acquaintances; and, as to enemies, he seldom has any—for he finds it easy, as well as profitable, to make friends in his way—and does not omit the opportunity. Inured to constant exercise and exposure out of doors, he is hale and rugged in health, stalwart in limb, and stout of heart. In linsey-woolsey frock, slouched hat, and cowhide boots, with steelyard upon his arm or shoulder, he traverses the rough hills of Vermont and New Hampshire, or threads the roads and by-ways that course through the Connecticut Valley, with one keen eye on the shrewd stock-raisers in those regions, and the other upon the daily price-current, which he consults with amazing regularity and care.

Having thus gathered his herd or flock, he approaches Brighton upon "market-day," confident that his toil will be compensated, as it certainly well deserves to be. Here he is esteemed for his apt business qualities, and no less for the goodness of his disposition; and, though educated in a rough school, and continually exposed to the harshest of weather, as well as other rude treatment in the course of his weary journeys in the saddle or afoot, his countenance is always cheerful, his manner of speech raw but becoming, and his general intercourse respectful. Your drover marries early, whistles admirably, works briskly, eats voraciously, sleeps soundly, deals honestly, and lives as happily as the average of human kind. He very rarely becomes rich—as his profession is the general "beating of the bush," while others carry off the bird. Without the drover's address, however, and the results of his widely extended labors, market-day at Brighton would present but a paltry show.

Another character inevitably to be met with, at this place, on these occasions, is worthy of mention—belonging to the *genus* "b'hoy." Though he aspires to compete with his more aristocratic namesake of the Bowery, in his habits and deportment, yet he simply apes the other, and does not possess the peculiar talent requisite to become a *Mose* or a *Sykesy*. He may be found (without the searching), upon every Thursday in the year, in and out of the hotel, or lounging around the cattle-pens, on the look-out for a "job." He always wears a pleasant face, when employed, and is by no means to be flouted, for he is exceedingly useful, in his humble way. He will take charge of your horse, if you "ride up"—point out the lions to you, if you are a stranger—find you a customer, peradventure, if you have any thing to sell—show you the fastest crab out, if you wish to buy a nag—knows just exactly the gig you were looking for, if you name such a matter in his hearing—has a "jewel of a harness" to match, which he will sell extr'onerry low, *to you*—knows every body in town, from selectmen to hog-reeve, and every body knows him, except by name—has traveled the world over, and "run with the machine"—so he says—understands himself, and the crowd, and you, and the rest of mankind generally, to a dot—will do you any little favor of any kind nameable, at all times, for a very trifling consideration, and, if you are inclined, will "take a drop" (at your expense) and a cigar, more or less—just as often as may be agreeable to you or any other "gen'leman."

Happy, careless fellow! He doesn't live any where, so he declares. He is "round about," here to-day, there tomorrow. He is the Brighton Fair locomoting *vade mecum*, and every body's *factotum*, for the nonce. Forever joking, laughing, rollicking—but with a constant eye to business upon market days—for this is his weekly harvest-time. He sports a half-jockey, half stable-boy suit of drab corduroy or fustian, and an intensely pink-striped calico shirt with Byronic collar, the bosum of which is adorned with a trio of Attleborough studs. A brace of high-top boots, a white felt, with its narrow black band, and a short riding-whip, complete his costume.

In all the "free fights," which will occur, occasionally, at such gatherings, this young gentleman "goes in" without an invitation; and is the frightful owner (undoubtedly) of the whitish-yellow dog, with one black eye and a most curiously constructed under-jaw, which attends him, whenever the pretty creature is not chained up, out of sight. This canine friend of his may have his faults (as who has not?), but I desire it to be expressly understood that *I* know nothing to this animal's prejudice. On the contrary, it is not to be doubted that he is a good dog, and everyone who approaches him is respectful, and even complaisant in their attentions to this beauty. I say nothing against this dog with the harelip. His portrait—taken from life—is presented, without comment further. His master, the indefatigable man-of-all-work to the Brighton public, is with him—a handsome pair.

Among the better grades of stock sent hither for sale may be mentioned the consignments of young horses from the North and West, and occasionally an animal of mettle—worse for wear—from the neighborhood or the city beyond. A stray Canadian pony may sometimes be had here "for a song," comparatively. But Brighton market has long since been decided upon as *not* the choice of marts at which one should purchase a horse.

Mr. Pleasanton, however, from the rural districts, has not been apprised of the state of public opinion upon this point (or he disregards the caution *in toto*), and, moreover, he "knows what he's about." And so, Mr. P., who is really a very respectable man and all that, goes to Brighton to procure a good "family beast." He has heard that occasional opportunities offer there for obtaining a valuable nag at a low figure. Mr. Pleasanton knows the points of a horse, and he smiles at the hint of his friends in reference to his chances of being deceived! Indeed, it would seem to please Mr. P. very much to meet with the individual who is competent to take advantage of *him* in a horse trade.

In the course of the day there is an impromptu trial of speed among such of the sale horses as are able to "show foot," a performance which varies the monotony of proceedings, and which comes off upon the fine level road a few rods beyond the hotel, usually under the auspices of the accommodating owner of the dog with the harelip and distorted under-jaw, aided by other *habitués* of that immediate ilk. After the trot the animals are mostly brought to the hammer, and, if sold at all, are knocked down to the highest bidder by the village auctioneer.

The road is lined with a heterogeneous mass of idlers, countrymen, villagers, boys, horsemen, spectators, and strangers, and the exhibition of the horses is vastly enjoyed by the eager crowd. A worn-down roadster, that has turned his mile within three minutes in better days, finds himself under whip and spur beside some puny pacing Canadian, urged to his uttermost over the "half-mile course" below the hill, only to be sadly beaten, first by his opponent in the heat, and subsequently by his rider for permitting what he could not prevent. The jockey "goes in" without entrance-fee here; the stable-boy trumps up a "game 'un," with which some fancy dealer may chance to be present, and which he may desire to offer for sale; the Vermonter, in his French cart, exhibits his tiny Morgan; the family horse, the hack, the cob, the pelter, the comely and ugly—all join issue in this transient exhibition, thus giving the buyers an opportunity to pass judgment upon the merits of the different animals to be disposed of.

"Gentlemen," observes the auctioneer, blandly, as the horses are brought up to the stand finally, and he surveys the collection of miscellaneous faces upturned around him, "we shall offer you a few exc'lent animals here, to-day, such as it is not our good fort'n to meet with upon these grounds or'narily. And among them, gentlemen, is a superior specimen, nine years, comin' ten, sound an' kine, well on his feet, been used by a gen'lemen, capitle driver in saddle or harness, sold for no fault, owner no further use for him, a substantial family beast—there he is—and how much am I offered for the horse?"

The auctioneer wipes his face, takes breath, and Mr. Pleasanton, being a listener, feels that he is in luck, and that this is just the animal he wants—for he has seen him travel, and heard a subsequent good account of him from one whom, in his innocence, he deems entirely disinterested in this particular animal.

"How much, gents?" continues the knight of the hammer. "Gimme a bid—start him where you please—he is to be *sold*, gen'lemen. How much did I hear? What for that fine animal? Look him over; judge for yourselves; you have seen him move; he's a good 'un. How much for the family horse?"

Mr. Pleasanton witnessed the trot but a few minutes previously, and he ventures upon an offer of forty dollars.

"Forty dollars!" exclaims the auctioneer; and, laying down his hammer, he comes to a pause, as if the proposition were a very absurd one on the part of Mr. P. or anybody else. He looks around upon the crowd, with a martyr-like expression, and finally continues, "Forty dollars only am I offered for that superior animal! Will gentlemen of intelligence stand by in silence, and permit this sort of sacrifice? Is there no one here that will start him at a hunder'd?"

Mr. Pleasanton is delighted, and the more so when he observes that no response is made to this appeal.

"Very well, gentlemen; I have said 'he is to be sold,' and we trade here on the square. But this is altogether *too* bad. Forty dollars I'm offered for this horse. Forty dollars—forty, forty, forty, forty—who says fifty? gimme fifty? shall I have fifty? forty only, goin at forty—did I hear fifty dollars for the horse? gimme five, then? somebody say five—forty dollars, only, I am offered—*will* you say the five?"

Another pause—another gaze of astonishment upon the listless and gaping crowd, and the auctioneer, having observed the nervous expression of Mr. P.'s face, ventures himself to advance a dollar.

"Forty-one! forty-one! forty one, one, one—"

"Two," says Mr. Pleasanton, quickly, "forty-two."

"Forty-two," continues the seller; "forty-two—thank you, Sir; cheapest bargain you ever got in your life. Forty-two, forty-two; gimme three—forty-two; who says three? forty-two, forty-two, forty-two—remember gentlemen, we *warrant* no horses that are sold at less than fifty dollars. Forty-two; shall I have three? Gimme a half, somebody. Forty-two—did I hear a quarter? Forty-two only; if that's the best bid, down he goes now. Quick, or you lose him. Forty-two dollars only; forty-two, and—he is yours, Sir."

Mr. Pleasanton advances, pays his money, half-a-dozen anxious individuals rush up with offers of halters at twelve shillings each, and Mr. P. gets away with his "family horse," which has been previously sold five times at least, within as many weeks on account of his utter viciousness and intractability—and which he also is glad indeed to be rid of, at the very first opportunity!

By this time the signal is given for dinner, and if there is any one matter than another to which the Brighton community is willing and eager to render justice, it is this. A simultaneous rush is made from all quarters of the grounds for the hotel; and piling in, upon, and over, each other—the drovers, market-men, butchers, strangers, and boarders make for the readiest seat in the great dining-hall to secure an early chance at the smoking and hearty viands prepared for their by-no-means over-fastidious palates.

The accustomed routine of this interesting process is rarely interrupted, except through the occasional increase of the crowd on especial days—in the busier seasons. Upon one occasion, however, at the witching moment when the stomachs of the throng most earnestly yearned for contact with the savory edibles in readiness to be discussed—just at the ringing of the bell—as the multitude poured in at the side entrance of the hotel, a huge ox bellowing with pain, came dashing suddenly down by the piazza at a furious pace, followed closely by a three-year-old colt that appeared to be having it "all his own way," in this novel and exciting chase.

The tail of the maddened ox he held firmly clenched between his jaws, and following sharply upon the tracks of the annoyed and desperately frightened bovine fugitive—away rushed the twain to the infinite merriment of the witnesses of this singularly ludicrous and entirely original exhibition. Passing around the hotel, and up to the vicinity of the pens again, they separated; and the lower portion of the tail of the ox was subsequently found to have been nearly bitten off during this race.

It turned out that this ox and colt were strangers, and had been placed in intimate proximity during the morning, but had conceived a dislike for each other. The colt finally bit at the haunch of his neighbor, who, in turn, planted his heels in the young stallion's face—whereupon the latter seized a mouthful of the tail of the ox, which act induced the other to set off at full speed down the path around the hotel as he did, yelling with pain, while the vicious colt clung to his hold with the tenacity of a bull-terrier. The young horse seemed in the end amply content with his revenge for the insult, and became perfectly peaceable a moment after the ox escaped him.

Dinner over, and the transfer of the cattle and sheep and swine is concluded. Knots of contented and quiet men stand about in the cool shade of the house, enjoying their pipes and cigars, after the generous repast they have just enjoyed with such exceeding gusto. The state of the markets, the prospects of the season, a dash at politics, and the finishing up of contracts, affords the *materiel* for an hour's easy and friendly intercourse among the now lessening crowd, prior to the final adornment of the gathering.

A renewed activity ensues at the pens, and the purchasers are now moving off with their little flocks of sheep, their brace of cattle, or single animals, selected during the morning. Mr. Pleasanton has already gone with his family horse; the old brindled cow, which is warranted to have given (at some earlier period) such fabulous quantities of milk, is in tow of her new owner *en route* for his little snuggery in the adjoining village; the fancy farmer who resides at the fine villa in Brookline, and who is now in the enjoyment of a fair income and his "first season in the country," is just departing in his natty wagon with a pair of those genuine Suffolk pigs for which he has paid *only* thirty-two dollars—scarcely half a dollar a pound; a trade which he will certainly make money out of—if nothing occurs to prevent it; the young man who has been standing at the roadside all the day with his pair of young steers has just induced a straggler to try them at a reduced figure, and is in the act of pocketing the proceeds; the boy with the cosset heifer in the morning is lounging beyond with hands in pocket and a saddened countenance, for "Buttercup" is disposed of, and his occupation's gone for the time being; the tongue of the auctioneer has ceased "going," for his auditory have vanished, and the stand is deserted; our friend with the calico shirt and felt hat is enjoying a stirrup-cup with a young gen'leman to whom he has just sold a four-year-old colt "of fine figure and action, thoroughly broke to saddle," and which the present owner can easily break to harness—very likely, in the course of time; the drover is preparing to depart, his herd having been cleared out at remunerative prices; the money-lender has long since disappeared, as it is now far past his hour of business; the Vermonter with his little French cart and wiry pony is higgling with a stranger at the corner, who has cantered him for his nag; buyers are now getting scarcer; the din which has filled the air for hours is more subdued; the occasional shout or bleat is more distinctly heard, and is less frequent; the dilapidated horse-frames have been drawn away, and the jargon of their impoverished masters no longer offends the ear; the dusty roads in all directions are teeming with life—the crowd retiring in vehicles or on foot—and a general breaking-up of market-day now transpires.

The stable-boys have had their full share of toil during the morning, and young "Jake" has been alive since day-break with brush and comb. The last horse has now been brought up, and the great barn-floor has been swept down for the day. The drover's assistant—a youth of fourteen—is awaiting the pleasure of his master, who is dallying with the Cambridge butcher over a final bargain for the remains of his flock till now unsold, and Jake, seated upon his upturned bucket, is displaying the half dozen coins he has been the recipient of, in the way of perquisites, since sunrise, a peculiar smile of satisfaction pervading his honest ebony countenance, while he recounts to his less fortunate temporary companion the prospect of his becoming a "gem'man" some day, and of rubbing down a crab of his own.

The crowd lessens. The busy knots of men have departed from the grounds, and a dozen or two of the more unsuccessful traders and villagers only are assembled within the limits of the office or bar-room of the hotel, enjoying a cobbler or parting pipe, and still harping upon fat wethers, fair beeves, and good store 'ogs, yet on hand.

Another opportunity offers, however, on the succeeding day; for a similar fair is held every week at Cambridge—but four miles distant—and so the sharpers hold on for original figures. The latter location is excellently well situated, and thoroughly appointed, under the superintendence of the famed Porter, formerly and for a long period proprietor of the Brighton establishment. But the original market can never be superseded, and fortunes will continue to be made upon these well-managed grounds, in spite of all competition.

The cars of the Worcester railroad run directly through the town of Brighton from Boston, connecting with the Springfield and Albany roads, upon the western terminus. Great quantities of live stock are thus readily brought in to this point, by rail, every week—a desideratum with dealers in and around Boston at all seasons of the year, and an arrangement of vast convenience to the first purchasers at a distance from the grounds.

An hour before sunset the pretty town of Brighton resumes its accustomed tone of quiet, and the multitude of beings who have made up for the mob during the previous twelve hours are far away from the tumultuous and exciting scenes of which they formed a part, and which are to be renewed upon each succeeding Thursday in the year, so long as people insist upon enjoying the sirloin of beef and the saddle of mutton....

10. THE ALABAMA STATE FAIR

HARPER'S WEEKLY, NOVEMBER 27, 1858

The Fourth Annual Fair of the Alabama State Agricultural Society was held in Montgomery, the capital of the State, between the 1st and 6th days of November, 1858.

The grounds are beautifully located upon the banks of the noble Alabama, occupying a large, level, grassy plain, to the north of the city. The space inclosed is ample, and the facilities afforded for display are on a scale commensurate with the rapidly improving interest of this young and flourishing State. In addition to a large number of well-arranged stalls for cattle, hogs, and horses, there is a finely graveled training course: a grand amphitheatre for the examination of stock, and for the exhibition of hippodromic performances; a commodious two-story edifice for the proper display of mechanical contrivances, as well, also, for the use of exhibitors in the department of the fine arts; a substantial gin-house, for the purpose of testing improvements in the preparation of our great southern staple, together with fixtures for pressing and baling cotton already ginned.

There are characteristic points of difference between a show of this kind in the Northern, and such a display as we are now describing in the Southern States. In the former, distinctive prominence is given to those mechanical appliances which represent the interests of the mighty grain-growing countries of the North and the imperial Northwest. The eye is bewildered by the multiplicity of inventions for reaping, garnering, thrashing, fanning, and grinding the exhaustless products of the cereal regions. There, too, are to be seen the infinitely varied modifications of machinery by which the numberless processes of manufacturing operations are carried on. There are more perfect planing apparatus; simpler contrivances for drilling, or boring, or filing; a new cog-wheel; a trifling, yet important readjustment of ratchets and pinions; some novel methods of printing calicoes, or weaving domestics, or spinning cottons; a new valve in an old piston-rod; an ingenious key, or an unassailable lock. There are men from the sooty forge and the clanking anvil; men from the dusty flouring-mill and the odorous laboratory of some noted perfumer; men whose ears are daily stunned by the whirr of spindles and the clatter of looms; men who listen forever to the groanings of ponderous wheels and the incessant puffings of busy steam-engines.

At a Southern Fair, on the contrary, the eye at once discerns the habits, taste, and pursuits of a people wholly given to agricultural and pastoral employments. But few machines are on exhibition, and those relate exclusively to the interests of the farm and to the homely duties of the planter. Here is, perhaps, a cornsheller and separator, and there is a bit of mechanical ingenuity applied to the grinding of corn and the crushing of the cob. Not only does the visitor discover at a glance that the tillage of the soil is the noble vocation of the sturdy and happy yeomanry around him, but he sees with equal readiness that the one great, engrossing, controlling idea is the growth and culture of cotton. On every hand, in every variety of phase, is this one absorbing topic represented. Here is a long row of beautifully ginned and securely packed cotton bales, with their fleecy samples exposed to view. Read the label on this plow. It is intended for the cultivation of the young cotton plant. Stop to observe this vociferous old man, who industriously plies an ungainly wooden machine to and fro all the day long. "What is that concern fur, Mister?" "That is Carter's Cotton Planter, the outbeatingest contrivance for evenly drapping and kiverin cotton seed in the world!" What is the use of all these cogs, and spirals, and files? The answer shows us how young Elliot goes to the planter's gin-house, takes his broken, useless gin saws, and in a few hours makes that busy file reset and rewhet every tooth to its pristine sharpness. The crowd rushes toward the discordant creaking of some huge fixture on yonder side of the Fair grounds. I run too, and am "in at the" packing, tying, and discharging of a beautifully packed cotton bale, weighing six hundred pounds. I see a fellow sedulously bent upon twirling a crank for an admiring crowd, and thrusting my spectacles through some cranny in the living wall, I find a man explaining how some cute Yankee, way up in Varmount, is trying to "do" the Alabama planter with a cotton-packing contrivance, full of wheels, and screws, and levers. Thus it is on every side; you see the enshrinement of the mighty staple in the central fane of this great, warm, throbbing, Southern heart....

...A word about this year's exhibition. It was declared by those entitled to know to be a decided success, a marked advance upon former shows of the kind in this State. Very many fine cattle were on the ground, chiefly Devon, Durham, and Ayrshire breeds. Milch cows fetched at the sales from $60 to $155. Berkshire pigs were sold at $30 per pair. Several fine stallions were in the ring, one valued at $4100. Another splendid Morgan horse, the property of Colonel Ferrell of East Alabama, so closely contested the premium with his costly competitor, that skillful judges required time to discuss their points.

But lest you might take it for granted that Alabama is devoted wholly to grosser pursuits, I am constrained to refer to a fine collection of pictures in oil, crayon, and pastel, together with several credible specimens of industrial art, such as designs for wall paper, carpets, table-covers, dress goods, etc., all furnished by the pupils of the Tuskegee Female College. This is the first effort to develop this application of artistic pursuits in the Southern country in connection with a literary institution. As an evidence of the favor with which it was received, the executive committee made a special presentation of a splendid silver pitcher to the College, through its President the Rev. Dr. A. A. Lipscomb.

A new product of the laboratory also took a prize before a special committee of scientific men. It is a disinfecting agent, superior, they say, to Labarraques French liquor. The fortunate discoverer is Professor John Darby, of Auburn, Alabama, a man of scientific acquirements of a high order.

In fancy needle-work, in embroideries, in patch-work, in home-made counterpanes, quilts, and similar goods, in leather work, wax and fruit ornamentation, in all these departments our fair Alabamians were tastefully represented....

11. THE COUNTY FAIR

by Nelson Lloyd
SCRIBNER'S MAGAZINE, AUGUST, 1903

The Wise Man of our Valley stood before the tent of the dancing girls. He had been called there by the tall showman, who was pacing up and down the platform, and in tones now soft and pleading, now thundering through a megaphone, was gathering a goodly company to hear his persuasion. Persuasive the show-man was. He was matching his glib tongue against the muffled beat of horses' hoofs on the track, against the music of the hurdy-gurdy in the merry-go-round, against the puff and purr of the traction engine exhibiting close by, against the shrill cries of a score of barkers along the white street. He was winning. The clang of tambourines, the boom of bass-drums, the redoubled shouts of his rivals failed to turn the tide that had set toward his tent. Behind him stood his company, two women, one in green, the second in pink, bold figures for the glare of the early afternoon, and a background of shimmering canvas. Before him was a motley gathering. The Dunker and his mild-eyed wife had paused out of curiosity, and stayed to stare and listen. The had come wittingly, to look upon the world and the devil. They had found them. And now, fortified by the poke-bonnet and the wide, flat hat, they were gazing upon them solemnly and critically, and yet without envy or guile. Whether or not they looked in condemnation could not be told, for the Dunker face is impassive, and the Dunker eye seldom flashes except when the spirit is stirred by religious emotion. Pressing closer about were young men from the town—dashing fellows with pink shirts and large watchchains; their less fortunate and staider brothers from the country, baking in their winter blacks, heavy garments, redolent with camphor; old men whose beards seemed to act as weights by which the mouths were kept open without effort. Here and there were women—the plain women of the country, the gay women of the world—of that smallest and yet biggest of worlds, the county town. On the outskirts hovered the small boys, from the dignified youngster with a little sister in tow and a quarter to spend, to the ragged, barefooted urchin who had dropped from the clouds and had a care not to fall near the ticket-taker's gate.

"The dancin' girls—the dancin' girls," thundered the show-man.

Then resting his megaphone on a chair and leaning gracefully on it, he took up his discourse.

"The show we offer you is an education in itself. It is the show that made the Midway in Chicago famous. It is the show that drawed the ay-lite of Paris to the Exposition there. It is the show that will be the feature of the St. Looey Centennial that is to come. And why? The lady on my right hand, who I now interduce, is the world-famed Little Egypt." The celebrity in green kissed her hand to the audience and smiled languidly. "There ain't a lady or a gentlemen here to-day but what has heard of this famous Egypti'n. She has danced before the crowned heads of Europe; she has been petted an' dined be the ay-lite of the world's capitals, an' is now on her way to appear in the opery-house in New York. That you have a chance to see her is be special arrangement. Havin' a day off, she has consented to appear here that you, ladies an' gentlemen, may attend her amazin' performance."

The girl in green stepped to the front of the platform, and with a languid smile and a few curtseys and steps gave a hint of that wonderous grace of hers. Then she leaned against the tent and watched the clouds. The dancer in pink lounged forward and stood on one foot, with arms akimbo, looking away off somewhere, over the midway, over the field, over the hills.

"Alvarita," cried the show-man, with a wave of his hand. "Cousin of the world-famed Carmencita, an' herself a Spanish lady of high birth. She is known in every quarter of the globe. His Royal Highness the King o' Englan', then Prince o' Wales, seen her dance before the London court an' sent her a boket of flowers. Of her a poet has said, 'Fairer than a lily, nimbler than a fawn.' To see her in her performance alone is worth double the money we ask—one dime—only one dime, to see the world-famed ladies in their beautiful entertainment."

The Wise Man of our Valley stroked his beard. From the show-man, now passing ticket after ticket to the line before him, he looked at a silver coin which twirled in his hand. From the coin he looked at me and smiled grimly.

"It is an education," he said. "What would us farmers do without this annual schoolin'? I come here to-day a pore, ignorant feller, an' be the judicious use of a dollar I've seen things I'm blessed sure I've never see in any other place. Mind the mermaid—the pickled mermaid down there. What a wonderful thing that was to stedy, an' for anly five cents. An' the wild man from the Filipinos! We hear a heap o' them Filipino Island these days, an' it's a special treat to see a feller from them parts a-caperin' round a cage, an' to see them feed him—only I wish they wouldn't 'a' spoiled him be tattooin' an eagle on his arm. Still, they is rumors that he was a barber before he become a Filipino, an' that it's the captivity that upsets his mind most, but it's well worth the money to watch him gnaw an' roar. They'll to tell you these fairs is dyin' out—that they ain't so good as they used to be. Nonsense! As long as the human race is cravin' information the county fair'll be an institution. Where else could we see a lady an' a gentlemen box like the two there in the tent be the wheel of fortune? Not seen it? That's well worth a dime. You might supposin' they was married, the way the lady hits the gentlemen. You might—"

"The entertainment is about to begin," shouted the show-man.

He seemed to address himself entirely to the worthy standing before him, hesitating and still twirling the coin.

"Little Egypt is now ascending up on the stage." The megaphone was aimed point-blank at my wise friend, and to add to its persuasion the twang of the banjo sounded from the tent.

"It's an education," said the old man, and, joining the line, we went in.

To the clink of banjos the girl was dancing. We saw her over a bank of hats, a black foreground for the green figure swinging to and fro in the pinkish light of the tent. And there was a personality about those hats. Each seemed in itself a spectator and the man beneath it a mere useless appendage. There were hats with brims of dandyish curl and crowns at a dashing tilt; *blasé* fedoras, drooping in a melancholy fashion that spoke a soul sated with the world and living art; solemn hats, God-fearing headgear with straight brims, refusing to look devil-may-care, however abandonedly slanted; bulky hats, crowning ponderous figures and hiding, it seemed, heavy eyes and wide-open mouths. Before them, backward and forward over the little stage, flashed the bold figure. Hers might have been a dance of Egypt, of Spain, of Ireland—perhaps it was a little of them all—but dance the girl did. There was a rugged grace in her movements; there was life and spirit.

Little Egypt? So the show-man called her. Little Egypt, the omnipresent! I saw her again that very week, down in a country called Egypt also. There Happy Joe Robinson presented her to a company of the drooping folks of lower Illinois. Her hair was red, and she wore pink, and timed her little steps to a wheezy melodeon. Happy Joe, too explained that this same girl had made the Midway famous, and it was by the merest chance that he had been able to add her to his galaxy of stars, then touring the Mississippi in the greatest show under the sun. We met again at the street fair in Missouri—at least the glib show-man, pointing to a buxom woman in black, declared that, on the "bond of this guarantee," it was the celebrated dancer; yet that very month, in blue plush, she danced on Fireman's Day on the shore of the Sound—Oh, Egypt! Egypt!

But what would our county fair be without her; what without the mermaid, or the lady boxer, or the wild Filipino gnawing at his beef-bone? My Wise Man told me that day, when Alvarita had made her closing bow, that he had picked too many apples in his time to drive six miles to see one simply because it was particularly big. His position seems just.

When since the break of winter you have been plodding your fields; when at last you have shaved your acres clean and stuffed your barn until no room is left even for the pigeons; when you have sent your little ones over to their aunt's and gathered your medium ones about you in the spring-wagon on the promise that they will not stray from their mother's sight; when you have headed your team for the county fair, the prize pumpkin, the fattest hog, or your neighbor Lizzie Lumpkin's beautiful hand-painting in the art-gallery, are not likely to prove of very great drawing power. These are the things of your workaday life. If you are a bachelor, sentimental and anxious to make a deep impression on a certain young woman, the vital question is not whether she wishes to see the latest style harvestor or the Perry Brothers' exhibit of Plymouth Rocks. It is rather, does she want an orange or a tintype. If you are particularly wealthy, you may even treat her to having her eyes examined by the oculist in the tent by the lunch-room.

The exhibits of live-stock and machinery are the reason of the being of the county fair. From them we may learn the plain truths of the agricultural gospel. In the music of the merry-go-round, in the rattle of the shooting gallery, and the shouts of the show-men we have the ritual. It is these that give life and light to the day and perhaps as we wander along the tented street, with every sense sated, the eye with color, from the red pop-corn to the green dancer; the ear with the crash of the hurdy-gurdy, the whine of the band, and the cries of the barkers; the taste with a half-green banana or a bit of patent taffy, there may by chance be driven into our dull minds some truths as to the value of lime on clay ground or oyster-shells in hens.

There is life at the county fair, whether it be along the shores of the Sound, among the fat farms of the Lebanon Valley, in the groves of Egypt, or on the rolling fields of Kansas. So I found it. Long ago John Gay caught the spirit:

> The mountebank now treads the stage and sells
> His pills, his balsams, and his ague-spells;
> Now o'er and o'er the nimble tumbler springs,
> And on the rope the vent'rous maiden swings;
> Jack-pudding, in his parti-colour'd jacket.
> Tosses the glove, and jokes at ev'ry packet
> Of raree-shows, he sung, and Punch's feats.
> Of pockets pick'd in crowds, and various cheats.

Were the poet turning his verses to-day he might add a few lines embodying the moving pictures, the glass-blowers, and the balloon. But had he wandered with the Wise Man among the people of our valley, had he set beneath the canvas of Happy Joe's Greatest Show under the Sun, or watched the baby-show in the Kansas grove, he would have felt that, after all, he had covered the ground very fully.

The county fairs, North, East, South, or West, are alike in the main points. In the people themselves the chief differences are found, and these, for the most part, are tonsorial and sartorial—in the cut of the beard and the cut of the coat. The cut of the brain is pretty much the same everywhere. So much is this true that in taking stock of gatherings of this kind it seems wrong to exclude the horse-show in the Madison Square Garden. What is it, after all, but a county fair stripped of its side-shows? The people find themselves entertaining enough to do without them. The exhibits do differ, but about as many persons are there to watch the horses as go with the Wise Man to see the prize pumpkin. It is a great social rendezvous. And right here we have the key-note of the success of the fair. At all of them we have the smart set. In the Garden it looks bored and sits in a box. In Kansas it is a bit less bored and it sits in a newly painted buggy. In Egypt it rides a mule. At all we have a middle-class and all the other classes which according to the Declaration do not exist. For does not snobbery work from the bottom up rather than from the top down?

I endeavored to explain this similarity to our Wise Man that day as we leaned over the rail by the track watching some horses being worked before a race. It was difficult to point out to him how there could be any interest in a fair where the people constituted themselves the show. When he heard how the great ones and the little ones of the land walked around and around, gazing at one another, he smiled gently.

"Say," he said, "don't you s'pose it kind o' tickles the angels to watch 'em?"

There was no time to reply. But if angels do smile they must have at that moment.

The race was off. A minute—and it was sweeping by us! We clambered on the rail and leaned madly over to get a glimpse of the finish. Two black bonnets and two broad black bodies shot out to obstruct our view. We knew them. We had seen these same Dunker sisters with a tall, pious brother in the poultry show discussing in low whispers Black Langhams, Buff Cochins, and Brown Leghorns. The tall, pious brother was gone, but we suspected that he might be found at the other end of the grand-stand taking a clandestine view of the sport.

This racing is a terrible thing! Right before our eyes, across the track there, a lot of young men are struggling and shouting in a mad scramble for gain. Dollars risked on the speed of a horse! A week's earnings wagered on a single contest! Just two Sabbaths ago at the big bush-meeting, Brother Pulsifer, with this very day in mind, inveighed strongly against the race and the wine-cup. But Brother Pulsifer is near-sighted! Brother Pulsifer is deaf! He knows not the music in the muffled thunder of the bunch as they swing around the bend; in the shrill Hi! Hi! of the jockeys; in the roar of the grand-stand. Brother Pulsifer is a pious man and learned, but we wonder if he has read what the Good Book says of the ostrich, "which leaveth her eggs in the earth, and warmeth them in the dust, and forgetteth that the foot may crush them: God hath deprived her of wisdom, neither hath He imparted to her understanding. What time she lifteth up her herself on high, she scorneth the horse and his rider."

Hold fast, sister! hold fast! Here, take a hand and climb on the second rail—you can lean over further. They're off, sister! They're off! For the horse "saith among the trumpets Ha! Ha! and he smelleth the battle afar off, the thunder of the captains, and the shouting."

It is the broad felt hats, the poke-bonnets and the buttonless Amish garb that give a distinctive tone to our Pennsylvania fairs, just as the fireman in his red coat and helmet, with a few extra caps suspended like canteens from his belt, stands out as the boldest figure in the county gatherings further "down East." Again, you will notice a nautical cut in the beards near the coast. In the farmer you will find just enough of the bowl of the sea, and in the sailor just enough of the stride of the furrow to make it a grave question as to whether to address a stranger as "Friend" or "Captain." They affect a peculiar style that is misleading. Studying a group of men perched on a fence watching the "exempts" go by, preceded by a bibulous band and followed by a rattling hand-engine, I have found it impossible to tell which kept summer boarders, which farmed in legitimate fashion, which sailed an oyster-sloop or was master of a stout clipper. Their clothes would have served equally well in a lumber-camp or a nor'easter.

Move westward, and this problem will never perplex you. Where he appears at all, the fireman is relegated to a minor place, and the veteran comes to the fore. The old soldier is the most sociable of his race. His age and honors give him time to spend four days at the fair, where the rest of us look on one as dissipation. So in Ohio, in Indiana, in Illinois, when in doubt you say "Comrade." But usually the veteran is unmistakably stamped by the faded blue uniform, the G.A.R. hat, and the large umbrella he invariably carries to protect them. To him the fair is no real treat. It is a side-show, indeed compared to the dedication of a monument or a regimental reunion. He has seen too many of them to rush about throwing baseballs at babies or tossing rings over canes. He is *blasé*. He plants himself in the shade of the band-stand, with a few of his cronies gathered about him, and discusses things in general.

My friend the Editor down in Egypt introduced me to a grand soldier—a little, brown man, with a uniform, the hat, and the umbrella. He had served in the Two Hundred and Something Illinois. The Editor made note of his presence for a local, and learned that he had just spent a week at the gathering up the road, and would have been in Washington that day at the great reunion had not his wife been took down with malary. He had come to the fair so as not to disturb her. Strolling with him along the line of booths and through the stocksheds, we fell in with a dignified, middle-aged man in black—a large black derby, black tie, black-striped shirt, and a very close fitting and shiny black suit. This person confided to us that he was a stranger and had crossed the river from Missoury with the two-fold purpose of picking up a span of mules and seeing a lady friend. Together we wandered about the sunless grove, now venturing a guess on the weight of a hog, now tickling a colt with the drover's buggy whip, now pausing to watch a party of young men in the rifle-gallery.

I thought of our Wise Man and our fair. How out of place he would be there! How uninteresting he would hold it! This was a region that the Wild Filipino, the lady boxer, and the heaviest actors in the world had not discovered. The Editor had apologized for it. It was mainly a social gathering, he explained, as we stood at the gate and he pointed across the road and into the woods where several families were camping in canvas-covered wagons.

In our valley they wear their hats on the back of their heads on these feast-days. Here they pull them down over their ears. In our valley hat-brims, hair, beards, elbows point in every direction in an untrimmed, merry way. Here they all droop.

This drooping strikes one very forcibly when he leaves the plain of central Illinois and meets the first outpost of Egypt leaning against a pillar of the store porch, not even blinking. The hat-brim droops, almost hiding the face; the corners of the eyes droop; the long, thin mustache, the shoulders, even the trousers over the boot-tops, droop, droop, droop. He looks as though he were being continually rained on. Even his mule seems to catch this dejected spirit. In the hills this oddity is still more marked. Further on in the open country near where the rivers meet the impression will not leave you. That day as I passed the gates into the grove the trees seemed as staid as the people. The heavy oaks almost shut the sunlight out, and in the cool shade the good folks of Egypt stood in little knots, exchanging greetings and discussing timely topics. On every stump there was an old man, or a woman with a baby. A thin stream wandered through the art-gallery, among the stock-pens, and back past the booths where the young men were spending their nickels with royal recklessness, but the centre of interest was the gate, for here you could see who was coming and going, and this was a social occasion.

As we sauntered about, the Veteran talked of up the river and down the river, and of his wife's folks in Arkansas; the Drover spoke of his own country on the Missouri side, and the Editor explained that this was his first year away from the water. I ventured to remark that even if a bit inland the country was charming and the people most interesting; they carried one back to Huckleberry Finn.

"Huckleberry who?" inquired the Editor, putting his hand to his ear.

"Huckleberry Finn," I shouted. The Veteran shook his head.

"Finn—Finn—Finn," he said, slowly, groping around the back of his neck with his hand, as though he had expected to find some information there.

The Drover allowed that the Finns lived either on this side or down the Arkansas. The Editor shook his head.

So natural was the way in which they disclaimed Huckleberry, it began to seem possible that in their wanderings they might have run across Judge Thatcher or the Wilkses. Mutual acquaintances of this kind are sometimes embarrassing. Recalling a New York man who had met Mr. Pecksniff several times at his club—or was under the impression that he had seem him there, at least—now it seemed wiser to change the trend of our conversation by suggesting the matinée.

Happy Joe Robinson's show was eminently refined. That was his drawing-card. Standing before his tent he introduced us to one after another of his company—to Merry Jim, the negro impersonator; to Professor McGonigle, the juggler; to Little Egypt and the McChider children—and between each little speech he was careful to reiterate that their performance had been given in many towns under church auspices. This might easily have been true. If Merry Jim's buffonery was a bit rugged, if Professor McGinigle had the air of Chicago, and Little Egypt suggested the chorus, the songs and dances of the McChider children were worthy of the Sunday-school cantata. Happy Joe himself taught a great lesson when he sang to the accompaniment of a melodeon. Every long song has a moral. In this case it was repeated at the end of each of the twenty stanzas—Remember you have children of your own. Half of the audience was made up of small boys and girls; there was present a goodly proportion of babies in arms, but that made no difference. How could they forget the tall figure in the long purple frock-coat and the low waistcoat, with a great brown hat crushed in his hand, and swinging rhythmically to and fro! One could not but feel that in after years, when they did have children of their own, the admonition thundered at them that afternoon would be remembered.

The Veteran said that it was a grand song, and I agreed with him. He declared that the performance as a whole was well worth ten cents. The Drover had been to St. Louis, and so intimated that he would be charitably silent. The Editor explained that it was as much as we could expect so far inland. But over along the river—

Yes, over along the river things are different. There is more life there. So many boats go up and down, and floating shows and all that. Six miles is a long way inland, and these are primitive parts, but when you have come from Kansas they are restful. For Kansas is different, too, and there is life there. Here you do the fair in an hour, and retire to a stump, and doze and talk. There before the baby-show is over the races have begun, and when they have been run, the football game is on. Nightfall sends you to the International Hotel, and you just have time for supper, and hurry back to the grounds for the opera.

Life in Kansas in fair times is very wearing. If you are resolute, though, and forego the races and the football game, you will find things to see. In the morning you can watch the judges looking over the live-stock on the track enclosure, but there are so few people about then that it is dull. By noon it is livelier. The Minister and I reached the scene just as the afternoon boom had begun. We had a light luncheon in the tent supervised by the ladies of Zion Church, and started out as the band in the grand-stand opened its patriotic concert. Of the races we saw little or nothing, of course. We had a few sly glimpses of the pacers, and saw all of the mule and chariot contests from a secluded spot at the end of the track. But we missed the running and trotting. For myself, I had wearied of these things and of the side-shows so abundant in the East, and was content to be led through the pens and sheds where I could see what the rolling country about us was producing.

The agricultural implements alone were an artistic treat. For is there anything more beautiful than a binder fresh from the factory; anything more inspiring than a plough with its bright red beam and glistening share; anything more powerful than the mighty steam thresher! Unless you have farmed and discussed with your next neighbor the advantage of this cultivator or the defects of that mower, you'd better watch the races. If you are an artist, longing for what you hold life's higher things, go to the gallery and gaze on some bad copy of nature. But here is where we find the best art! Cunning hands must have laid the red and green on this harvester, turned that projecting iron into a duck's-head, transformed the cross-bar into a golden rib. So light and dashing it looks, we almost fancy it, horseless, gliding through the grain. The sulky plow, the self-acting hay-rake, even the humble potato-lifter, seem to be tugging at their tethers. These machines, in the glory of their paint, are too beautiful to use! They should be collected in some gallery where we could wander among them, tying knots on imaginary sheaves; planting corn on a smooth, clean floor; listening to the music of the sheller crunching but the choicest ears; dozing to the swish and roar of the thresher as the dustless straw beats through it. It is like a hanging a Van Dyck on a fence to send them into the field.

The Minister agreed with me. He believed in the old system of gleaning and winnowing. For the purpose of illustrating a point in the sermon the biblical methods were infinitely superior. Picture Ruth following a binder! Having found this line of thought, he started on a careful survey of it, but by good fortune our wanderings had carried us to a large pavilion.

Standing outside on a little elevation, we looked down on a field of bonnets, which seemed to muffle a mighty buzz, now dying, now swelling again, now silent as a clerical-looking man stepped to the edge of the platform at the distant end.

"Lot 56," he cried, reading from a catalogue in his hand. "Lot 56—best boy baby over one year and not exceeding one year and six months—shown by mother. Prize, $2. Twelve entries."

The buzz became a roar. Twelve mothers lifted themselves from the chaos of bonnets and climbed to the platform. From that moment the clergyman and his fellow judges were lost to our view. At rare intervals we could catch sight of a bit of black coat or a bald head, but they were quickly gone again.

My Minister mopped his brow. "I was a judge last year," he said.

A meek little man was standing close by, and we heard him chuckle.

"It is remarkable the woman go in for it," he exclaimed. "Why, it'll take 'em a month to get over the decisions, and for the rest of their lives them judges won't have any reputations for eyesight or sense. I know how it is with my wife. She put Emily in with the best girls under one, last year. The child wasn't even placed. This year she has William in Lot 55, and I s'pose she's busy this minute explainin'—"

He stopped. He made a rush for a little woman who was forcing her way out of the crowd. She was holding a baby so high in the air that we could see a blue ribbon on his arm. It was William.

Several times that afternoon we saw the same young gentleman, and on every occasion he was reposing on the arm of the meek, scoffing little man, and he so reposed that the blue ribbon could not be missed.

While the baby show may be a source of much dissension in a community, it serves one good purpose. This is the time to visit the Palace of Art, for when the competition of the infants is on, this distinctly feminine side of the fair is deserted. So we found it. We wandered almost alone about the big hall, and with that privilege a long journey is repaid. But you can see much the same thing in our valley. Kansas may grow taller corn than we do, but our neighbor Lizzie Lumpkin's "Bit of the Susquehanna" equals, at least, this prize-winning blue grove. Her "Storm Off the Atlantic City" far surpasses that "Moonlight on the Ocean." We can show you some beautiful fruits, both in oil and water-color in our valley, but in crayon and pencil we are far behind these. We have not surpassed the horse and cow class. Some day, perhaps, our Miss Lumpkin will give up blue and green for black and white, and we shall be able to do something in "after Gibsons" and panels full of cranes.

Kansas may boast of her corn and her cattle, but in the fine arts our valley holds her own. Leave the pictures and move along the hall. That embroidered frame is striking. I saw nothing like it at our fair, but down in Egypt there was a patch-work quilt, a mosaic in cotton, that makes that great one there look like a solid piece of material. That is an exquisite splasher—the one beneath the handmade dress—and it's a prize-winner, too, but against those yellow slippers I'd match the pair Miss Lumpkin's mother crocheted for Mr. Lumpkin, and I'd win. The embroidered pillow-shams, the paper flowers, the best-dressed doll and the honorable mention whisk-broom holder are well enough in their way, but we hurry by them, being men.

Being men, we pause again. From art in hand-painting, we have soared into art in cake-baking. Before us on long tables rise rows of monuments to housewifery—chocolate-layer and cocoanut, marble, mountain, sponge and snow, angel-food and jelly-twist. How fine they must have looked on the first day! Now they seem a bit depressed. From each one a triangular slice has been cut. It lies wearily across the top, and a crescent hole in its corner shows where the official teeth have been. The cake has been judged! There is no need for it to swell up. So it sags.

The best dried corn, the canned cherries, the preserved tomatoes, the candied pears and strawberry jelly look the same North, East, South, and West, but they are as essential features of the county fair as the races and the livestock. They lift it above the street-fair's level.

In some part of the West they will tell you that these street-fairs are driving out the fine old county gatherings. It can never be. The street-fair is altogether a commercial venture, designed by the small merchants to gather in their town a crowd that will spend its money freely. Several large companies supply the attractions, and for a consideration from the associated store-keepers and saloon-men, they take over the village, block its thoroughfares with cheap shows, and make day and night hideous with the blare of their bands and the shouts of their barkers. The company gets the dimes taken in at the score of gates. The merchants make their profit from the crowd. The crowd flocks from show to show, and eats pop-corn and shouts as though it were having a mighty good time.

From the bright, trim Kansas grove, and the shade of the Egypt oaks, I dropped into the dusty streets of a Missouri town when it was crowded with these cheap shows. It soon was wearisome. There were no stumps to sit on, no trees to lounge under when one tired of listening to the barkers. And that was all there was to do, for the best of the shows was on the outside. The show-men themselves were far more entertaining than any other performances they had to offer within their gates, and in their particular line they were wonders. Our Eastern barkers are mere tyros beside these fellows. A few here did simply lie roughly. The bullet-headed man that managed the snakes, allowed me to look, free of charge, at the boa-constrictor's teeth, and shouted at me that within there were seven hundred and fifty wrigglin' reptiles, and that I had his personal word of honor that the charmer before me had been two years in the Smithsonian Institution and had been declared by Government experts to be immune from a rattler's poison. I simply did not believe him. But the little fellow in the frock-coat, a derby, and a white bow tie, looking every inch a Sunday-school superintendent, took me into his confidence, and explained it was high time I left the old farm and saw the world. I had heard of that storied city of the Bible, Cairo, and he had brought it to my very door. Here was an opportunity for me to see how the streets and houses looked; how the people lived, how they prayed to their strange gods, and how they fought. He was so kind and confidential about it that I felt really disappointed when I paid my dime and found in his tent a camel, a donkey, and a few Chicago Arabs.

With the memory of this fresh in my mind I stood listening to a handsome bronzed man before the animal show. He told us stories of life in the jungle, of the battles of lions and tigers, of the intelligence of the elephant and the cunning of the wolf. He had about him large pictures of all the beasts, and made his lecture clearer by referring to them with a long, pedagogic pointer. He told us of the lessons in fortitude, patience, and love that we could learn from the jungle people, and closed with a few words on the triumph of mind over brute force as it would be illustrated when the lady in pink stepped into the den of roaring lions. Had I paid my money and gone away it would have been well spent. The fellow was so gentle and yet so masterful that you believed in him in spite of yourself. And when you went within to see one lion, a few parrots, and an intellectual pony, the bullet-headed man with his seven hundred and fifty wriggling snakes seemed truthful beside this master of their art.

But street-fairs must differ. Some of them must rise to the plane of the county fair. Some must fulfil the promise of the posters. One I have heard of, and I hope to go back to that Indiana town and do it from end to end with my friend the Chief of Police. It was he who told me of it. Our acquaintance thus far has been very limited, but when we parted it was with the promise that we should meet again. And when that promise is fulfilled he is to show me things well worth so long a journey.

WILLIAM L. SLOUT

We met in the early morning on the platform of the station. I had slept that night in the Palace Hotel. The hotel is in the station. This being a junction point my room was bounded on two sides by railroads. By midnight it seemed as though the house was the hub of a great spoke-work of tracks. The train East was due at four o'clock. The clerk, with kind precaution, awakened me at three. Outside on the platform I found a solitary man sitting in the glare of the electric light. It was easy to tell by the helmet perched on top of his head and by the brass buttons on his blue castaway coat that he was the police-officer of the town on night patrol. The proper thing to do on meeting the police-officer of a small place is to address him as "Chief." In this instance the proper thing was done, and the Chief waved me to a chair at his side.

There was a silence which at a time like this could be broken only by a cigar. It was offered with an apology for its character.

The Chief held it up under the light and gazed at it from afar off. "It looks as if it'll smoke," he said.

He spoke as though the act of smoking was to be voluntary on the part of the cigar, but in reality he helped it along by puffing very hard.

"Goin' East?" he asked.

"New York."

"Comin' back October 9th, of course?"

"I think not."

"No? Now I tell you it 'ud be well worth your while," he cried. "By crickety! it would. You just otter see our street-fair."

"Oh, is that all?" I said.

"All! Ain't that enough? You've never seen our street-fair, man, have you? Well, once you've seen it, you'll come regular. Now, to give you an idee—" he paused and smoked.

"To give you an idee, we have—" He smoked again. Then he fired it. "We have a Queen!"

"A Queen?" said I, getting at last waked up to the importance of the thing.

"Why, we crown her," he exclaimed. "You see it's this way. We vote for two weeks proceedin' the crownin'. Every vote costs five cents. I know one feller in this town who has already spent forty dollars ballotin' for his lady. Whoever gets the most votes is Queen, an' we give her a diamon' ring worth $150—think of that."

"What does the Queen do?" I inquired.

"Do?" he replied, sharply. There was a note of disgust in his tone. "Do?" he repeated. "Why, man, she's a regular Queen—she don't do nothin'."

Truly this was a fair worth seeing! I told him how I felt, and he smiled. I told him that I wanted to hear more about it, and he smiled again. Tilting his chair back on two legs, he rested his head against the wall, and with his elbow on the chair-arm and the cigar smoking itself between his fingers, he was comfortably fixed to describe the glories to come.

All the Little Egypts in the world dance at that fair, and a hundred brass-bands make the streets ring with martial music. A thousand little boys in blue velveteen drag the Queen's chariot, and a thousand little girls in white dresses, white stockings, white shoes, and pink ribbons follow it, singing carols. How the diamond flashes in Her Majesty's crown! Down Main Street she goes—past the bank, past the court-house, past the post-office. Before the Presbyterian church the royal coach halts, and a mighty chorus sings an anthem. A thousand sopranos trill the high notes. A thousand basses go "arum-arum-arump." Graciously the Queen bows. And the diamond flashes again. The little boys shout and fall to the ropes.

On they go! by the drug-store; past the hotel. All the eloquent barkers in the world are in this street, but when the Queen comes they are silent. All the snake-charmers in the world show their teeth, too. The mermaids set up a terrible splashing and try to get out of their tanks, for they hear the roar in the streets and see the people rushing out of the tents. There are a great number of Professors McGonigle, and they all begin throwing knives at once, and it looks as though somebody will surely be hurt, but nobody is. There are only two McChider children in the wide world—Happy Joe told us so—and now they are piping their little song at double the regular speed. There is only one Happy Joe in the wide world, too, and when the Queen comes he catches her eye. He raises his right hand, folds back his long purple frock coat, and hooks his thumb in a waistcoat pocket. His left hand goes to the brim of his brown fedora, and it sweeps from his head as he bows very low. The Queen has passed. The royal coach rolls on until it reaches the railroad track and doubles back into Indiana Avenue. We see Her Majesty no more.

Night comes. The ghostly tents glow in the moonlight. The street is deserted save for a single figure moving slowly to and fro across the square. He halts beneath the arc-light and stands there swinging his club. By his helmet we know him. It is the Chief. He is watching over them all—over the Queen and her court, over his town and his fair.

WILLIAM L. SLOUT

12. THE SPECTATOR (*AT THE FAIR*)

OUTLOOK, NOVEMBER 2, 1907

It has long been a favorite theory with the Spectator that in nothing does the character of a community show more plainly than in its play-days. The times of relaxation are a good index to the real aspirations and ambitions of the people, as they are of the individual. Opportunity to visit a Middle West county fair was welcomed as offering an insight into the modern farmer's relation to the larger affairs of life. The county fair is always a farmer's gathering. The Spectator remembered it back East as a place for the congregation of clumsy lumber-wagons and displays of huge pumpkins. So there were farmers at this county fair out in the plains country; but where were the rattling wagons and the clumsy-footed horses? Hundreds of teams drove up the dusty road to the gate of the fair grounds, but they are hitched to smart surreys, double carriages, or citified buggies. Over on the farther side of the grand stand where the hitching-places had been provided were actually acres of farmers' rigs, and not a half-dozen wagons among them. At the livery stables in town were hundreds of other rigs, and these too were buggies, surreys, and rubber-tired carriages. The farmer of to-day gives his family some real comforts in the way of transportation.

Nor was this all. Here and there came an automobile, and the disregard of the machine shown by the farm horses gave evidence that this modern luxury has become common throughout the land. "Yes, a good many farmers have motor-cars," explained the gatekeeper. "Most of them are runabouts, but there are probably a dozen touring-cars in the county outside the towns. The finest car around here is owned by a young farmer twelve miles from town. There he comes now," and he pointed to a handsome forty-horse-power machine that had just made the run over the prairie roads, its bronzed-cheeked owner at the wheel. With smooth highways nine months in the year, no stones, and few hills, it is little wonder that motoring proves fascinating. The farmers' wives and daughters were well dressed, cheery, and seemed to be enjoying life. Altogether it was a very satisfactory and typical American crowd that filed into the grounds.

The exhibits of grain, live stock, and domestic productions were no doubt much the same as of old, but what most interested the Spectator was the class of amusements offered. Of course the perennial and perpetual merry-go-round was there, though it had a different name and some new-fangled appliances in its mechanical organ and jumping horses. The same old hot-air balloon that is scheduled to go up at four o'clock and does not do so until six-thirty was present. But along with these was a new sort of amusement feature, a product of modern invention. In a black tent was a moving picture show—how our fathers and mothers in their youth would have marveled at this wonderful production! In front of the grand stand as a free attraction were vaudeville artists performing on a trapeze. A scantily dressed lady made a "high dive" into a shallow pool of water. A children's flower parade attracted more attention than did all the other features of the day. Some illusion shows, minstrels, and similar entertainments lined the "warpath"—the name that has everywhere succeeded "pike," as that did "midway." But nowhere on the grounds was "Bosco" who "eats 'em alive"; nowhere was the gaudy group of dancing girls—it was throughout a clean, wholesome, decent sort of entertainment that commended itself as worthy of a sturdy, well-to-do, farmer-like community.

"It is the kind of amusement that pays best," explained the manager of the fair, philosophically. "We probably are not too good to have the other kind if it would attract bigger crowds—but it don't. The county fairs tried that after the Chicago Exposition. All over the West they had reproductions of the Midway, with all the Streets of Cairo novelties then introduced. It was looked on as a drawing card and there was rivalry as to which could go the farthest and not invite a visit from the police. In the end it killed many a county fair. The decent folks would not go—and after a while the managers woke up to the fact that there are more decent folks in any community than any other kind. More than that, they are the ones who have the money and influence. So the county fairs and the street carnivals and other things of the sort began looking for clean shows fit for every farmer's wife and daughter, because it is that class that makes the fair a success. The town folks can't do it alone. When we did that, the fairs began to be popular again, and now hundreds of Western counties are having them when six or eight years ago they looked up the grounds in discouragement. People come to the fair to be amused, and they care very little for speeches and instruction unless they are greatly out of the ordinary. For instance, last year we brought a milking-machine run by a gasoline engine and milked cows on the ground. It took eight policeman to keep back the crowds. That was something that both amused and instructed, and every farmer and his family longed for a similar equipment."

We used to hear a great deal about the sad and lonely fate of the Western farmer's wife, but there was little evidence of loneliness in the appearance of these woman who surrounded the quilts and fancy-work in the Domestic Arts building. They seemed as much at home in discussing modern adornments of the home as the women from town, and there were evidences of a social life far beyond the limits of the municipalities. One whole section was devoted to the work of a club of women living ten miles from the county-seat town, and on farms. They met every fortnight and kept abreast of the times. When the Spectator came across some old friends and was invited to a picnic dinner on the grass near the race-track, it was found that modern cookery is not less expert than that of earlier days. The array of eatables was fully as abundant and as appetizing as ever grace the old New York State dining-table; and if the laughing company did not do it full justice, it was solely because of lack of time. Who could linger long at a lunch of this sort with two bands, a phonograph, and a steam-animated piano all playing within a dozen rods?

At this fair one hundred dollars in several prizes was offered to the boys who raised the best samples of corn. That was not remarkable. Another thing was unusual: one hundred dollars in a number of prizes was offered to the girls who brought in the finest flowers. It seemed to the Spectator that this marked a distinct advance in the Middle West's viewpoint. In all its previous existence it has been lauding the corn, wheat, alfalfa, herds, and flocks. To give deliberate reward to flower-raising means that the ethical influence of beauty is making itself felt even in the most utilitarian of commonwealths. To place flower-raising on a level with corn-raising, to give the same reward for one as for the other, means a healthy appreciation of the advantage that grows out of encouraging adornment in the home. The effect of several score competitors for the prizes, with their carefully tended flower gardens scattered over the county, pleasing all who saw them through the long summer, could but be beneficial to the aesthetic development of that section. Now that the fruits were gathered, it was a personal satisfaction to note that more admirers surrounded the gay bouquets than were gathered before the neatly arranged rows of corn.

Anything that brings people together in friendly intercourse is good for a community. The older one grows, the more one appreciates the beneficial effect of a broad community life. The county fair is a civilizer in this, that it brings realization of the good things possessed by others, and leads away from introspection and toward the larger affairs of life. The tendency of the modern exposition is less to encourage fierce rivalry than to get the people together for a harvest home visit. This was the sentiment of the fair ground throng. Those who had lived in the county when fairs were devoted chiefly to horse-racing and a few doubtful entertainments rejoiced at the change, and praised the new condition of things. They said it had taken years to build up the fair sentiment on the right basis, that it had been expensive at times and often seemed likely to fail entirely. In the end, perseverance won, and the result was helpful in both a business and a social sense. Other counties adjoining had been less successful, but were trying to conduct annual shows on a similar plan—which simply goes to prove that the county fair, homely and apparently simple as it is, depends for its success, like other public gatherings, on the intelligence and the grasp of correct principals possessed by its managers.

THE GREAT EXHIBITION AND ITS VISITORS

IV.

WORLD'S EXPOSITIONS

The success of London's Crystal Palace Exhibition of 1851, in which Prince Albert took such an interest, encouraged other cities to host international fairs. New York responded quickly with a smaller Crystal Palace in 1853 which was essentially a failure. It took a national commemoration in 1876 and the Centennial Exhibition at Philadelphia to set off a plethora of fairs throughout industrializing America—at Atlanta, New Orleans, Buffalo, Denver, Louisville, and other enterprising communities. But it was the Chicago World's Columbian Exposition of 1893 which, profiting by earlier examples, epitomized America's place in world industry and commerce, summarized the progress of the nineteenth century, and gave notice to the country that Chicago was ready to become a major metropolis.

There, the inclusion of an organized amusement area alongside the fair proper, thereby eliminating a peripheral settlement of disreputable entertainments outside the fairgrounds as had occurred in Philadelphia, established the famous Midway Plaisance from which the Ferris wheel and "kooch" dancer became national symbols of fun and frolic. Further, it created the idea of a collective amusement association, or more commonly, the traveling carnival, which perpetuated the "midway" and the Ferris wheel and debased the enchanting "kooch" dancer for all time.

13. THE GREAT EXHIBITION AND ITS VISITORS

PUTNAM'S MAGAZINE, DECEMBER, 1853

The throng of strangers in our streets for some months past, the season during which our regular denizens are more than decimated by summer travel, would have suggested to a chance observer who had known the city in former years, some peculiar attraction, some new wonder or pleasure; a fresh excitement, or a lately opened avenue of gain. "Has Jenny Lind found a successor?" he might have asked; "or are National and Whole World Conventions being held, for the establishment of Women's rights, or Men's rights (lately worse threatened): for the discrediting of spirituous drinks, or the encouragement of spiritual visitors? Has the Sea-Serpent come in through the Aqueduct, or a new *danseuse* been imported by Niblo? Has Mr. M'Clure traced the Auroral light to fields of pure silver surrounding the Pole, or Comstock invented a plough that will lay bare the entire resources of our Californian fields in a single week?"

We know of no compendious answer that would at once account for the concourse, and show our questioner that his conjectures had not run altogether wide of the mark, so well as these little words—"The Crystal Palace"; the cognomen of that harmonious and lovely stranger; that powerful World's Convention for the benefit of every body's rights; that irrefragable Temperance sermon; that grand Congress of Rapping, Ringing, and Table marvels; a Sea-Serpent in size, an Ellsler in grace, an Aurora of illumination, a Californian in industrial promise—is it not a worthy and sufficient cause for this grand convergence, that makes our young city seem, for the time, a very London?

Far back in the country, while yet the burning weather lasted, the thrill of this splendid novelty was felt; in sober villages, in lonely farm-houses, in log-huts still haunted by deer and the prairie-wolf. Even then, preparations were making, excuses devised, and pence put by, for a visit to New York as soon as the harvest should be housed and the heat abated. "The Crys-*tial* Palace" was the universal theme, the moment any one appeared who knew any thing about it. How big was it? And what color? And when would it be ready—quite ready, with all the grand things in their places? Many of us citizens were a good deal mortified that the satisfactory answer to this last query was necessarily so long delayed; but perhaps that only gave a greater *prestige* to the thing, the getting up of which took even New York so long to complete. But some spoke of the delay as if it were a personal injury, even though their own visiting time was yet far off. Their imagination resented any blanks in the picture which occupied so much space. Others thought that if the new reaper, and the latest threshing machine, and fanning mill, and corn-sheller, with their kindred, were on the ground, other things did not make any important difference, only that mother, and Jane, and Debbie-Ann wanted to see the finery, so it was necessary to await the final signal. It was especially curious to observe the interest of the elder people, old ladies in particular, who one and all declared they would "see *that*, if they never saw anything else!" The combined notion of splendor, variety, and extent, warmed up every imagination that was not utterly extinct, and raised every head not wholly "subdued to what it works in," till difficulties dissolved or were thrust aside, and not a "huddle" but sent its quota of gazers, wonderers, and most amusing critics.

Meanwhile those with whom knowledge was more abundant and money not quite so hard to come by, all who had travelled or meant to travel, or who had read other people's travels in the splendid olden world, were already astir, waiting for no harvest-garnering, or work-finishing, or even for the filling up of the immense spaces of the House of Glass, rather pleased to have less of distraction for the first view, so often to be repeated before a rational curiosity could be satiated. Our hotels can bear witness to the floods of silk and broadcloth, from all points of the Union, that filled their halls to unexampled overflowing, even while the summer was yet fierce. New York being on the way to Saratoga, to Newport, to the White Hills, to Quebec and the Saguenay, to every where, in short—even the ultra-fashionable, not famed for rational curiosity, did not disdain to bestow a passing glance on the Industry of All Nations, dignified as it was in their estimation by the Art and Elegance of All Nations....

But, when the Palace was at last pronounced finished, what was the vision that greeted the unsophisticated, as they entered its airy courts for the first time? At first dazzle; a thousand sparkles and rainbows; light and movement undistinguishable for a while; then, as the eye settled, order emerging here and there; beautiful forms and colors developing themselves one by one; vast climaxes of Art, Industry, and Invention, extending away and away in long perspective on every side; whole avenues of wonders, distracting choice; and, overhead a soft, silvery sky, with many lights, a mimic firmament of delicate cerulean, from which we might almost expect falling dews, so well does its flecked azure counterfeit the heaven-hung arch that spans all. From that centre point where stands the image of the majestic form our American eyes love best to look upon—the grandest of Nature's models—we look, on all sides, down radiating line of display, in which various national emblems and devices suggest the world-wide interest of an Industrial unity....

...The picture-gallery, so full of wonder and delight, has revealed a sixth sense to many a fascinated eye and heart. O, how enchanting it must be to traverse it, without having ever before seen a fine landscape, or a life-like scene from history! What sympathy of passion have we watched in faces that staid spell-bound before Washington crossing the Delaware! Many a fair cheek has flushed in rivalry with another beauty on canvas; many an eye has been surprised into moisture by pictured woe or heroism; and we are mistaken if the glow of pleasure has not lighted in some hearts the flame of high resolve, or warmed into life the seeds of honorable ambition. Indeed we could hardly be persuaded that every day in the Crystal Palace does not see the dawn of thought that will one day shine out over the land in modes of beauty and benefit. Stupid starers enough there are, doubtless; incredibly stolid, troglodyte remarks that reach our ears occasionally prove this; and we are credibly informed of things that show ignorance "deeper than ever plummet sounded."

...One of the pleasantest moments at the Palace is that in which the roof-lights begin to look black instead of white against the sky, by reason of the fading of the day-light and the dawn of the gas, and when the great dome begins to emerge again, in a new yellow glory, and the long, lighted avenues to remind one of the Boulevards and the Champs Élysées. The scenic effect of this juncture is unsurpassable; and when the lighting is at its full, and fine music begins to enchant the air, and the unappreciating crowd become, all unconsciously to themselves, a part of the show, their gaudy colors and swaying motion, enacting a great *parterre* under the vagaries of a fresh breeze, we feel that we need not cross the ocean to see one of the most magnificent indoor spectacles in the world.

The police of the Palace make no inconsiderable feature in the show, with their neat uniform, marked caps, and erect, gentlemanly bearing. They are well-drilled and ready; but with an American crowd, largely composed of women, they have little strictly professional duty. But they have done important service in one direction, by showing, on a small scale, the value of a uniform dress for functionaries whose official character is their strength. They are like some of those powerful and brilliant pumps in the Machine Arcade, that never

"*Up and down their tedious arms do sway,*"

but quietly, and without sputter throw water with great force—right back into the place it came from, just to exhibit the principle. What they do is not much, but it is nonetheless evident what they can do upon occasion. To our rowdy-ridden city the model is one of the most valuable in the whole collection. Whether granite-colored caps of office, that seem to hint an incipient fossilization, would be of good augury in city-guardians, seems open to question. These head-pieces give the C.P.P., with the solemn silence which is part of the wearers' duty, something of a Druidical air, and help the picturesque of the Palace, considered as a great Temple of Industry. When the oracle jaws do open, at the adjuration of spasmodically courageous waifs, it is for utterances which may be deemed Druidical for brevity and sternness, and Delphic for mystical enwrapment. But this is all in character, and helps the *prestige* no doubt. Human nature is always salutarily impressed by judicious official snubbing, within the limits of civility.

As ten o'clock strikes, every bell in the edifice (brazen) strikes back, and there ensues such a terrific tintinnabulation as has not been heard since poor Poe's time. What a verse he might have added to his song of the "Bells—bells—bells" if he could have heard this belligerent dismissal. The noise is to the ear what the flaming sword of the first Paradise was to the eye, and has a familiar effect—that of causing every human occupant to flee....

...One cannot help thinking what a splendid crown it would make to the list of wonderful inventions in machinery here exhibited—inventions that do all but breathe and talk, and certainly double man's life by the addition of power and economy of time they offer him—if one had been contrived that would give us, in one view, the thoughts, fancies, motives and hopes of each exhibitor. In looking over the catalogue, one seems to catch glimpses of far off interiors; household scenes, as well as dark, oily workshops, and cold and dreary attic *ateliers*; silent, anxious night watches, as well as rattling looms and grating of saws and mill-stones. There is one class that touches our curiosity and interest above all: "Specimens of fine needlework"; "Octagonal silk quilt, of 6500 pieces"; "Fancy bed-quilt, highly ornamented with designs of birds, fruits, and flowers"; "Black apron of knitted silk, with bead embroideries"; "Rag hearth-rug"; "Worsted work, Auld Robin Gray"—dozens more of just such things, done in our neighboring country towns, and in close and reeking streets of our own city, by female fingers; "Specimens of Irish pearl, tatting, etc., by Sophia A. Ellis, Kildernoc Rectory, Louth, Ireland"; "Doylies embroidered with views in Ireland, by the Countess of Clancarty and Lady Anne Butler, Ballinasloe, Ireland"; "Vestments, embroidery, flowers in lace, etc., Sisters of Mercy, Kinsale, Ireland"; "Crochet-work, from the Industrial Poor School of The Ursuline Convent, Black Rock, near Cork, Ireland"; "Crochet and knitted articles from Breslau, Prussia"; "Fine embroideries, Miss Brasch, Bremen"; "Embroidered Cushion, and newly invented toys, Charlotte Paulsen, Hamburg" (the noble-hearted woman who has been the life and soul of the great ragged schools there, persecuted and almost proscribed by the government, who could not tolerate the catholicity of her views); "Cassava Starch, Mrs. McClintock, Demarara"; and a "Bird's Nest," from the same place; "Poems," by a lady at St. John's, New Brunswick; "Various specimens of embrodery, by Signora Madalina Tedeschi," whose whereabouts we need not doubt of; and so on and on, through all the courts, the modest and elegant contributions of women appeal to the eye, carrying the imagination back to the homes where these things are contrived and labored over, and the hopes and the honest pride with which they were dispatched to the Great Exhibition. It makes one almost shudder to think that every item, in all that vast array of offerings, from men and women, poor and rich, obscure and famous, has hopes behind it. We pass by a thousand things to look at one; we give to that one hardly more than a passing glance; yet there are garnered lives every where, and human hearts interested in every pause we make. Who knows whether the artist himself, poor and depressed, is not at our elbow, seeing our indifference, or hearing our contempt? He has been toiling in silence for years to perfect that little implement, which is to the careless eye as the small dust of balance amid the grandeur all around it; to his thinking, the ingenuity, or the utility, or the elegance of *that* is as conspicuous as it could have been in a form ever so imposing, yet, host after host, day after day, sees no lighted eye, no lingering footstep near the life-product. The sculptor, some stranger from the other side of the ocean, who brought to the New World the statue which seemed to him unnoticed at home only because it was surrounded by Art's perfected pearls of all time, understands English enough to be stung by the "Horrid!" of the pert young lady, or the uplifted eyebrow of the cool critic.

It is a mistake to forget the human background of that immense show, which looks, at first sight, like the triumph of Materialism. The people whose brains contrived and whose hands made all, are greater than the things made, and the hearts and hopes and happiness of that multitude are bound up in and under the public reception and appreciation of the various works there presented. If we could see, in some special "Arcade"—(it would need to be longer than the Machine Arcade, which is *only* 450 feet!) the entire army of artificers, with all those who love and who depend upon them, ranged in order due, it might be only a smutched and grimy host to the fastidious observer, slightly relieved, here and there, by a more genteel specimen of humanity. Keen eyes there would be, and expanded foreheads; pale cheeks, and hard hands, and travel-soiled feet; men of all climes, from China to Peru, women of all complexion, the Anglo-Saxon predominating; little children, too, for no small amount of the work, is, in some cases, done by such as are hardly old enough to be trusted out of the mother's sight—the silver and gold filagree of Genoa, for instance (of which the statuette of Columbus is an exquisite specimen); all this were to the lover of his kind a moving sight; to God who made and loveth all, an array of life most worthy and precious; a host of workers in His service even better than they know of; helpers of His plan by the natural and legitimate use of the powers and faculties He gave them; rolling on the great Car of Improvement towards the supernal goal to which all that is good and true must tend—the assimilation and reunion of man with his Maker.

> Men, my brothers, men the workers, ever reaping something new,
> That which they have done but earnest of the things that they shall do.

Strange, that a novelty so grand, a sight so splendid, an enterprise so humane, should not have stirred to its inmost core the great metropolis which was its natural and proper seat. Strange that men far-reaching and high-souled, who see in their own commerce something above and beyond the pelf which the vulgar suppose to be their only aim, should not at once have joined hand in hand, to exalt and dignify a display so entirely in concordance with their own comprehensive views of the advancement of our country, in all that she yet lacks to bring her to the highest level of the nations, in arts, as she has already proved herself in arms. Strange, passing strange, that the advocates of Peace, so numerous here, should not have seen, in this consent of foreign lands in a general exhibition and competition of their choicest products, a foundation and an earnest of that condition of things, when the ledger and not the sword shall decide the relations of countries to each other; and when the loom shall be more potent that the cannon in settling national difficulties. Strange above all is it, and sadly laughable, that there should have been heard even a whisper that the Palace was to be slighted as a "money-making scheme!" This sounds like a joke and a bad one; such an objection, it would seem, could never have been even whispered in New York, that great common sense city, which has long ago discovered that the thing that "won't pay," isn't worth doing....

...And out of that grew a poor attendance of the very people who ought to have given the earliest impetus, the cultivated and enlightened inhabitants of the city of New York. The great deficiency of the Exhibition has been in the people; "*live critters*," as the old lady said; not exactly quadrapedal but bipedal, and not only bipedal but endowed with heads with brains in them. Multitudes from the north and from the south, and from the east and from the west, have flocked to the shrine of our bright wonder; but those who, above all, should have done it and themselves honor by an intelligent interest, having almost disowned it. There was no Prince Albert at the foundation; no Queen and Archbishop to grace its opening with regal splendor; republican simplicity was the only glory of the ceremony, and a citizen yet new in the presidential chair, its only marked dignitary. Yet it has risen, slowly but surely, and taken its due place in the estimation of the community. Its avenues are crowded more and more, and whoever can speak and write in our land begins to feel its inspiration. As the year wanes the throngs increase; the promise of a whole winter's access was hailed with acclamation. The Crystal Palace is at last the fashion, and its projectors, builders, encouragers, abettors, and contributors, have quietly ascended to the position due to their liberality, discernment, skill, faith and courage. May their light never be less!

14. A SENNIGHT OF THE CENTENNIAL

by W. D. Howells
ATLANTIC MONTHLY, JULY, 1876

The Centennial is what every one calls the great fair now open at Philadelphia. "Have you been at the Centennial?" "How do you like the Centennial?" Some politer and more anxious few struggle for logical precision, reflecting that you cannot go to a Centennial, anymore than you can go to a Millennial. These entangle themselves in International Exhibition, or talk of the Exposition. The English, who invented it, and have a genius for simplicity (in some things), called the first international exhibition the World's Fair. But this simple and noble name does not quite serve us, since our World's Fair means the commemoration of our hundredth national anniversary; and so, at last, Centennial is the best name, in spite of its being no name at all.

The Centennial is so far peculiar in other ways that one may fitly give one's self the benefit of a doubt whether it is wholly advantageous to have seen the other world's fairs in order to have an intelligent appreciation of this; whether, in fact, it were not better never to have seen anything of the sort before. We will assume, for the present writer's purpose, that this is so. We may even go a step further and suppose that one's acquaintance with the Centennial is to be most fortunately formed upon a dull, drizzling day, somewhat cold and thoroughly unpleasant, like the 17th of May, for example. On that day, a week after the opening of the show, the first impression was certainly that of disorder and incompleteness, and the Centennial had nothing to do but to grow upon the visitor's liking. The paths were broken and unfinished, and the tough, red mud of the roads was tracked over the soft asphalt into all the buildings. Carts employed in the construction came and went everywhere, on easy terms alike with the trains of the circular railway whose engines hissed and hooted at points above the confusion, and with the wheeled-chairs in which ladies, huddling their skirts under their umbrellas, were trundled back and forth among the freight cars of the Pennsylvania Railroad. At many points laborers were digging over the slopes of the grounds and vigorously slapping the sides of the clayey embankments with the flat of their spades; and ironical signboards in all directions ordered you to keep off the grass on spaces apparently dedicated to the ceramic arts forever. Even if these grassless spots had been covered with tender herbage, there seemed not enough people present to justify the vigilance that guarded them; but I think this was an illusion, to which the vastness of the whole area and its irregular shape and surface contributed. There were probably fifteen thousand visitors that day, but many thousands more dispersed over the grounds and scattered through the different buildings would have given nowhere the impression of a crowd. With my simple Bostonian experiences as ground comparison, I had been diffidently thinking that Mr. Gilmore's Jubilees possibly afforded some likeness to the appearance of the spectators at the Centennial; I am bound to say now that the Centennial at no time and in no place gave any such notion of multitude. From day to day the crowd sensibly increased, but it never struck one as a crowd, and it hardly ever incommoded one, except perhaps in the narrow corridors of the Art Hall, and the like passages of the Annex to that building; these were at times really thronged.

If we had been the most methodical of sight-seers we could hardly have systematized our observations on a first day. It was enough if we could form a clear idea of the general character of the principal features and their position. Even this would not at all do. We wandered quite aimlessly about from one building to another, and, if we ever had anything definite in view, gave ourselves the agreeable surprise of arriving at something altogether different. Nevertheless from these desultory adventures some distinct impressions remained—such, namely, as that of a great deal of beauty in the architecture. The Agricultural Hall we did not see till next day, and we therefore did not see what I believe is considered the best of the temporary structures; but the Main Building has a lightness, in spite of its huge extent, which is as near grace as it might hope to come; and the Machinery Hall has the beauty of a most admirable fitness for its purpose. The prospect of the interior is very striking, and much more effective than that of the Main Building, where the view, from the floor at least, is more broken....

...We had time the first day for hardly more than a glance at the different buildings. We went next to the Machinery Hall, through the far extent of which we walked, looking merely to the right and left as we passed down the great aisle. Of that first impression the majesty of the great Corliss engine, which drives the infinitely varied machinery, remains most distinct. After that is the sense of too many sewing-machines. The Corliss engine does not lend itself to description; its personal acquaintance must be sought by those who would understand its vast and almost silent grandeur. It rises loftily in the centre of the huge structure, an athlete of steel and iron with not a superfluous ounce of metal on it; the mighty walking-beams plunge their pistons downward, the enormous fly-wheel revolves with a hoarded power that makes all tremble, the hundred life-like details do their office with unerring intelligence. In the midst of this ineffably strong mechanism is a chair where the engineer sits reading his newspaper, as in a peaceful bower. Now and then he lays down his paper and clambers up one of the stairways that cover the framework, and touches some irritated spot on the giant's body with a drop of oil, and goes down again and takes up his newspaper; he is like some potent enchanter there, and this prodigious Afreet is his slave who could crush him past all semblance of humanity with his slightest touch. It is, alas! what the Afreet has done to humanity too often, where his strength has superseded men's industry; but of such things the Machinery Hall is no place to speak, and to be honest, one never thinks of such things there. One thinks only of the glorious triumphs of skill and invention; and wherever else the national bird is mute in one's breast, here he cannot fail to utter his pride and content. It would be a barren place without the American machinery. All that Great Britain and Germany have sent is insignificant in amount when compared with our own contributions; the superior elegance, aptness, and ingenuity of our machinery is observable at a glance. Yes, it is still in these things or iron and steel that the national genius most freely speaks, by and by the inspired marbles, the breathing canvases, the great literature; for the present America is voluble in the strong metals and their infinite uses. I have hinted already that I think she talks too much in sewing-machines, but I dare say that each of these patents has its reason for being, and that the world would go mostly unclad without it. At least I would not like to try to prove the contrary to any of those alert agents or quick young lady attendants. Nevertheless, a whole half-mile of sewing-machines seems a good deal; and *is* there so very much difference between them?

Our first general impressions of the different buildings were little changed by close acquaintance. What we found interesting in the beginning, that we found interesting at the end, and this is an advantage to those whose time is short at the Centennial. You know and see continually more and more, but it is in the line of your first enjoyment. This is peculiarly the case in the Main Building, where the contrasts are the sharpest, and the better and worst most obvious. In the case of some of the nations (notably Russia, Turkey, and Spain) no judgment could be formed, for there was as yet nothing to look at, when we first came, in the spaces alloted to them....

...Our second day at the Centennial began in the Main Building, where after a glance at the not very satisfactory Italian department we found ourselves presently amid the delicate silver-work, the rich furs, the precious and useful meat, as the artistic representations of national life of Norway. It was by far the completest department in the building, and for that little country, winter-bound in paralyzing cold and dark for so great a part of the year, the display of tasteful and industrial results was amazing....

...The Main Building is provided with many fountains of the soda sort, and one large fountain for the unsophisticated element, all of which were pretty, and contributed to that brightness of effect which was so largely owing to the handsomeness of the show-cases and pavilions. The finest of these were American. We were thought to have sometimes dimmed the lustre of our jewels by the brilliancy of the casket, but the general display gained by this error. In the middle of the building a band played many hours every day, and over all, with his *baton*, and both arms extended, perpetually triumphed the familiar person of Mr. Gilmore, whom one fancied partially consoled for his lost Coliseums by the bigness of the edifice and the occasion, though, as I said before, the multitude was in nowise comparable to that of our Jubilees. The sparseness of the visitors was more apparent than real, as seen from the organ loft at the end of the building or from the galleries overlooking the central space, but it was worth while to suffer the illusory regret produced by this appearance in order to enjoy the magnificent *coup d'oeil* which was to be gained only from those heights.

In the afternoon we made the tour of the State buildings, of which, generally speaking, it is hard to detect at once the beauty or occasion. Doubtless the use could be discovered by public or representative bodies from the various States. The most picturesque building is that of New Jersey; that of Massachusetts was comfortable and complete, which most of the others were not. The Michigan building promises to be handsome; the Ohio building has some meaning in being of Ohio stones, and it is substantially and gracefully designed; the West Virginia building is observable for its exterior display of native woods. But really the most interesting of these not apparently well-reasoned structures is the Mississippi house, which is wholly built of Mississippi woods, the rough dark bark logs showing without, and the gables and porch decked with gray streamers of Spanish mosses. A typical Mississippian, young in years but venerable in alligator-like calm, sits on this porch (or did there sit on the afternoon of our visit), with his boots on the railing and his hat drawn over his eyes and sheltering his slowly moving jaws as they ruminate the Virginian weed. He had probably been overquestioned, for he answered all queries without looking up or betraying the smallest curiosity as to the age, sex, or condition of the questioner. Being tormented (I will not name the sex of his tormentress), concerning the uses of a little hole or pouch (it was for letters, really) in the wall near the door, he said that it was to receive contributions for a poor orphan. "I," he added, "am the orphan"; and then at last he looked up, with a faint gleam in his lazy eye which instantly won the heart. This Mississippian was white; another, black, showed us civilly and intelligently through the house, which was very creditable every way to the State, and told us that it was built of seventy different kinds of Mississippi wood. We came away applauding the taste and sense shown in the only State building that seemed to have any characteristic to say for itself. But in a country where for the most part every State is only more unrepresented in its architecture than another, it is very difficult for the buildings to be representative.

In their neighborhood were the foreign buildings, the most noticeable of which were the English, Japanese, and Canadian. The English were stuccoed without, showing the wooden anatomy of the building to some extent, and suggesting the comfort of country or suburban homes; the Japanese was like the pictures of all Japanese houses; the Canadian was a sturdy stroke of poetry. It was all built of Canadian timber and lumber. Rough saw-logs formed the stalwart pillars of the portico; boards and planks piled upon each other defined the shape of the building, which had something immensely gratifying and impressive. To be sure, no Canadian could go there for entertainment, but no Canadian could look at this great lumber lodge without thinking of home, which the profuse tiles of the New Jersey house or the many-shingled sides of the Massachusetts building could never suggest to a native of those States....

...It was not till our third day that we went to the Woman's Pavilion. Those accustomed to think of women as the wives, mother, and sisters of men will be puzzled to know why the ladies wished to separate their work from that of the rest of the human race, and those who imagined an antagonism between the sexes must regret, in the interest of what is called the cause of woman, the Pavilion is so inadequately representative of her distinctive achievement. The show is chiefly saved to the visitor's respect by the carved wood-work done by ladies of the Cincinnati Art School. Even this, compared with great wood-carving, lacks richness of effect; it is rather the ornamentation of the surface of wood in the lowest relief; but it is very good of its kind, full of charming sentiment; it is well intentioned, and executed with signal delicacy and refined skill. It is a thing that one may be glad of as American art, and then, if one cares, as women's work, though there seems no more reason why it should be considered more characteristic of the sex than the less successful features of the exhibition. We did not test the cuisine of the School of Cooking attached to the Woman's Pavilion; the School of Second Work was apparently not yet in operation: if it had been in a Man's Pavilion, I should have thought it the dustiest building on the grounds. It seems not yet the moment for the better half of our species to take their stand apart from the worse upon any distinct performance in art or industry; even when they have a building of their own, some organizing force to get their best work into it is lacking; many of those pictures and pincushions were no better than if men had made them; but some paintings by women in the Art Hall, where they belonged, suffered nothing by comparison with the work of their brothers. Woman's skill was better represented in the Machinery Hall than in her own Pavilion; there she was everywhere seen in the operation and superintendence of the most complicated mechanisms, and showed herself in the character of a worker of unsurpassed intelligence....

...A beneficent Sunday in our country retreat interrupted our sight-seeing: a Sunday of rural scenes and sounds, when trains forebore to chuckle to and fro on the Pennsylvania Railroad in exultation at Pennsylvania prosperity, and the rich landscape throbbed under the gathering heat. The meadow-lark sang everywhere; the redbird's voice was mellow in the dense woods; the masses of the dogwood blossoms whitened through all the heavy foliage. It was a land of blossoms and of wavering grass, and a drive over the country roads in the afternoon, past thriving farms and thrifty villages, showed it a land of Sabbath-keeping best clothes, clean faces, neat hair, and domestic peace on innumerable front steps and porches, where children sat with their elders, and young girls feigned to read books while they waited for the young men who were to come later.

Monday was hot and abated our zeal for the Philadelphia spring by giving us a foretaste of what the Philadelphian summer must be. The sun fried the asphalt pavements of the Centennial grounds, and a burning heat reverberated from them, charged with the sickening odor of the cement. That was a day for the stone interior of the Art Hall, but to tell the truth we found none of the buildings so hot as we feared they would be. It was very tolerable indeed both in the Main Building and the Machinery Hall, and in the United States Building we should not have lost patience with the heat if it had not been for the luxurious indifference of that glass case full of frozen fishes there, which, as they reposed in their comfortable boxes of snow, with their thermometer at 30°, did certainly appeal to some of the most vindictive passions of our nature; and I say that during the hot months it will be cruelty to let them remain. There are persons who would go down from Massachusetts to join a mob in smashing that case on the 4th of July, and tearing those fish to pieces. There are also people of culture in this region who would sign a petition asking the government to change the language of the placard on the clothes of the Father of his Country, which now reads, "Coat, Vest, and Pants of George Washington," whereas it his honored waistcoat which is meant, and his buckskin breeches: pantaloons were then unknown, and "pants" were undreamt-of by a generation which had time to be decent and comely in its speech. This placard is real drawback to one's enjoyment of the clothes, which are so familiarly like, from pictures, that one is startled not to find Washington's face looking out of the coat-collar. The government had been well advised in putting on view these and other personal relics, like his camp-bed, his table furniture, his sword, his pistols, and so forth. There are also similar relics of other heroes, and in the satisfaction of thus drawing nearer to the past in the realization of those historic lives, one's passion for heroic wardrobes mounts so that it stays at nothing. In one of the cases were an ordinary frock-coat of black diagonal, and a silk hat such as is worn in our own epoch, objects which in their character of relics we severely summoned what veneration we could, while we searched our mind for association of them with some memorable statesman. We were mortified to think of no modern worthy thus to hand down a coat and hat to the admiration of posterity, and in another moment we should have asked whose they were, if we had not caught sight of a busy attendant in his shirt-sleeves and bare head, just in time to save us from this shame....

...I have to leave in despair all details of the government show of army and navy equipments, the varied ingenuity and beautiful murderousness of the weapons of all kinds, the torpedoes with which alone one could pass hours of satisfaction, fancifully attaching them to the ships of enemies and defending our coasts in the most effectual manner; the exquisite models of marine architecture; the figures of soldiers of all arms—not nearly so good as the Danish, but dearer, being our own. Every branch of the administrative service was illustrated, so far as it could be, and the bribes almost sprang from one's pocket at sight of the neat perfection with which the revenue department was represented. There was manufacture of Centennial stamped envelopes, which constantly drew a big crowd, and there were a thousand and one other things which every one must view with advantage to himself and with applause of the government for making this impressive display in the eyes of other nations.

After paying our duty to these objects, we took our first ride on the narrow-gauge railroad, of which the locomotive with its train of gay open cars coughs and writhes about the grounds in every direction, with a station at each of the great buildings. I believe this railroad has awakened loathing in some breasts, and that there has been talk of trying to have it abolished. But I venture to say this will never be done, and in fact I do not see how the public could get on without it. The fare is five cents for the whole tour or from any one point to another; the ride is luxuriously refreshing, and commands a hundred charming prospects. To be sure, the cars go too fast, but that saves time; and I am not certain that the flagman at the crossings are sufficiently vigilant to avert the accidents whose possibility forms a greater objection to the railroad than mere taste can urge against it. As we whirled along, a gentleman next to us on the transverse seat entered into an agreeable monologue, from which we learned, among many other things, that they had in the Agricultural Building the famous war-eagle, Old Abe, whom a Wisconsin regiment carried through the war; and the next morning we made haste to see him. We found him in charge of one of the sergeants who had borne him through thirty battles, and who had once been shot down with the eagle on his perch, and left for dead on the field. The sergeant was a slim young fellow, with gray eyes enough like the eagle's to make them brothers, and he softly turned his tobacco from one cheek to the other while he discoursed upon the bird—his honors from the State government of Wisconsin, which keeps him and a man to care for him at the public charge; his preference for a diet of live chicken; his objection to new acquaintance, which he had shown a few days before by plunging his beak into the cheek of a gentleman who had offered him some endearments. We could not see that Old Abe looked different from other bald eagles (which we had seen in pictures); he had a striking repose of manner, and his pale, fierce eye had that uninterested, remote regard said to characterize all sovereign personages. The sergeant tossed him up and down on his standard, and the eagle threw open his great vans; but otherwise he had no entertainment to offer except the record of his public services—which we bought for fifty cents.

We were early on the ground that morning, and saw the Centennial in some aspects which I suppose the later visitor misses, when the crowd becomes too great for social ease. The young ladies in charge of pavilions or quiescent machinery, and the various young men in uniforms who superabounded at nine o'clock, gave the Machinery Hall the effect of a vast *conversazione*, amidst which no one could wander unconscious of a poetic charm. I am sure this was blamelessly pleasant, and if the Centennial did nothing but promote all the multitudinous acquaintance, it could not be considered other than a most enormous success. These happy young people neglected no duty to the public; there never was on this continent such civility and patience as that of the guards and policemen and officials of the Centennial, and the young ladies would leave a word half-breathed, half-heard, at the slightest demand of curiosity concerning anything they had in charge. In the midst, the Corliss engine set an example of unwearying application to business, and even while one gazed in fond approval, innumerable spindles began to whirr and shuttles to clack, and a thousand *tête-a-têtes* were broken up as by magic....

...We thought it well during our week at the Centennial to lunch as variously as possible, and I can speak by the card concerning the German Restaurant, the two French Restaurants, and the Vienna Bakery; the native art in cooking we did not test. The German Restaurant and the Lafayette Restaurant are very reasonable in their charges, less expensive, indeed, than most first-class city restaurants. The Trois Frères Provençaux is imprudently extortionate. Not that dishes cooked with so much more sentiment than any you can find elsewhere are not worth more, but that there are absurd charges for what Americans ordinarily pay nothing for: bread, butter, and service at double and quadruple the Parisian rates. But it is even worse at the Vienna Bakery, where they have twenty-five cents for a cup of coffee, and not good coffee at that—not at all the coffee of Vienna. Happily, no one is obliged to go to these places for sustenance. There are a hundred others within the grounds where you may lunch cheaply and well, or cheaply and ill, which most of our nation like better. There is, for instance, a large pavilion where one may surcharge the stomach with pie and milk at a very low price. There is an American Restaurant, there is a Southern Restaurant (served by lustrous citizens of color), there is a restaurant attached to the Old Colony House; there is no end to them; and I am very glad to say of them, and of all other American enterprises for the public comfort, that their opportunity has not been improved to the public ruin. The extortion seems to be all by the foreigners—unless sixty cents an hour is too much for a wheeled chair. I think it is; but the chairs will doubtless be cheaper when the cars of the circular railroad have run over two or three. All stories of the plundering of strangers by the Philadelphians may be safely distrusted. Probably never before in the history of world's fairs has the attitude of the local city towards its guests been so honest, so conscientious, so generous.

The grounds of the Centennial are open twelve hours every day, and your payment of fifty cents admits you for all that time to everything there. No account, however close, however graphic, can give a just conception of the variety and interest of the things to be seen. The whole season would not exhaust them; a week or a month enables you to study a point here and there. Yet if you have but a single day to spend, it is well to go. You can never spend a day with richer return.

A very pleasant thing about the exhibition is your perfect freedom there. There are innumerable officials to direct you, to help you, to care for you, but none of them bothers you. If you will keep off those clay slopes and expanses which are placarded Grass, there will be no interference with any caprice of your personal liberty. This is the right American management of a public pleasure.

The muse at all minded to sing the humors of a great holiday affair could find endless inspiration at the Centennial; but there are space and the reader to be regarded. Yet I must not leave the theme without speaking of the gayety of the approaches and surroundings; the side shows are outside here, and the capacity for amusement which the Centennial fails to fill need not go hungering amid the provision made for it by private enterprise. It is curious to see the great new hotels of solid and flimsy construction near the grounds, and the strange city which has sprung up in answer to the necessities of the world's fair. From every front and top stream the innumerable flags, with which during a day in town we found all Philadelphia also decked. Yet it is an honest and well-behaved liveliness. There is no disorder of any sort; nowhere in or about the Centennial did I see any one who had overdrunk the health of his country.

Not the least prodigious of the outside appurtenances of the Centennial is that space allotted on a neighboring ground to the empty boxes and packing cases of the goods sent to the fair. Their multitude is truly astonishing, and there is a wild desolation amidst which I should think the gentlemen of the Centennial Commission, in case of a very disastrous failure of the enterprise, would find it convenient to come and rend their garments. But no one expects failure now. Every day of the week there saw an increase of visitors, and the reader of the newspapers knows how the concourse has grown since. The undertaking merits all possible prosperity, and whatever were the various minds in regard to celebrating the Centennial by an international fair, no one can now see the fair without a thrill of patriotic pride.

15. IN AND OUT
OF THE NEW ORLEANS EXPOSITION

by Eugene V. Smalley
CENTURY MAGAZINE, JUNE, 1885

    The common way of going to the city to the Exposition is the one-mule car. There were plans for steam transit at first, and something may come of them before the fair closes; but the only charter granted fell into the hands of some speculative persons, who had no money to build a road themselves and demanded fifty thousand dollars for the privilege. As I wrote in February, the fair-time being already one-third gone, the only alternative to mule transit is the steamboats on the river, which are too far away for most visitors to make use of. The mule-car is not a bad conveyance, however. True, the track is rough and the seats are hard, but the little animal clatters along at a lively pace over the plank roadway in the middle of the street, pulling his load with ease, for the ground is so level that the water in the deep ditches seems in doubt which way to run, and usually ends by standing still and hiding itself under a covering of green slime. In a few minutes the car gets beyond the business district, and thence on to the Exposition gates it runs through green and fragrant suburbs, where the date-palm, the magnolia, and the orange shade delicious little inclosures, half garden and half lawn, which look as if their beauty was quite unpremeditated, and came from nature's own generous moods. Handsome mansions, with pillared fronts, alternate with pretty one-story cottages, and a little farther out are the red and green houses of the negroes with their projecting hood-like roofs. There is no crowding of population into tenement houses in New Orleans. The poorest laborer that rolls cotton-bales on the levee can afford a three-room cottage for his family, where there is plenty of light, air, and shade. In hut and mansion life goes on with open doors all year round, and even in December and January, when fires are kept up, the children play on the thresholds, and you get glimpses of the interiors as the car jogs past. The winter in New Orleans does not seem to be the death of the year, but only a brief sleep filled with dreams of the summer's luxuriance of leaf and blossom. Most of the trees, such as the live-oaks, the water-oaks, the oranges, and the magnolias, do not shed their foliage, and the roses seem not to know when to leave off blooming. I found the rainy season in January, of which there was so much complaint in newspaper correspondence, not altogether disagreeable. The frequent warm showers, and the spring-like feeling in the air, made the weather seem like an English May.
    In the street-cars there is less reserve than in such vehicles in Northern cities. Strangers open conversation with you from mere expansiveness and friendliness of feeling. There is a deal of chatting about the city, the weather, and the fair. Children are noticed and petted, and babies create a general sensation. In every other car smoking is permitted. If ladies get into the smoking-cars, which are plainly distinguished from the others, they are expected to make the best of the situation and not glare at the men for finishing their cigars. Sometimes there are outspoken protests against this custom. A party of ladies entered a car one day in which a Creole gentleman sat in placid enjoyment of his cigar and his morning pa-

per. The windows were shut and the air was thick. The ladies began to make half-whispered remarks about the "horrid air." Then something was said about "no gentleman smoking in the presence of ladies where they came from." Still the smoker was obdurate. He puffed away with increased vigor. He had a right to smoke, and he evidently did not intend to be intimidated. Various sarcastic comments were made with less and less pretense of undertone, until the attention of all the passengers was attracted to the struggle. Finally, one of the woman said, "Let's offer him five cents for his cigar." "Of course he'll take it," said another; "he could buy two of the sort he's smoking." This shot finished the poor Creole. He threw his cigar out of the window, scowled at his tormentors, but was too polite to make any retort.

The steamboat route to the Exposition starts from the head of Canal street. It's very odd, this going uphill to get to the water side of the city, and finding all the open drains flowing from the river instead of toward it. During the sail, which lasts nearly an hour, you pass along the greater part of the river frontage of the city and get a strong impression of the extent and variety of its commercial activity. There are dozens of cotton-steamers, flying English, French, Spanish, Dutch, and Italian flags, steamers from Mexico, Cuba, and South America, fruit-schooners with fragrant cargoes from the lagoons of Yucatan and Honduras, black brigs laden with logwood and mahogany, and all sorts of queer, non-descript sail-craft from bays and bayous bringing fish and oysters, sugar and rice. The river steamboats do not make as great a show at the levees as they did years ago, the new railroad running parallel to the Mississippi and Red rivers, or crossing the Atchafalaya and the many navigable bayous that help carry to the gulf the abundant waters of those great streams, having seriously impaired the river trade of late. There is an amusing irregularity in the movements of the Exposition boats. If they have a time-table, they pay no attention to it. The gang-plank is not hauled in as long as a possible passenger is in sight on shore. Two boats will lie for an hour on the wharf, keeping up a terrific din with bells and whistles as if just to pull out. Each has its runners ashore soliciting passengers, the rival captains standing by the gangplanks and shouting, "First boat for the city—Start in one minute—Giver her another toot, Jim—Stand By, there, to cast off that line—This way, gentlemen—go half an hour before that other boat." Meanwhile, the passengers who have come aboard at the advertised time of leaving do not grumble. It's the custom of the country. Nobody is in a hurry; nobody cares to be on time. Even the restless, impatient Northerner soon falls in with the ways of the natives, and finds it delightful to enter into the easy-going spirit of this lazy land, "wherein it seemeth always afternoon."

The city of New Orleans was in need of the invigorating influences of the Exposition. Its trade has been at a standstill of late. The Eads jetties at the mouth of the Mississippi and the building of new railroads gave it a fresh impetus a few years ago; but these new forces seem to have culminated. The place is not decaying, but it is not advancing. I noted but two conspicuous new buildings that have been erected in the business quarter since my last visit, six years ago. The receipts of cotton have not averaged as many bales during the past five years as in the five years preceding the war. The heaviest receipts in the history of the city were in the crop year 1859-60—2,139,425 bales. The receipts for 1883-84 were only 1,529,188 bales. Besides, the profit arising from handling the staple is much less than formerly, owing to the establishment of steam-presses at various points in the interior which compress the bales ready for shipment to Europe, so that there is nothing for New Orleans to do with them but transfer them directly to the ocean vessels from the cars and steamboats. The sugar crop of Louisiana was 221,515 hogsheads in 1883, and was 449,324 hogsheads as long ago as 1854. The grain movement to Europe by way of New Orleans is not increasing, notwithstanding the enormous expansion in recent years of the Western wheat crop. The gains achieved for the general business of the city appear to have come from the building of the railroads and the consequent bringing of the surrounding country within easy reach of its trade. The important new roads—all built with Northern capital and managed by Northern men—are two lines to Texas, connecting with the Southern Pacific system, a line north-eastwardly into Alabama, forming a part of one of the through Northern routes of travel, and a line following the general course of the Mississippi to Memphis. In 1880 the census showed 216,000 people in New Orleans, a gain of only 13,000 in a decade. The present population is probably 225,000, not including the people brought here by the Exposition. These figures do not, however, convey a correct idea of the importance of the city as a center of commerce, for the reason that it is commerce alone that makes New Orleans, the multitude of manufacturing industries which would be found in a Northern city of any considerable size being almost wholly absent. Besides, New Orleans is great by comparison. In all the South-western and Gulf States, the next largest city had only 43,000 inhabitants in 1880. That was Nashville, Tennessee. The gap between 216,000 and 43,000 is a wide one. After Nashville came Memphis with 33,500, Mobile with 29,000, and Galveston with 22,000. The prominence of New Orleans is explained by the fact that it is from five to ten times as large as the other principal cities within the circuit of its trade relations.

There is much complaint of the city government and the lethargy of the business men. At a *café chantant* one night I heard a popular song criticising the mayor, the aldermen, and the merchants, because of dull times, diverted trade, and unemployed labor, and the refrain to each verse was: "Stick a pin in them and see if they're alive." The Exposition sprang from the conviction that the future growth of New Orleans depends on securing a larger share of the trade of Latin America. The idea back of it is that the shores of the Gulf of Mexico and the Caribbean Sea and the islands of the Antilles should exchange their products here for the manufactures of the North. If this idea bears important fruit, it must be through the accession of fresh Northern blood and capital to the business circles of the Crescent City. This is what it is hoped the Exposition will accomplish, by bringing Northern enterprise here to see the opportunities open to the southward for commercial activity. New blood is needed, because the old stock becomes lethargic through the enervating climatic influences. Rarely does the successful merchant who comes as a young man from the cooler latitudes leave a son who inherits the father's energy. One generation is enough to change character. The long, hot, moist summers of the Louisiana lowlands are fatal to vigor. A city that lies below the level of the river which washes its wharves and only a few feet above the poisonous swamps surrounding it, and which has six sweltering summer months, must always continue to draw upon the North for new men to carry on its larger business activities....

...Among foreign nations Mexico has taken the most active interest in the New Orleans World's Fair. Her government has formed an admirable exhibit, which presents a faithful epitome of her natural resources and her industrial life. The aim has not been to display a few articles of exceptional merit, but to show the whole range of useful products and native manufactures. One is surprised at the number of things the Mexicans make, and make well. Their cotton fabrics are good, and of tasteful patterns; their woolens are well woven; their leather-work, especially in saddlery, is wonderfully fine; their pottery is quaintly original; they prepare a multitude of food products and wines. Many articles show ingenuity and a great deal of patient labor. The little painted clay statuettes made by Indians, and representing phases of Mexican life—the beggar, the fruit-seller, the priest, the country gentleman, the fisherman, etc.—and the bird-pictures made from the feathers of the birds they represent, show the genius of close imitation, of patient handicraft, and to some extent of original conception, and seem to indicate an industry, which could be much developed by training. After spending an hour in the Mexican courts one marvels that a people who can produce all these things should make so small a figure in the sum-total of the world's civilizing forces.

In the Horticultural Hall Mexico makes a remarkable display of the different species of the cactus plant. This odd freak of the vegetable kingdom assumes no end of fantastic shapes. There are cacti like enormous pincushions, as big as barrels; cacti like giants' clubs, standing thirty feet high; cacti with thorns a finger long; cacti covered with beautiful pink blossoms; cacti with big roses growing among their spikes; cacti in pods, in bulbs, in branching candelabra. This cactus show alone is worth a visit to the Exposition. After seeing it one understands why the Mexican infantry soldiers wear high-topped boots. I have spoken before of the Moorish Building erected for the display of Mexican mining products, and of the barracks for the Mexican soldiers and the military band. The band has enlivened the fair through all its stages, furnishing music on every ceremonial occasion with never-failing courtesy and good-nature, and with a cosmopolitan impartiality, playing Dixie or Hail Columbia, Gounod, or Rossini, or Mozart, or Strauss with equal good-will, or singing the songs of love and patriotism of their own country. To these swarthy musicians, sixty of them I think in all, and representing most of the types of Mexico's much mixed races, the Exposition is greatly indebted.

Near the great tower of green sugar-canes which serves as a beacon to guide the visitor through the mazes of the Government Building to the Louisiana section, and beneath the rice-thatched pavilion, is a placard with the following legend: "Louisiana wants more men and women of brains, energy, and capital. Her lands are the most productive and the cheapest of all the Southern States." Close at hand, on one of the white pillars which show the sources whence the United States draws its supplies of sugar, and the comparative amount furnished by Louisiana, is a statement in black letters that "only one-twentieth of the land in Louisiana available for sugar is now under cultivation." These two inscriptions provoke inquiry. Here is one of the oldest settled portions of the Union, which could show a flourishing agriculture and a considerable commercial city when such States as Illinois, Iowa, and Wisconsin were peopled only by savages, and such cities as Cincinnati, Chicago, and St. Paul had not even a name, setting up claims for immigration in competition with those of Dakota and Oregon. How does it happen that there are still great areas of rich land untilled in the Mississippi delta? The first answer to the question is, that these lands largely require protection from overflow by levees, and that the present population has all it can do to maintain the old embankments, and cannot afford to build new ones to redeem more soil from the swamps. The second is, that the social organism is based on agriculture, and agriculture in all the lowland districts is based on negro labor. As many white people are now living on the labor of the negroes as that labor will support. The small immigration from Europe and the North goes to the towns and engages in trade. There has been very little influx of new blood in the country districts. The negro labor is probably in the aggregate as productive as in the days of slavery; but a smaller share of its results goes to the white land-owners, and a larger share to the blacks themselves. Thus the whites always speak of "the good old days before the war," and were, no doubt, as a class, in better circumstances then now, though the aggregate annual wealth-production was not as great. Of the three special staples of Louisiana agriculture, cotton, raised in the uplands north of the Red River, shows some gain in its annual yield; sugar is variable in quantity, depending greatly on the seasons, and requiring large capital for its culture; rice, which is especially a black man's crop, has increased steadily, beginning with 20,978 barrels in 1865, and without a single setback advancing to 498,138 barrels in 1883.

The time is not far distant when land will be too valuable on this continent for large areas of the warm, bountiful soils in Louisiana to be allowed to remain idle, and when the Mississippi delta, with its interlacing rivers and bayous, will be a semi-tropical Holland, as well diked and as thoroughly utilized as the thrifty, populous country in the Rhine delta....The visitors themselves are as well worth seeing as the show. To sit on a bench on one of the broad aisles of the Main Building, or better still beneath the spreading arms of the great live-oaks on the grounds, and observe the passing throng, is to my mind the best part of the sight-seeing at the fair. The first broad division one makes is between Northern and Southern people. The energetic tread, the business-like air, and the evident disposition to do up the exhibition thoroughly and speedily, betrays the man from the North, as well as the cut of his coat, his Derby hat, and the unnecessary overcoat he lugs about on his arm, incredulous as to May weather lasting long in February. The Northern woman is more fashionably dressed than her Southern sister, has a quicker gait, a better complexion, a nervous, eager manner, and an appearance of being in quest of information quite essential to her well-being. The Southern visitors saunter and chat a good deal; they seem never in a hurry. The women affect black in preference to colors, and are not particular as to the forms of their bonnets. The Hebrew clothing merchant, who has pervaded the entire South since the war, has nearly driven out the black broadcloth suit which was once the regulation garb for gentlemen, and it is not much worn now except by the older men, but the soft slouch hat holds its own. There are more distinct and recognizable types among the Southern population than in the North. The large-boned Kentuckian or Tennesseean, reared on a limestone soil, differs widely from the inhabitant of the malarial lowlands of Mississippi and Louisiana. The Georgian can be told by speech and look from his neighbor in South Carolina. The Texan is a big breezy fellow, with a long stride and an air of owning half the universe. The Creole Louisianian (by which term, let it be explained for the hundreth time, is meant, not a mulatto, but a native white of French or Spanish ancestry) is short of stature, slight of frame, with a curious mixture of languor and vivacity in manner, carefully dressed, very polite, and with small interest in the doings of the world outside his own State.

The odd characters at the fair are the terror of the exhibitors. A Cincinnati furniture-maker discovered a country-man from Arkansas whittling a handsome mahogany cabinet "to see what the wood was like." The man's knowledge of furniture was evidently limited to articles which could not be damaged by a reasonable use of the jack-knife. Another exhibitor, who had fitted up a room with the finest specimens of his art, was horrified to find an old lady eating her lunch of fried chicken seated in one of his satin upholstered chairs. "What's the cheer good for if it ain't to set down in?" she placidly remarked, in reply to his earnest request that she would go somewhere else with her victuals. The same exhibitor one day found that some visitor to his alcoves had left a token of his approval on the polished surface of a costly mantel, in the words "This is pretty good" scratched with a knife.

The Turks who sell olive-wood, beads, and other trinkets "from Jerusalem"—all made in Paris—are picturesque additions to the permanent personnel of the fair, though their genuineness, like that of their wares, will not always bear inspection. An amusing scene occurred one day at one of these Oriental bazaars. A tall man, with a rural air, stopped before the stand and appeared to take a lively interest, not in the goods, but in the features of one of the salesman in scarlet fez and baggy trousers. He surveyed the Oriental in front and in profile, and then, slapping him on the shoulder, exclaimed, "Hello, Jake, when did you come from Indiana?"

The Turk from Indiana acknowledged his old acquaintance and begged that he would not "give him away."

...The old Liberty Bell, which stands in the Main Building upon the car built to transport it and its guard of stalwart policemen from Philadelphia, appears to awaken a sentiment of nationality in the breasts of the Southern visitors to the Exposition. Their patriotic feelings do not always extend to the national flag, however. It is rare to see the Stars and Stripes in New Orleans save on the shipping and the Government buildings. The people are fond of bunting, and to gratify their taste for color they devise many strange banners. Visitors are puzzled to make out the meaning of these combinations of red, purple, green, yellow, and white floating from flagstaffs on stores and hotels. To the frequent question, "What sort of flag is that?" the answer is, "Oh, that don't mean anything in particular. It's just a fancy flag," or more often, "That's the flag of Rex, the King of the Carnival." When the Bankers' Building on the Exposition grounds was decorated, a photographer from Philadelphia, who had been taking a picture of the throng, called out from his platform as the Stars and Stripes were unfurled from the roof of the structure, "Three cheers for our flag!" There were a few cheers and almost as many hisses. The Exposition will, unquestionably, do much toward stimulating the growth of the national idea in the South. A study of the enormous aggregation of products, arts, and inventions in the Government Building classified by States cannot fail to produce an enlarged conception of the greatness of the republic, and a feeling of pride in its magnificent resources. Opposition to the national emblem is only a sentiment in the South, and is fast fading into tradition. There is not the slightest desire for separation. The Southerner does not want to hurrah for the old flag, simply because he thinks that to do so would be to show unfaithfulness to the memory of the cause for which he or his kindred fought—a memory which to him is sacred.

The Centennial Exhibition at Philadelphia was held when the business of the country was deep down in the rut of depression into which it had been settling after the panic of 1873. The exhibition seemed to be the turning-point. It set people in motion and broke the spell of lethargy. Hard times are a mental disease. At the outset a necessary reaction from the fever of speculation, they become a chronic condition prolonged far beyond the time needed for restoring wholesome conditions to trade. People grasp their money tightly, become overcautious, draw back from the most inviting enterprises, and retrench expenses beyond reasonable economy. The malady affects even those whose incomes have not in the least suffered. The rich grow penurious without themselves knowing why. Thus the consumption of products of all kinds diminishes and manufactures and trade languish. A great exhibition encourages people to travel, interests their minds by its display of inventions, processes, and products, and thus lifts them out of the old grooves of inactivity and causes them to loosen their energies and their purse-strings. Perhaps the New Orleans fair is destined to do the same good work in breaking up hard times as was done by the Centennial. It is a pity that its magnitude and attractions did not become earlier known to the country at large. It took about two months to educate the country up to an appreciation of the Philadelphia Exhibition, but afterwards came the pleasant fall weather, most inviting to travel and sight-seeing. Unfortunately, the summer will begin in New Orleans about as soon as a knowledge of the merits of the "World's Industrial and Cotton Centennial Exposition" is widely diffused. If it were practicable to hold the great show together and reopen it in the coming autumn, its benefits would be much increased, and the wise plan of its projectors of bringing together within its gates for better acquaintance and mutual profit the peoples of all the North American republics and colonies might be more fully realized.

16. AT THE FAIR

by M. G. Van Rensselaer
CENTURY MAGAZINE, MAY, 1893

Two years ago Chicago was beginning to put up the buildings for her Fair. "Absurd!" cried America; "ten-acre, twenty-acre lots roofed in—how can they ever be filled?" Yet, of late, up and down the land has gone the cry of the disappointed exhibitor, shorn of his hoped-for quantum of space. The East has called out to the West, "You are keeping it all for yourself;" the West has replied to the East, "You want to crowd us out entirely;" and the fact is that there has been no space at all for many claimants, and not nearly enough to satisfy the more fortunate. The mass of offered exhibits has surpassed the utmost anticipations of the organizers of the Fair; and indeed they would have been a great deal happier if it had been a great deal smaller.

And now has come the time for the crowd of spectators. Long ago we stopped asking, "Who will wish to go to a Fair at Chicago?" To-day the question is, "What may we best do, what may we best choose to look at, when we get there?" Of course no one can see the whole of a Fair like this, inside and out; and time, energy, and disappointment will be saved if a plan of campaign is prepared in advance, and the mind is trained to feel that it must be followed.

It is not easy to follow any plan in such sight-seeing if one has the usual American mind, as alive with mere curiosity as it is with a craving for instruction—pleased to be looking at anything, discontented only to think that other people are seeing things with which it cannot make acquaintance. But a plan, and the power to stick to it, will be your only safeguards from disaster if, beneath your shifting, purposeless wish simply to see, there lies a genuine desire to profit by sights of a certain sort. If you are going to enjoy your visit to the Fair in the way that will leave the best residuum, that will best satisfy you when the prickings of mere rivalry in sight-seeing have died out, when the excitement of the crowds and vast architectural panoramas will have faded, when the temptation to sit in the shade on a plausibly marble bench under a deceptively marble colonnade, and watch the sun shine on fluttering flags and party-colored awnings and reaches of shining water, will seem, in retrospect, to have been a devil's drug narcotizing your sense of duty—if you are a conscientious person with a real practical interest in any one department of the Fair, you must take at least part of your pleasure in the Fair very sternly.

I know whereof I speak, for I went to Paris in 1889 with an insistent need to acquaint myself with modern art. I stayed five weeks; I did not go every day to the Fair, but I went very often; I tried to do my duty, and I did devote myself especially to the art galleries: but while I hardly saw the contents of any of the other buildings, and did not even set foot within so vast and varied and interesting a one as the Palace of the Liberal Arts, I left Paris with a sense of shame and defeat. I did not really see the pictures and statues; I did not really learn about modern art.

Nor, at Chicago, will you learn about the things which are dear to you unless you are very wise and steady, patient and self-denying. Take a day first to satisfy your curiosity to gratify your sense of wonderment and your love of beauty, to get your bearings and discover how much exertion you can support.

Go all over the Fair grounds, and to the top of at least one of the big domes or towers. See the Fair, as a Fair, from its various centers, and from different parts of its circumference, especially from the lake. I think you can do this in one or two days, if you start early and end late, if you are strong, and if you have yourself conveyed by all available means of conveyance—encircling railways, boats, and rolling-chairs—and if you do not step inside a single building except for the ascent in search of your bird's-eye-view. Then go home, stay in bed the following day, if you are wise, and the next day spread the wings and stiffen the spine of your conscience, and go in search of the things you have come to study—steam-boilers or roses, fishes or stuffed birds, needle-work or statistics of idiot asylums, methods of slaughtering men or cattle, or of preserving human life or edible fruits. Stay at this task until you have finished it, or until it has exhausted your powers of applications. Then release and relax yourself. Go to see something else—palms if you have been studying plows, pictures if you have been studying electric motors. The things you know least about, and care least about, will then seem delightful, for you will have purchased the right to idle, and only its purchasers know the whole of the charm of idling. There are few pleasures like looking at things in which one feels no concern after looking with profit at those which concern one deeply. There is no exultation like the cry of the spirit when, tired but self-approving, it says to itself, "It doesn't matter an atom whether I understand this or not, whether I remember it always or forget it to-night." If you take your idling first and your working afterward, you will miss, I say, the fullness of the pleasure of desultory looking, and you will probably never get to your working at all in such an idler's paradise as our Fair will be.

Of course, after what your rustic fellow-countrymen would call a "good spell" of idling you will be ready to come back, refreshed, to your work again. Or, if you have completed it, you will go home with the satisfactory feeling that you have enjoyed both sides of the Fair, its instructive side and its mere pleasure-giving side.

One more word: While you are trying to work—to learn, to appraise, to remember, to profit—be by yourself, or be sure that your comrade is exactly of the same mind as yourself. The Fair will be a safe place, and there will be so many people in it that no one individual will be annoyingly observed. You need not fear to part from your wife for a time, or, on the other hand, to let your husband part from you. Each of you has special tastes, special curiosities; and if you try, hand in hand, to examine ethnological antiquities and dolls dressed to represent the changes of fashion, or sporting goods or kindergarten methods, neither of you will see what you should as you should, and both will be dissatisfied. Every woman knows that two women shopping together do not "accomplish" half as much as though they had shopped separately, while their tempers are doubly tried. The crowded galleries of the Fair will be like colossal shops with the counters for different wares sometimes a mile apart. If you want to accomplish anything there, you had better try by yourself. It is delightful to study interesting things just as one chooses; but although I have experienced both fates, I do not know which is more exasperating—to drag an unsympathetic soul about with you while examining anything, or to be an unsympathetic soul dragged about by some one else.

Most Americans, I think, will go to the Fair with some serious purpose before them—if not to study carefully any of the collections, then to make a careful general survey of the Fair itself, as illustrating the present condition of our nation from many points of view, and likewise its promises and prospects for the future.

The desire for self-instruction is a very broad, bright thread in the mixed fabric of the American temperament, and the organizers of the Fair have done well, even from the advertiser's standpoint, to lay particular stress upon its educational possibilities.

Nevertheless, not all Americans have minds which are eager for knowledge. There must be many who do not intend to visit Chicago because of any profit they may gain. They are going because they hope to amuse themselves. They, too, will have their reward. They, too, have been prepared for in manifold ways. Perhaps they will spend less time within the true boundries of the Fair than in the great annex called the Midway Plaisance, where a merely commercial ingenuity has been allowed fuller sway. Here, however, they will see many amusing, strange, or beautiful sights, some of which have hitherto been visible only in far odd corners of the world, while others have never before been seen at all. Here, I say, the most frivolous may disport themselves well; and they will carry home some instruction, if only in the shape of a wider knowledge of possible kinds of entertainment.

But even these two classes do not include all Americans. Some—chiefly born at the East, I think—have voices which refuse to join in the general chorus of anticipation. Although never so well assured that the Fair will be a "great success," they declare that the last thing they want to do is visit it. They profess themselves *flâneurs* by nature—or by diligent cultivation. They know all they need to know about the world's progress in all directions, or they think that further knowledge would be bought too dearly by a long journey, probably discomfort, much fatigue, and a constant mingling with crowds. When their daily tasks do not claim them, what they crave is repose, refreshment, freedom from mental no less than from physical effort. When they seek their summer pleasuring they want to take their ease in the world's great inn, and so they think longingly of one of its quieter chambers. It tires and distresses them even to imagine this vast *table d'hôte des nations*, where preparation has been made for the daily entertainment of some two hundred thousand guests.

Perhaps they visited "the Centennial" in 1876, and found it crude and ugly, confused and confusing, tiresome as well as tiring. Perhaps they visited the Paris Exposition in 1889, and found it so gay and charming that, they think, no other exhibition can give them new emotions of pleasure. Or perhaps it is only on general principals that they say they dislike big exhibitions, hate sight-seeing, detest the name of a catalogue, and think any object deprived of its charm by being placed in a collection. But in any case they protest that the Fair's chief value in their eyes is the value of a huge magnet which will draw off the crowds from other places, leaving them more in peace for their peaceful pleasure-seeking.

Often such people take great pride in their apathy. They think that it is banal to want to do what everyone else is doing; and they say to themselves that it is not lack of intelligence which keeps them away from Chicago, but an especially keen degree of intelligence; they say that they can amuse and instruct themselves, and therefore need not try to profit by the biggest object-lessons, the showiest illustrative panoramas, the most emphatic lecturing to the eye, the most stupendous variety-show, that the times afford.

But such people, if they are true *flâneurs*, will make a great mistake in keeping away from Chicago. Of course there are dawdlers of an inferior sort, people who are simply stupid, and can enjoy nothing but doing and thinking nothing; and it makes no difference whether these go to Chicago or stay at home. But your true *flâneur* feels a genuine interest in one thing—his own capacity for the reception of such new ideas and emotions as may be received without exertion of any kind. He does not crave knowledge, but he delights in impressions. He likes to idle in the city because, if he keeps himself purely receptive, the city prints each instant a fresh picture on his brain; or to idle in the country because nature, or the contemplation of his own soul, more slowly does the same. He loathes the thought of Chicago, because it suggests hard work at sight-seeing, and his ideal is the easy work of holding himself passive yet perceptive.

But he loathes this thought either because he does not know what the Fair will be, or, more probably, because he has some little shred of the true American intellectual conscience in his make-up. It is hard for an American to get wholly rid of the feeling that he ought to improve himself. If his intellectual conscience is not potent enough to turn him into a worker, it suffices to hamper his pleasure as an idler. He is perfectly happy only where every one else is idling too, and, therefore, much more often in Europe than at home.

But, if you belong to this guild, you had better stifle your mental conscientiousness altogether for a time, and go to the Fair. Certainly it will torment you if you take any last remnant of it with you; but if you go in perfect freedom, you will find such an idler's paradise as was never dreamed of in America before, and is not equaled anywhere in Europe today.

If, I say, you go wholly conscienceless—not like a painstaking draftsman, but like a human kodak, caring only for as many pleasing impressions as possible, not for the analyzing of their worth—you will be delighted in the first place by the sight of such crowds of busy human bees, and the comfortable thought that, thank heaven! you are not as they. And what a setting for these crowds! What a panorama of beauty to drink in and dream over, and to carry home, in general views and bits of detail, for the perpetual adornment of your mental picture-gallery!

You need not avail yourself of all the quick means of getting about. You can hire a little boat for yourself, if you choose, and drift slowly around all day in this new white Venice of the West; or, when sun beats too hot through your awning, land on the island, be refreshed by green shrubberies, and fancy yourself lolling in true gardens of Japan. Or, not caring whither you go or when you get there, you can saunter about on foot, on sunny marble *quais* or canopied bridges, in sound of splashing fountains, along great shadowy arcades of columns, pausing at last under palm-trees beneath the tropic dome of Flora's temple, or in the veranda of some little rest-house on the esplanade where the brilliant stretches of Lake Michigan will give your imagination room and verge enough to convince you that you have passed out of the old workaday world altogether—that you are looking from this great palatial bit of fairy-land into a further realm of mystery and marvel. If the beautiful in nature especially appeals to you, Lake Michigan will indeed furnish you with fine emotions, exquisite sensations. There is no water like it in more eastern regions. It has twenty moods for one that the ocean shows; and compared with the famous lakes of Europe, it is like a string of many precious stones—beryls, opals, amethysts, aquamarines—compared with a single sapphire.

But if you like best to win from humanity your changing vague delights, you will have it before you in great plenty and variety, against astonishing piled-up backgrounds of commercial products, mechanical marvels, artistic elaborations, which you can placidly contemplate as backgrounds, not trying to appraise their monetary, scientific, or artistic worth. Or if you care particularly for esthetic impressions, these you will get in wonderful reaches of architectural magnificence, emphasized by the shifting lights and shadows of a variable but sometimes almost tropic climate, accented by gay passages of color, enlivened by the flutter of a myriad flags and awnings, and everywhere doubled in beauty by their reflection in the waters which, after all, are not the waters of Venice, since they are pure and blue; and these marvelous panoramas, again, you can accept at their high pictorial worth, not troubled, like the critic or the student, by the need to appraise, consider, and recollect.

Something of what you, a happy idler, may perpetually enjoy at the Fair our artist has tried to show, telling of its colossal effectiveness by night as well as by day, and giving glimpses from those quieter points of outlook which will stand in picturesque contrast to the showier, gayer panoramas. If, this artist tells us in his pictures, Turner would have found good material in certain places, Corot would have found as good elsewhere. Indeed there is no artist concerned with interminglings of natural and architectural beauty, or with human beings of modern types, who would not be enchanted by the opportunities of our Fair. One wishes only that during its short six-months' life it might be painted by as many hands as, in the last four centuries, have painted the Italian Venice; and one feels sure that no two painters who may attempt the task are likely to paint the American Venice in identical ways.

I have always wished for a chance to celebrate a certain friend of mine who, with great trouble, got himself a holiday and journeyed from the far West to see the Centennial Exhibition. He arrived on a very hot day; near the entrance of the grounds he found a Hungarian band playing delightfully in a delightful little restaurant; there he sat down for mental and physical refreshment; there he sat all day; and thither he returned each subsequent day during his hard-earned week of leisure, and sat till eventide. He saw no more of the exhibition than this, but he still declares that he got "more good" out of it than any one else, and looks back upon it with feelings of unmixed self-approval.

He, indeed, was a true *flâneur*. People of his kind will probably be tempted at Chicago to do a little more than he did at Philadelphia; there will be so many enchanting spots for placid contemplation that they will not remain for a week in one. But if they are really are of his kind, they will not be tempted into over-exertion or disturbed by the conscientious activity of others; and the longer they stay, the oftener they pitch their mental camera on a new spot, the richer will be their feeling of pleasure and self-approval in after days of retrospection.

V.

AMUSEMENT PARKS

Summer gardens, constructed on the grounds of former estates, began as early as the 1790s having popular appeal for the thousands of laborers, tradesmen, and shopkeepers who were unable to seek their pleasures far from their homes and their work. There, confectioner-impressarios dispensed punch and ice cream in bower-like settings, and provided musical concerts and pantomimes, along with dazzling displays of fireworks. With most of the regular theatres closed during the hot summer months, the gardens benefited from the seasonal entertainment lag.

The success of these small, city oases fostered larger commercial pleasure parks along the outskirts of the major urban areas, located on more spacious grounds, which catered to summer excursioners and groups of holiday revelers. Possibilities for fun included everything the smaller gardens offered, along with facilities for athletic contests, marksmanship, bathing, boating, picnicking, and innumerable booths and stalls for hawkers, conjurers, and other purveyors of entertainment.

From these sources grew the more familiar amusement parks. By the end of the nineteenth century they were complexly mechanized and excessively merchandised versions of the other pleasure places, with additional features borrowed from circus, fair, and theatre. With the extension of city trolley lines, allowing inexpensive access to the rural parts, these parks grew and thrived, until recently, when many have been swallowed up by expanding city boundaries, and destroyed by the same urban enigmas that are a common plague to numerous enterprises. Still, a new genre of "theme park" has replaced these gaudy examples of the turn-of-the-century; and, judging from the success of Disneyland and a host of imitators, the public is as insatiable as ever for the bustle, noise, joy, thrill and throb of these behemoths of American amusement.

17. NIBLO'S SEEN BY A CHILD

NEW YORK CLIPPER, APRIL 28, 1874

What delightful remembrances are mine, tinged with the sadness of regret, when I think of the Niblo's Garden of my childhood! Joyous time, never to be recalled but in memory's pleasant fancy. Then there *was* a garden, and such a garden! What a paradise, to my young eyes, it was! The plants and the flowers, and the gayly lighted refreshment saloon beyond, where I catch a glimpse of the well-known figure of a lady superintending all, and whom I point out to my little companions as I proudly communicate the fact that this is Mrs. Niblo, that I have been introduced to her, and that she has sometimes treated me to ice-cream. My companions are sufficiently credulous, but my claiming such distinction as this staggers their belief. And here are smart waiters, in snow-white aprons, hurrying to and fro with little trays of that ice-cream. *Such* ice-cream! Have I ever since tasted anything to compare with it? In it I invest my ten cents, or fifteen at the most, held ready in my hand through half the little vaudeville, "The Miseries of Human Life," that I have just seen performed within the theatre. As yet, my experience of the miseries of human life is limited, and I have no sympathy for Mr. Croaker—though admirably acted by Mr. Chippendale, the present manager of the Haymarket Theatre, London—and much prefer to hear the band play, as, seated at a little table in the open air, I eat ambrosia, while there, high above my head, with the real moonlight falling on her, a charming creature—to me neither Madame Javelli nor Madame Axel, but a beauteous fairy glittering with dew-drops—issues from a little pagoda on to a rope that extends some distance across the Garden, and thereon performs evolutions so graceful and daring that I stare upward spell-bound and open-mouthed, in awe and admiration, till, amid a blaze of fireworks, she has with her own fair hand showered down on mine and many older heads bright bits of colored paper from the basket she holds, and thereupon has vnaished! The intermission is over, and I eagerly run up a flight of broad of wooden steps leading to the Theatre, and encounter a gentleman with rosy cheeks and smiling face, who pats me on the head as he passes me. I turn breathlessly to my companions to ask: "Do you know who that was? That's Mr. Niblo!" They have had ocular proof that *he* noticed me, and from that moment I am an eminent boy in their estimation. Up another flight of steps, and we gain a second gallery. Opening onto this second gallery are windows whose blinds are jealously closed; but the gaslight streams through the interstices, and I and my companions, a bevy of little Peeping Toms, are tempted to peer (guilelessly enough, Heaven knows!) down through them at the pretty fairies dressing there. Charming to linger here, though I catch but a glimpse of the hem of some fairy garb, or hear merely the ripple of their laughing voices; but if I stay I may not get a seat, for I hold no coupon. Does anyone? No; fifty cents is the general price of admission all over the house, and no reserved seats—first come, first served. Think of it—the whole Garden and Theatre free to range in! I can sit down in the parquet, if I like; or in the first tier, if I like; or in the second; or up in that place beyond, that looks to me like a wide pulpit. But upstairs is best to see from, and here I scramble to a seat, just in time; for the leader is giving the signal tap with his baton. Is the leader

Monsieur Fenelon or Signor La Manns, Monsieur Guerin or Monsieur Gilles? To me not one of these, but a magician, who by a wave of that little wand causes the curtain to rise and show me wondrous things indeed! Now it is an old man who is standing at a desk, when suddenly a closet-door opens, and a skeleton stalks forth and stands at the old man's elbow. Stretching forth its bony arm, the skeleton rapidly substitutes the sandbox for the ink-bottle, and laughs grimly when the old man pours the contents of the latter over the parchment before him, while the old man, catching sight of his ghastly tormentor, falls down upon his marrow-bones, paralyzed with fear. Now it is Harlequin and Columbine, who, to escape the pursuit of this same old man, go through a wall, and in the opening through which they vanished a giant appears, gnashing his teeth, whereupon the old man jumps clean through the giant's stomach, which evidently disagrees with the giant, for he totters forward in great agony. In a trice it is a gloomy graveyard, and ghosts (on whom are dancing-slippers) rise from their tombs to awful music, and stalk about with measured tread. Presto! change! and it is a carnival—a dazzling scene, all illuminated. There are ringing bells, and jingling of tambourines, and gay music to which madly whirl a myriad of gorgeously dressed dancers, whose ghostly coverings have vanished into the sky. Again it is Harlequin and Columbine, rapidly descending a rocky pass, still pursued by the same wicked old man, when a hermit suddenly appears and delivers a speech to Mr. Henry Wells and Madame Marzetti, i.e., to Harlequin and Columbine. I know the hermit is Jones, for Jones is the only speaker in all the pantomimes; and a bold speaker he is, who rolls his r's and his eyes, and whose voice seems to come from the pit of his stomach. I consider myself an authority in acting, and think Jones a fine tragedian. His speech (which is pretty nearly the same thing in every pantomime—referring to the wise use the lovers must make of the talisman he presents them with, warning them of the dangers they will have to encounter, and blessing them) comes rather abruptly to an end, for Jones is suddenly jerked down a trap, and is seen no more. Harlequin taps the ground and a little box rises; the lovers are quickly dressed in pilgrims' garb, and provided with long staffs—all produced in a twinkling from the miraculous little box. They are ready just in time; for here comes the cruel father and the White Knight, stumbling and threatening down the rocky way. Quickly the scene changes to a hall of brazen statues, when lo! in an instant every statue descends from its pedestal, and all join in a solemn dance—a series of jumps, resembling "The Cure" of later date. Suddenly we are in China, with lanterns and mandarins and pigtails, and a grand ballet with umbrellas. And here is the princess—so tiny a creature!—personated by Miss Flora Lehman; and Ventilataw the English traveler, in the person of Gabriel Ravel, who shocks Chinese decorum by investigating the ladies' bathing establishment while the dear creatures are in the bath. Heavens! how they scream; and here they come flying out *en déshabillé*, running for their lives!

Ah! dearly remembered "Kim-Ka" and "Magic Pills," "Mazulme," "Asphodel," "Raoul," and "The Green Monster!"—seen and seen again, and with renewed delight every succeeding time. And the comic pantomimes! "Godenski," with the wonderful skaters; and "The Milliners," with the marvelous Hungarian mirror-dance; and "Jeanette and Jeannot," in which the soldier who beat the drum so dexterously little dreamt, perhaps, that he was destined to own miles of vineyards in Spain, and be world-famed as the great "Blondin"; and "Monsieur Dechalnmeau"—ah! here comes the old gray mare, with Monsieur Jerome Ravel upon her back, and his stupid valet, personified by François Ravel, perched on the crupper behind him; and "Robert Macaire," with Mr. Antoine Ravel, the very prince of Robert Macaires; and "Jocko!" Poor Jocko! who saves Le Petite Jules, the dear little boy!—oh, how I envy him in his possession of so delightful an ape for a friend!

But Jocko, alas, is dead, and the curtain falls; and I am groping my way, holding tightly by my father's hand, through a dim passage-way, where the gas is already turned off.

I am behind the scenes. What hallowed ground to me! What a world of never-ending mystery! But there is Jocko, alive again, with his head on a chair beside him.

"Who—who—is that?" I stammer.

"That is Monsieur Marzetti, the gentleman you saw just now playing Jocko."

I see that Monsieur Marzetti's face is flushed, that drops of perspiration are streaming down it, that he is panting as if he had been running, and that the lady who stands beside him, fanning him with a palm-leaf fan, holds a glass of some restorative to his lips. And I hear somebody say: "Warm work in July for a man in that hot dress and mask!" and I see it all. I believed in a *real* Jocko, and I am cruelly undeceived. The ape is only a man! I suppose I look bewildered and strange, for Monsieur Marzetti, catching his breath as he speaks, laughs, and tells me in broken English that Jocko knows me, and then I am called by name; and I am told, moreover, that Jocko is going to have a benefit in two or three weeks, and if I come to his benefit he will climb the boxes and come round to me. I don't know whether I feel elated at this intelligence or not. But Jocko is as good as his word, and *does* climb the boxes on that eventful night, and gives me his paw to shake, at which I feel that all the eyes of the audience are directed at me, and I blush to the roots of my hair.

But the stage is cleared, and a rope is stretched across it, and the tight-rope performance begins with Le Petit Amour, whose baby-steps along the perilous cord are guided by Monsieur Antoine Ravel. The little act is over; Le Petit Amour is kissed and runs laughing off the stage; and now Monsieur Gabriel Ravel enters in sailor's costume, and, without a balance-pole, yet with velocity and grace that would put to shame many a dancer upon the boards, executes a sailor's hornpipe. There is a tremendous burst of applause, a lull, a pause, and here comes, shambling on, an awkward looking man. When he salutes the audience, a smile passes from face to face, his action is so *outre*; he goes flying at the rope as if it were his bitter enemy, whom he had determined this night to conquer, or else to die himself. He performs several feats cleverly, yet he is continually falling, only to quickly pick himself up and go at it again like a Trojan. A violin is brought him. In the midst of an aire he turns a somersault, playing as he revolves, landing on his feet on the rope, and finishing the aire without having missed a note. This gentleman's name is Gravelet—Blondin Gravelet. As it is thought that Blondin sounds better, perhaps read better on the playbills, Blondin he has become on the bills, and Blondin he is to-day. With him the tightrope performances close, and the curtain falls.

The orchestra plays, and mingling with its music I hear another orchestra, playing faintly in the distance. It comes from the adjoining building—Niblo's Saloon. Communication is had between the Theatre and the Saloon by means of a door, passing through which I look down upon a very aristocratic audience. They were listening to "Ernani! Ernani!" sung by a lady—Mrs. Bostwick. As yet I care little for *prime donne*—above all, for an American *prima donna* of the amateur type—so I close the door softly, and return to the realm of pantomime and ballet.

Mlle. Bertin is dancing. She is graveful and dignified, has a prettily shaped head, and dances well; but not so well as that fragile nymph Celestine Franck, noiseless and light as a snowflake. And here is Monsieur Paul Brillant, the most indefatigable of ballet-masters, and a prince of dancers, who, with languishing eyes bent on the premiere, makes desperate pantomimic love. I have not arrived at the languishing age, and, considering him and the whole race of male dancers ridiculous bores, am glad when he gets off and the funny man comes on. There is charming dancing in the Ravels' ballets: "La Sylphide," Le Diable Amoureux," "Le Diable à Quatre," "Ondine," "Miranda," and many others, with the beautiful Adelaide Lehman, the very flower of the troupe.

Ill-fated girl! I see her now in her peasant-dress, leaning from the cottage-window, smiling and kissing her hand to her lover below, in "Le Fête Champêtre." A moment more, and she disappears from the view of the audience, never to come before them again. Bright with youth, beauty and hope, in an instant she is torn from the ladder on which she is standing, enveloped in flame, burnt and blackened. It is Christmas-Eve, and there is a strange silence behind the scenes, broken only by whispers and a hurrying of people to and fro; for the Angel of Death is hovering near. In one of the dressing-rooms above, a girl in bodily agony heroically and most patiently awaits the final summons. One long week of suffering, and on New-Year's Eve poor Adelaide Lehman, dutiful daughter, devoted sister, most irreproachable of women, is at peace and rest.

But the season is over, and the Ravels have flitted away to earn new laurels in other cities. And now new faces rise before the footlights of Niblo's Garden. I will briefly notice them as they appear as in a panorama of the past—a sea of faces, following from season to season. I cannot place them as they succeeded one another in rotation, but will speak of them as they severally rise in my memory. The Rousset Sisters—Caroline, Adelaide, Theresine, Clementine—who took the town by storm in "Catarina, Queen of the Bandits." Who that ever saw the four sisters can forget them in "La Manola," or "Giselle?"—in which Caroline Rousset surpassed all previous Giselles, even Augusta and Blangy. How wildly, how madly, she danced in that ballet! A dancer to whom applause came like the intoxication of wine, and who received more applause than any dancer I have since seen. Giselle, with the Prince of Courland, faultless in dress, but with little to do, but doing it very well. The Prince of Courland has become the Prince of Costumers, and reigns at Wallack's. Indeed, if I mistake not, I saw him on the stage there the other evening in the gambling scene in "Money." And now it is the French comic opera, and a little, pale-faced, black-haired lady is the *prima donna*—Mademoiselle Calve—and how she sings! But she fades from my sight, and is replaced by more dancers, imported from Paris by the enterprising stage-manager, Mr. John Sefton: Mlle. Leontine Pougand, fat, fair, and saucy; Señorita Soto, tall, majestic, a true Andalusian beauty, with arching instep and flashing eyes; Mlle. Lavigne, who can jump higher than any of her companions; Mlle. Melanie Drouett, who, I think, is homesick, but who eventually finds consolation in a happy marriage, and retires to private life; Christine Leeder, weak on her toes, but strong in the sailor's hornpipe; and lastly, Monsieur Mege, whose pirouettes are simply marvelous. And now it is a new songstress; Madame Anna Thillon, with her sweet face and brown curls, and faultless bust and arms, and light soprano voice, and pretty affectation of broken English. She is supported by a tenor, Mr. Hudson, who makes believe he can sing, and who carries it off with so gallant a bearing, and with acting so clever, that the audience freely forgive his vocal shortcomings. Just here I remember the performance of an old English comedy, "The Belle's Strategem": Doricourt, Mr. Charles Wheatleigh—his first appearance in America; Letitia Hardy, Miss Fitzpatrick. Miss Fitzpatrick's dressing is faultless, and she wears *real* laces and *real* jewels; but Miss Fitzpatrick's success isn't much to speak of. The fact is, the public have not yet begun to accept either real laces or real jewels as a substitute for talent. Indeed, I think the public appreciates much more heartily the efforts of the new French dancer, Mlle. de Melisse, who makes her debut between the acts of the comedy, and who doesn't wear real laces or real jewels—in truth, wears so little of anything, that Mrs. Grundy is scandalized beyond bounds.

Ah! But we arrive at a special, an eventful night. Niblo's is gayly decorated, and the auditorium is crowded with the elite of New York, on tiptoe of expectation. At last a gentleman, surrounded by his friends, enters one of the private boxes. It is Louis Kossuth. He bows his acknowledgment of the hearty cheers that greet him, and is seated. This is a benefit-night for the Hungarian cause, and the dancers wear the Hungarian badges on their breasts. They are Celestine Franck, Victorine Franck, Madame Marzetti, and Mlle. Natalie Tilman, the last named lady being now proprietress of one of the leading and most fashionable dressmaking and millinery establishments in New York. I remember that, at the close of the comedy, Mary Taylor reads or sings some verses in honor of the patriot present. The comedy is "The Rival."

But where is he to-day who was the centre of all eyes that night?—he who was greeted with cheers, the honored guest of the nation? In Europe, almost friendless—desolate and alone, earning a bare subsistence by teaching languages. And where are the Ravels, the joy and delight of my boyhood? Reposing happily beneath the shade of their vineyards near Toulouse, France. Shall I go on and tell you more? No; for here my boyhood's recollections end, the man's begin, and I bid *adieu* to the Niblo's Garden of my childhood.

18. SUNDAY IN JONES'S WOOD

HARPER'S WEEKLY, NOVEMBER 5, 1859

Jones's Woods are not Elysian fields. Romance and poetry dwell not therein. Tranquil delights have there no abiding place. Of sheltering shades, and balmy breezes, and languishing lawns, and other rural comforts which woodland and grove are popularly supposed to afford, there are limited supplies. Of bustle and tussle, and broil and hurly-burly, there are profusion and variety. You would perhaps expect nothing else in a place with such a name. Jones does not awaken hopeful expectations. There is nothing about Jones to appeal to your tender imaginations any more than about Smith, or Brown, or Robinson. Jones's Woods is simply a business-like title, meritorious in brevity, and exceeding apt in application; for Jones's Woods, especially on Sundays, is about the most business-like place you have visited.

It is the business of leisure that prevails—the labor of entertainment, the hard work of enjoyment. Of a Sunday morning you will find there are hundreds upon hundreds of straggling wanderers, toiling earnestly to experience amusements; laying themselves out with unflinching determination to acquire gratification at all hazards; often pervaded with firmest convictions that their purpose is in course of accomplishment, and that only a few more struggles are needed to perch them along upon a tolerably lofty elevation of bliss. To help them to this end, practical philanthropists, who have discovered that among a certain class of the community no luxury can equal that of a wild and aimless waste of money, have provided manifold means. Not an avenue but is flanked with booths and stalls, in which capital to any amount may be sunk to rise no more. Not a path but is thickly planted with traps for the absorption of unwary coin. There are numberless "shooting galleries," not unlike those of the beer gardens, in which men give their minds with grave intensity to the discharge of penny pop-guns. There are little tents, beyond all circulation, in which pictorial shows are displayed, and wooden figures put through courses of mechanism. There are gymnastic appliances, upon which sportive young men and women are invited to swing and hop, to tumble and see-saw, to wriggle on parallel bars, and to skim the air on edges of big wheels, revolving in somersaults and otherwise. There are wooden horses for timid infants to career upon, and live donkeys for the indulgence of more courageous youth. There are bowling alleys and billiard halls ever resounding with crash and click. Not least, if last recorded, there are countless and inexhaustible supplies of cheap refreshments, which never fail to find a ready market. As you pass, you are exhorted to pause and partake. "Sandwiches, Sir, sandwiches—very nice ones!" cries a salesman, anxious for your welfare; but sandwiches do not recommend themselves to our appetite, and you proceed. "Cakes, Sir, cakes—pies, pies, Sir—confectionary?" cries, inquiringly, another disinterested dispenser of unsubstantial food; but you are also unmoved to test the quality of his stock. Others direct their appeals not so much to individuals as to the public at large. "Lobsters here," says a purple-faced woman, behind a fishstand; "lobsters here, all ready for any gentleman with fine red claws;" and no sales are effective. Oysters, however, appear to find greater public favor, and the sizzle of fries and roasts salutes the ear, while steaming stews perfume the atmosphere.

It is possible that, somewhere in these sketches, allusion may have been made to Beer—that feeble hints of the fascination exercised by that fluid over the German soul may have been ventured upon—that intimations of the passionate and reckless abandonment of all other considerations in favor of that of beer, which characterizes the German spirit, may have been put forth. Even if so, revived allusions, hints, and intimations become necessary when Jones's Woods are the subject of discourse. Here beer reigns with supremest power. It drowns all other thoughts. Its flow is constant and unrestrained. Ever-gurgling spigots emit their steady streams. Tankards are tossed aloft with ceaseless energy. Beside the river which sweeps by the "Woods" staid Germans stroll, with mugs in hand, and gaze with calm contempt upon the inferior element that rolls below. They turn away, and with rapt countenances, and eyes half closed with quiet ecstasy, still sip and sip with smiles of saturated joy, as if in meditative dreams reflecting on a Paradise where cheese-and-sausage-bearing trees spring up in graceful clusters from the prolific soil of genial islands reposing tranquilly upon the bosom of a sea of beer.

The scenes at Jones's Woods are not monotonous. The eye meets always rambling groups of men and women, dancing children, lads and maidens illustrating young love influenced by beer, brisk operations of athletic tendency in swings and on ropes, and busy effervescence of trade in shops and stalls. Sounds of tumbling ten-pins, bullets tapping upon targets, hum of talk and laughing outpeals never diminish. Look, closely, and you will find, too, abundance of incident. See that family party. A young mother, it would appear, draws after her a wicker wagon, in which two infants, face to face, recline. The father, a fresh-looking German, walks carelessly at a little distance. His shaky step and wandering eye tell you he has been putting too much enemy in his mouth. The young woman is troubled more for him than for the children. People look into the little wagon and laugh, and turn jocosely to the mother, who half smiles, but languidly, not brightly. What can the joke be? You approach nearer, and then you find there is but one child, and a fat doll stuck opposite, with very flabby kid face, and countenance denoting many nursery struggles. Spite of its injured nose and absent eye, the baby leers fondly upon it, and makes passes at it through the air—surest sign of infantile affection. You think it a droll idea, this conjunction of stuffed image and young flesh, and take opportunity to inquire what it means. You learn, and then you do not laugh, like the rest, that the wagon once bore a pair of little Knaben, and that when the oldest languished and drooped to death the other sickened too, missing his crib-fellow, and could only be appeased by this kid and cotton-wool substitute, from which he never would be separated, least of all in his out-door rides.

While this is told you, the father has joined the merry sportsmen who find satisfaction in pop-guns. He has tried a shot. Some one claps him on the back and cries "Bravo!" He dilates a little, and essays another. He is incited to shoot for wagers. His wife murmurs dissuasions; but he tips her a grimace of deep import, as to say, "See, now, how I will fleece these fellows!" These fellows—dark-looking men, with oily hair, and hooked noses, and close-knit brows, and glaring costume—urge him on. Money is put up. The hooked-nosed men miss shabbily, and tipsy German wins. He thrusts the coins into his outer pocket, and drawing forth his handkerchief a minute later, unconsciously scatters them over the ground. Another match, and he wins again. Exultant, he boisterously consents that the stakes shall be greatly augmented. He collects all his possessions and deposits them. This time he loses every thing.

He withdraws, dejected, and rejoins his wife. She does not reproach him, but tells him he was deceived—that his first winnings were permitted only for the purpose of leading him on to larger risks. He doubts, but will have positive assurance. He stumbles up to make investigations and is repulsed. He persists, and is hustled off, a little bruised and much torn. He suddenly becomes repentant, and rejoining his wife, hovers round the wagon as she draws it away.

A little after noon the visitors evince a disposition to settle near the centre of the Woods. You learn that a tight-rope performance is to be provided. This must be seen. At an elevation so great that you have not before noticed it stretches the line—an airy nothing. People say, with evident complacency, that the last night's rain has made it so slippery that the danger is extreme. Presently the funambulist appears. He is clad in white shirt and trowsers, without coat or hat, and with slippers on his feet. You ask who he is, and are told his name is Chiarini, and that he appears thus simply dressed "out of respect to the day." You are convinced that the day will feel honored by this mark of Mr. Chiarini's respect.

He begins his evolutions, and the crowd applauds noisily. He skips about, and lies down flat, and elevates his feet, and in many other ways forsakes safety and invites danger. Now he daringly spins round, teetotum-like. But stop—he swerves, his foot slips, his balance-pole rushes through the air; will he fall? The crowd gasps and shudders, then rushes off a little to give him a good clear space to drop upon if he must come down. But no; he clings closely, and by a convulsive writhe restores his equilibrium. New and louder shouts encourage him, and he persists in more audacious efforts. At length, exhausted, he retires, and the throng dissolves to seek again fresh pleasures and fresh beer.

Thus pass the Sundays in the Woods of Jones.

19. THE TROLLEY-PARK

by Day Allen Willey
COSMOPOLITAN, JULY, 1902

The expression, "trolley-park," may not as yet have come into common use, but no explanation of its meaning is necessary. The oldest of the trolley-parks has been in existence but a few years, yet to-day these resorts are to be found in the outskirts of nearly every city in the land. The fact is that the street and suburban railway companies, realizing the profit arising by catering to the pleasure of the masses, have entered into the amusement field on an extensive scale. These breathing-spots are not confined to the cities, but are becoming popular as centers of recreation for clusters of small communities which may be linked by the electric current.

Originally, few, perhaps none, of the promoters of the trolley-route thought of it as a means of carrying the pleasure-seeker except to public parks. The main incentive was the business to be secured by transferring the throngs of toilers to and from the store, office and factory, and forming a means of communication between the different parts of the city. With the advent of the electric car came the opportunity to build homes amid more natural surroundings. Townfolk became more appreciative of the charms of the country, but trolley-riding for enjoyment, which has become a summer habit in the larger centers of population, was not thought of a decade ago. The companies were quick to note the increase in their revenues from this unexpected source, and naturally encouraged it by giving transfer-tickets from one route to another and allowing children to ride free or at half-price. As a result, people of all classes availed themselves of the opportunity to get a breath of fresh air and pass the long evenings enjoying the "trolley-breeze," for a rapidly whizzing trolley-car can stir a breeze in the stillest night of midsummer. The need of some place where one could alight and thus vary the monotony of the ride, led to the inception of the park scheme. From the few acres of grove, or possibly the open field with a tree here and there, some rough benches and a shed or so for protection from the weather, these pleasure-grounds have been developed into resorts some of which are far more attractive than the public parks of the cities where they are located. On a holiday one may see more than fifty thousand people gathered in some of the more extensive trolley-parks owned by companies in Philadelphia, Detroit, Minneapolis, Baltimore, and other centers of population, listening to the band-concerts, watching or taking part in the ball-games, boating on the lake and river, strolling along the shady walks, having a family picnic under the trees or enjoying the summer opera. Except for the nickel, dime or quarter which admits to the concert, rents the boat, or provides some other special amusements, the park is free to all, the company obtaining its reward in the fares which it collects. These parks, combining natural and artificial diversions, have become the Mecca on holidays and Sundays not only of what we are pleased to term the working classes but of the "middle millions"—especially those parks where no intoxicating beverages are sold and where other conditions are designed to encourage the patronage of the family.

The inventive genius has made a study of diversions for the trolley-park, which perhaps represents a greater variety of popular amusements than any other resort. He has constructed a miniature railway over which a pigmy locomotive makes regular trips drawing the "Overland Limited" with its dozen carloads of pleasure-seekers. The merry-go-round, with its gaily decorated horses and lions and dragons swinging around the circle to the music of the orchestrion, is another magnet of enjoyment for big as well as little folk, and the ludicrous efforts to spear the gold ring afford much merriment to all. Next to this may be the "aquarama," where you pay your dime to drift with the current along the mysterious river, passing an ancient castle with its frowning battlements, plunging into darkness as your craft goes through what seems to be a tunnel in the mountain-side. Then appears a vista of field and forest; next you may float through a desert of the Orient, on this wonderful tour. The "Railway to the Moon" takes you on another novel journey. The force of gravity is employed in the "up and down hill" line. Climbing to the top of a stairway, fifty feet or so, you enter a car which rushes down the incline with such speed that it ascends another elevation by its momentum. Descending this, it comes to the end of the road with sufficient speed to turn and run back to the foot of the stairway on the level track. The latest idea in the up-and-down railroad, however, is the "loop the loop," as it is popularly termed. The car moves along by means of small rollers on wheels sliding inside a grooved rail and runs down a long incline with such speed that it makes a complete circle or turn in the air, the motion being so rapid that centrifugal force keeps the occupants from falling out, though they are strapped to their seats as an additional safeguard. From Canada has come the thought of the water toboggan; but in lieu of the chute glistening with ice, an inclined platform forms the slide down which the boat with its crew rushes into the water with such force that for the moment the merrymakers are hidden in a sheet of spray.

When the family is weary of these amusements, there is plenty left to do. The boys can find a ball-game to watch or can get up "one-old-cat" with their companions, or exchange their pennies for the privilege of hurling a ball at the shining face of a negro, who usually manages to duck just in time to avoid disaster, but not too easily to destroy the hope of nailing him next time. And it is wonderful with what savage zest the small boy will take aim until his last penny has been handed across the board. Then he stands around hoping that some professional pitcher of a base-ball team will come up presently and get his money's worth.

Meanwhile the rest of the family spreads luncheon under the trees or embarks on a swan-boat or a barge, and pleasantly idles away the time until the lengthening shadows on the lawns and lakes makes it advisable to gather the clans preparatory to departure. In little groups they bustle out to the open cars and a quick ride through the country into the town or city completes the holiday. At every corner the tired pleasure-seekers wend their way toward home.

Of all the large trolley-parks, Willow Grove, in Philadelphia, is probably the most spacious yet laid out, though with the rapidly increasing number of such resorts no one can tell how long it will hold supremacy. It not only contains many of the amusements described, but it has a pavilion large enough to seat ten thousand people who listen to the music of such organizations as Sousa's, Damrosch's and Innes's bands, which are engaged by the month and paid by the railroad company.

One of the most interesting of the New England parks is known as Whalom, situated on the lake of that name in Massachusetts. It is a recreation-spot for the cities of Worcester and Fitchburg, and several smaller places on the trolley-line. An ornamental depot was built at the railroad terminus, as well as a band pavilion and restaurant. The grounds lent themselves naturally to the art of the landscape-gardener, but it was wisely determined not to lay out anything so fine and elaborate as to necessitate "Keep Off the Grass" and "Do Not Touch" signs, so the crowds roam at will over the lawns and through the groves. The lake, a beautiful sheet of water, has an excellent beach for bathing, and is also used for boating and sailing, while the zoo on its shore contains deer, moose, elk, and other forest denizens. The Whalom Theatre, perhaps the most notable amusement feature, was constructed in one of the principal groves. In it three thousand persons can enjoy the opera performances given nightly by companies of thirty to fifty people. All the scenery and stage-effects required for such productions as "La Grande Duchesse," "Said Pasha" and "Maritana" are introduced, the stage being fully fifty feet in depth. The rear and sides of the theatre are open so that the woodland at its back can be utilized for forest scenes if desired. The building is illuminated with four thousand incandescent lamps. Although the theatre cost thirty thousand dollars and the expense of maintaining it averages five hundred dollars weekly, the railroad company sometimes closes the season with five thousand dollars' profit, yet the highest price for a reserved seat is but ten cents. The popularity of the place is shown by these statistics. It is an interesting fact, however, that the fares collected on the railway during the park season amount to thirty-five thousand dollars more than during the spring, autumn or winter.

WILLIAM L. SLOUT

20. NEW YORK'S NEW SUMMER PLAYGROUND

by Theodore Waters
HARPER'S WEEKLY, JULY 8, 1905

I once took a trip to Coney Island with a professor of psychology for the purpose of studying the New York mob at play. "I am told that erstwhile dignified citizens indulge there in all sorts of childish antics," he remarked on the way to the beach. "Strange how people can so far forget themselves! It will be instructive."

It was. During the day I was edified at the spectacle of a doctor of philosophy astride a wooden horse, on which he rocked to and fro and at which he yelled vigorously in an effort to win a race against other wooden horses sliding rapidly down a metal runway. And before the day ended I had seen this same citizen "looping the loop" and "bumping the bumps," balancing himself on jumping stairways, throwing rings over canes, exclaiming at the beauties of scenic railways, and, in short, performing the same childish antics that every one performs, whatever his or her station in life, when on a visit to Coney Island.

The professor delivered a lecture, later, on the psychology of crowds, in which he used himself as an illustration of how the individual may be influenced by the mob; but there is more in Coney Island than mere mob influence. Time was when the place was shunned by ultrarespectable New Yorkers, who went instead to Manhattan Beach; but nowadays Coney is visited by all classes, and the demand for the peculiar brand of relaxation which it supplies has become so great that the concessions and the crowd have overflowed into Brighton and Manhattan Beach, with the result that the whole shore is being made into one great playground for the people of New York. The Boer War is being fought again daily back of the Brighton Beach Hotel; a Japanese village is being built against the Manhattan Beach Hotel, and the space between is being laid out for special concessions, scenic railways, a large new railway station, etc., and it will not be long before the place will bear about the same relation to old Coney Island that Greater New York bears to old Manhattan Island. It will be the most remarkable amusement-ground in the world, and by all odds the largest.

The reason for this popular expansion is obvious. If the visitor can divest himself of the tremendously compelling atmosphere of the place and view it dispassionately, he will find that there is hardly a concession on the ground which does not appeal directly to the emotions. In this the *concessionnaire* copies the method of appeal of great literary and dramatic masterpieces, but he goes a step further. A book or play appeals to the emotions through the intellect. One must sit and read a book and imagine the situations depicted; one must sit and witness an actor in the throes of strong passions. But in Coney Island it is the spectator, as it were, who is made to perform. To be sure, there are some concessions, such as the Galveston Flood, or Creation, which follow the traditions of the theatre by giving a show upon a stage, with special reasons therefor, but in the most successful shows the patron is himself juggled with, stood upon his head, or whirled through space, or shot up to the moon, or dropped into the bowels of the earth. It is the key-note of Coney Island's success; it is why over one hundred thousand persons go there Sunday after

Sunday during the summer season. The professor of psychology could sit unmoved during the running of a great horse-race like the Suburban, but the moment he found himself jostled about by the wooden horse in Coney's Steeplechase, with a prospect of beating his wooden competitors, he became at once a very elemental being, yelling and plunging and strenuously intent upon winning a little pink ticket for a free ride.

In fact, the *concessionnaire* is constantly on the look-out for some new way of exciting old emotions, and a trip over the Island means that a whole gamut of them will be played upon. The man who invented the scenic railway hit upon a principle attraction which has brought him a fortune. To sit in a car which passes alternately from light to darkness and darkness to light and makes sudden and dizzy descents of twenty feet or more is to have one's mental and physical sensibilities excited to the utmost.

The Trip to the Moon is nothing more than a mimic representation of just what one might expect to experience on a real trip to that planet. The crowd is ushered on to a slightly rocking platform fashioned like an airship, and is easily led to imagine that it is rising through space, because the star-laden scenic sky surrounding the ship is made to drop rapidly and silently, and the enormous wings of the ship flapping out horizontally prevent any passenger looking downward over the rail. A convenient storm obscures the view entirely after a while, and then the moon, a circle of extinct volcanic cones, appears near at hand, and you step out of the ship into a grotto, through which a dwarf leads you to the king and queen of the moon. These are two midgets, who are so glad to see you that they sing a weary song of welcome (for which no one should blame them, as they do it thirty or forty times a day), and conduct you to a dragon's mouth, which opens and allows you to walk into his stomach. The way is treacherous, for the floor rocks and the walls of his alimentary canal are clammy, so that the relief which one feels on getting out of him at last is sufficient to counteract the surprise of suddenly finding oneself out in a street on earth.

Now this show is utterly unreasonable from any scientific standpoint, but no one appears to think it strange that a king's grotto should be found on a burned-out planet, or that the dragon's tail should reach down to earth. There must be some climax, and perhaps that of being swallowed alive is as good as any, and the sudden exit into brightly lighted Luna Park is about as near a portrayal of a pleasant awakening from a bad dream as could be invented.

In the show known as Hell Gate there is a well-reasoned *motif* based upon an ancient and very human dread—that of the whirl-pool. Poe used it with fine effect long before the art of the *concessionnaire* was heard of. In an open-fronted building in Dreamland has been constructed a fifty-foot whirl-pool. The water swirls terrifyingly towards the centre, and boats crowded with passengers describe a constantly narrowing circle, until before the eyes of the astonished spectators they dive into the middle of the pool. It is a clever device, that of admitting all the world free to see the boats take the plunge, for every one is eager immediately to take the plunge for himself and see what happens beneath the pool. As a matter of course, it is very pleasant down there. The "pool" is merely a spiral trough made of wood and iron, through which the water carries the boats to the centre, where the slope suddenly dips and allows them to slip beneath the outer rims of the spiral into a subterranean channel which follows a tortuous course under the building. There are scenes by the way intended to corroborate the popular conception of the earth's interior, and these are about as true to nature as those which we found on the moon, so that by the time the spectators above are beginning to wonder what has happened to the boat, the passengers have had a surfeit of subterranean horrors, and are shot up through one side of the pool to the surface.

Coney Island is the apotheosis of emotion. "Shake 'em up!" yells the barker in front of the animal show (which the crowd patronizes in the hope that one of the lions will bite his keeper), and that is what they are doing all over the Island—"shaking them up;" actively when they loop the loop, passively when that same barker, dressed and painted to resemble an automaton on a music-box, suddenly begins to imitate the jerky motions of such a figure for the benefit of the gaping crowd. Every one in the crowd knows the man is human, and every one knows that every one else knows it, and yet each man peers into the face of his neighbor in the hope that some one may be fooled by it.

The crowd that spends hours in front of the "Bumps" knows well what will happen to any one who attempts the descent. Its knowledge, however, is not greater than that of the bumped, since they are recruited from the crowd, yet the insane joy that is exhibited when a man or a woman goes head over heels is based partly on the conscious delusion that the fallen ones did not know what was in store. The public may always be depended upon to help the *concessionnaire* deceive it. In fact, there is an axiom known to playwrights and novelists which holds that the expected may often be made more interesting to an audience than the unexpected.

The young people who flock past the "Flatiron" building in Steeplechase Park know well enough that a gust of wind from an electric fan will blow their hats from their heads and that they will be made ridiculous in front of the crowd, but the number of those who walk by the spot does not diminish for that reason. The crowds which gaze for a penny a look into the moving-picture machines bearing signs which deny the pleasure to "all persons under sixteen years of age," know well enough that there can be nothing on view to which Mr. Anthony Comstock could possibly object, but that does not ease their curiosity.

There is horse-play in the "Foolish House"—a mere maze of mirrors within-doors. There is religious awe embraced in the contemplation of "Creation," a panoramic spectacle illustrating the story of Genesis. No one could possibly help being affected by that vivid panorama of old earth in the making, accompanied by the solemn voice of the lecturer, who, with the showman's instinct for the verity that lurks in the incongruity, proves his case by adhering almost literally to the Scriptural account. Not even when Adam, in all the nakedness of a suit of underwear which wrinkles as he walks, is discovered by Eve, similarly attired, does the scene lose its spell. At least no one suggests that the spectacle has come perilously near to blasphemy.

The gambling instinct is played upon through the offer to the man with the weighing-machine, who engages to charge you nothing for his talent, or his lack of it, rather, if he fails to guess within three pounds of your weight. There is emotion in such scenes as the Galveston Flood and the Johnstown Flood; and I am amazed that some one has not attempted a reproduction of the horrors of the *Slocum* disaster. What an opportunity to give the *blasé* New-Yorker the sensation of his life by putting on a stage steamboat, letting it burn to the water's edge, and rescuing him at the last moment with a stage police-tug, while dummy passengers burn to death in real fire or drown in real water. I venture to predict that such a horror would be both denounced and patronized by all who were fortunate enough to escape from the real steamboat.

Something like this is surely coming to Coney Island if the appetite of the mob goes on increasing. The place has developed a sort of emotional Frankenstein whose desire for the bizarre is constantly on the increase. I visited several shows in which the audience had already begun to show signs of disappointment.

Instead of jostling his patrons about until their teeth rattled, the *concessionnaire* tried to appeal to their sense of the beautiful by means of a stage spectacle. One of these shows was a trip to far-off parts of the earth. New York Harbor, the ocean, and finally the "far-off parts" passed before our eyes in panoramic procession while we were seated comfortably. We were a small audience; but had we been placed upon the deck of a stage steamship which rocked while the scenery moved past us, if after a while we had been allowed to get off the boat and stand upon the shore of those far-off lands, there would have been more of us, even though we had been compelled to return to the United States *via* the stomach of a "dragon."

To be sure, such an arrangement would call for added ingenuity, and it would cost more in proportion, but ingenuity is the body pulse of Coney Island just as emotion is its nervous system; and as for the great expenditure, that is valued as an advertising asset. "Fire and Flames" and "Fighting the Flames" are moving pictures viewed from the front. The audience recognizes itself in the people who walk the streets, throng the shops, sit in the restaurants, lounge in the barrooms, sing in the church, and finally perish in the fire. But what looks quite simple from the front is complicated from the rear. The populace of these imitation towns is composed of hundreds of persons, all of whom must be drilled to act their parts. Some of these are mere members of the mob; others, as, for instance, the woman whose baby is rescued from the fire and whose heartrending screams set one on edge with apprehension, must needs be theatrical artists of no little talent. The dwellings themselves are constructed of fire-proof material filled in by parts which burn merely for the sake of the scenic effect. In each room of the houses is a huge powder-blower, operated by compressed air from the tank; so that when the flames burst from the windows they are not the result of haphazard chance, but part of a system which operates like clockwork and is the result of inventive ability on the part of the scene manager.

21. THE AMUSEMENT PARK

by Rollin Lynde Hartt
ATLANTIC MONTHLY, MAY, 1907

SIR JOHN LUBBOCK, in his quaint little philosophical mosaic *The Pleasures of Life*, entirely omits to mention those felicities which, selected and compounded with due discretion, fashion the amusement park. This delinquency argues no intellectual or emotional snobbishness on Lubbock's part. With insatiable curiosity he probed the activities of Battas and Cambodians, of Fijis, Bachapins, and Bouriats, and recounted them in *The Origin of Civilization and the Primitive Condition of Man*. With equal (perhaps analogous) concern, I fancy, would he have contemplated the joys of shrieking multitudes such as frequent the "scenic" railway, the "shoot the chutes," and the "house of follies." But *The Pleasures of Life*, appearing a score of years ago, came too early to admit of these fascinating considerations.

And yet, precisely at that period, Mr. Erastus Wiman was evolving the first amusement park, progenitor of the two thousand with which the nation is now beatified. To his iridescent electrical geyser at St. George's, you had access only by his Staten Island Ferry; to his Wild West, somewhere in the Hinterland, only by his Staten Island Railway; thus, whether by boat or train or by entertainment, it was always Mr. Wiman who transported you. And so remunerative became the dual rôle that later, when the trolley began its conquest, speculative genius snatched a leaf from Mr. Wiman's book; and you could scarce find a company unenterprising enough not to stimulate traffic by opening a grove or park supplied with alluring bears, irresistible simians, and the enticements of al fresco vaudeville. Meanwhile, the Saturday half-holiday and the Continental Sunday augmented the response vouchsafed by an adoring public.

It was commonly by milder measures than Erastus Wiman's that his disciples applied his theories. They judged that the town-stayed summer millions would yield up dimes and nickels gladly in purchase of idyllic and faintly sensational enjoyments. In this they had the wisdom of their day; and, as eras overlap, in pleasures as clearly as in creeds and philosophies, many charming examples of that somewhat placid, not to say languid, style of amusement park still survive. The people love them; love them better at heart, I believe, than they love the corybantic frenzies that seek to supersede them. Happier, though less frolicsome, than at Luna Park or Wonderland they taste the delights of restful contentment, comingled with a tempered and soothing gayety—the shade of radiant beauty; forest folk, in open-air cages, for things to pet and to wonder at; the theatre as at least a tolerable substitute for melody and humor; the river, with luscious wooded banks and glassy surface, for cruises in pretty launches or prettier canoes. Besides, there are swings, and a tiny electric fountain, and a "palace of electrical marvels," to say nothing of the paradise of bonbons, tinted drinks and peanuts; everywhere contentment, shining from sunny faces, particularly from the faces of wee children. Once, as it seemed to me, I saw the genius of such a place personified in a sweet little maid of three, who clapped her chubby hands in ecstasy before a bed of flowers as she cried, "Oh, see these pwitty, pwitty, *pwitty* woses!"

Nevertheless, there arose certain misguided schismatics who found the idyllic pleasures grow a trifle dull, or fancied they did. People don't always think what they think they think, even regarding their amusements; indeed, it is there, most especially, that they manifest their autoguillibility. This our perveyors of recreation have known from of old. Witness Barnum. Given, therefore, a populace prone to worship strange divinities, and capital will soon enough supply the altars. Here and yonder, springing up sporadically and without effort at organization, arose sierra-like funiculars, whirling death-traps, and mad, cyclonic—even seismic—bugaboos. Such won proselytes, who exhibited the traditional zeal of the convert, to the vast discomfiture of those who still confessed the fascination of bears and swings and peanuts. Folly, like would-be wisdom, has its poses, chief of which is sophistication; and what had been at first a mere inarticulate dissatisfaction with the tamer, but pleasanter, diversions became outspoken disdain. And all along, the charming grove had attracted many supercilious souls of the sort that affect to despise cheap amusement, as who should say, "Ah, yes, we went there, but pray don't imagine that's our notion of a lark!" It was, and they fibbed; and now the fib served to aid the propaganda of heresy.

Meanwhile capital, with ever an ear to the ground, had caught murmurs that set it thinking; why not kidnap the institution, cram it with heathen allurements, put it where the proletariat was already wont to go a-pleasuring, and make the reincarnated and expanded elysium independent, henceforth, of the broomstick train? In this there should be dividends! And just at this juncture, when speculative interests sat plotting, there arrived a concrete suggestion, brilliant and convincing.

Expositionism set in. It became epidemic. American cities were of two classes only, those that had had the distemper and those that wanted it; Americans likewise of two classes, those that had visited expositions and those that counted themselves debased and undone because they hadn't. If, therefore, a miniature exposition should lift its towers and opal-tinted minarets close to some enormous centre of population, it would pay for itself in a season or so. Sound logic, wanting only the revision that makes assurance doubly sure.

Problem: What features of the world's fair to reproduce? The most popular, of course. And which are they? To determine this, the capitalists studied expositionitis by isolating the germ. They watched its growth in the culture tube, and as soon as it got big enough for its name to be made out, they knew their duty. The Midway, as they had already guessed, was the *clou* of the exposition. Americans had owned themselves half-Latin in their zest for carnival; the gala mood, long held in abeyance by Puritan tradition, had leaped forth in a day, claiming and winning an uproarious recognition. Hence the reincarnated amusement park, while feebly imitating the exposition architecture and providing a garish replica of its illumination, gave the Midway a dominant rank—indeed, permitted nothing but Midway—and, in needless tremors lest the people might have tired of those somewhat familiar distractions, combed Christendom for supplementary felicities. The Middle Western street-fair, the Parisian *fête foraine*, the mardigras, the fiesta, the penny vaudeville, the circus, the dime museum, and the jubilant terrors of Coney Island, were rifled of their magic. Never was Midway so frantic, so extravagant, so upsetting, so innoculously bacchanalian!

Meanwhile an unsuspected economic secret had been disclosed. Whereas Wiman and the Wimanites had naïvely financed their own "attractions," the brazen Midway compelled its concessionaires to purchase the right to exhibit. Thus its expansion knew practically no bounds. It realizes the boast of the country circus, becoming literally "a stupendous aggregation of monster shows." The more numerous and effulgent those shows, the more multitudinous the crush at the general entranceway. So, what with tolls at the outer wickets and imposts at the countless little counting houses of vassal princes, you had here a scheme for money-making that would tempt investments till, according to *The Railway and Engineering Review*, the total capitalization of amusement parks in America has reached the great figure of $100,000,000.

On the other hand, economic law involved a limitation. Summer empties the town of the class that flung away money so riotously at the expositions; instead of a fifty-cent admission fee at the gate, the park humbles itself to be happy with a dime, and very modest must be the additional fees within. Its patrons, the residuum of the mountain-ward, shore-ward, and Europe-ward hegira, make up in numbers what they lack in opulence. Besides, knowing world's fairs chiefly by hearsay and the half-toned photographs in the Sunday newspapers, they are indulgent of sham. Have patience, then, with a world of short-comings well calculated to scandalize the classic Burnham and cause the great Roltaire to beat his breast. A hot board walk replaces the delicious lawns and shubbery, tinsel architecture the exquisite façades, a few plastic fol-de-rols the lavish sculpture-groups, a heartrending "lagoon" the iris-bordered waterways, a jargon of ill-combined hues the gracious harmonies of color, and a crudely magnificent illumination the sweet poetry of radiance that once—ah, so rapturously! turned plaster to opalescent glory. And yet, if you dismiss those visions of supreme loveliness, you call the place very pretty, while to those for whom it is particularly designed it represents a jubilant paradise of beauty. Indeed, it contributes not a little to aesthetic education. The people, like yourself, arrive at artistic appreciation through an ever-diminishing series of humbugs.

In its main purpose, though, this barbaric ensemble attains the very pinnacle of success. It expresses joyousness—sings it, shouts it, a hundred times re-echoes it. In cupolas and minarets, in domes and flaunting finials, in myriads of gay bannerets, in the jocund motion of merry-go-rounds, circle-swings, and wondrous sliding follies, in laughter and in shrieks, in the blare of brazen music and in the throbbing of tom-toms, it speaks its various language—joyous ever.

Yet somehow, amid those frisky multitudes, you detect traces of reaction. Aimless spirits drift hither and yon, wary and hesitant, "like green pigs far from home." With hilarities awaiting them on every hand, they are teasing their souls with such questions as, "Is it worth a whole quarter?" or "Should I come off alive if I tried it?" And this countercurrent of grimness results, I suppose, from a popular (and highly unpopular) fallacy. A dime takes you into the park, or pretends to. But you are never so emphatically outside it as when merely inside it. Upon that central space converge all its gaudy shows, and you aren't inside any one of them. Tantalus, I dare say, was a much-abused man in his time, but they didn't make him purchase his affliction. Unlike Tantalus, you may gain the delights that now torment you, yet vaguely you imagine that they should of right be already yours. You know in your heart that they should not; you know that the initial dime simply qualified you to pace the board walk, hear the bands play, watch the parades of show people—Indians, Arabs, firemen, and the rest—and witness the antics of your contemporaries. Nevertheless, you cherish resentment—the bitterer because of its lack of logic. How fallen your nature since you passed the metamorphic wicket! Outside it, you were Mark Tapley; within, you are Scrooge.

To unscrooge Scrooge, all the beguilements of the art persuasive are let loose at you through megaphones; for your mood has been anticipated, and a race of coaxers, wheedlers, spell-binders, and bamboozlers raise up to make attractions attract. Nothing can surpass their moral earnestness, granted you don't wink at them. They cry up the shows with passionate eloquence, sometimes even exhibiting the performers as a guarantee of good faith and a stimulus to zeal. "Esau here—the ape man—only specia of his kind in existence!" "Princess Fatima here, a full-blooded Bedoueen from the storied city of Nineveh, will dance the mystic anaconda dance, exactly as danced by Hypatia in Holy Writ!" "Don't miss the Fatal Wedding! Sixty laughs to the minute!" "Foolish House—cra-a-a-azy house—only a dime, ten cents, the tenth part of a dollar!" You'll ha-a-a-ave to hurry! The whale is about to enter the ring!" Zounds, what a hubbub!

Laugh, if you must, at their methods, but laugh much more heartily at the need of their being there at all. For nowhere else, save in that most absurd of situations, a battle, will you find the case paralleled. Ten thousand men strut gayly forth to annihilate ten thousand others; but, once arrived upon the field of glory, they don't know about that battle. That is why talented exhorters, called officers, have been scattered through the ranks to persuade the slayers to slay; without those subaltern cries of "Come on, boys!" there would be no battle. Likewise these pleasure-seekers, after braving the horrors of stifling railway trains and hideously overcrowded trolley-cars to reach the blessed portals, have now to be barked through them.

Within, there is generally a ripple of rather ironical comment, an exchange of I-told-you-sos. And as you wait, wait, dripping with perspiration, you analyze the economics that permit the modest charge for admission—walls of painted burlap, gaps where the wood shows through, perchance even confessions of that tarred black paper suggestive of huts for Italian ditch diggers. And all the while, the "ballyhoo" keeps baying the crowds without, as though the performance was "about to begin" and you "had to hurry." You declare that you are not so much before a stage as behind the scenes—that the real proscenium was the gorgeous entrance-way, the real performance a petty tragedy in which the over-borne hero (to wit, yourself) got robbed of his money. But actors draw their pay, and you shall yet draw yours, See! Yonder comes the chief showman—with some natural pangs you recognize him as the barker. Hound of a cheat!—yet away with anger; the curtain goes up, the frolic begins—full value for the dime. However, it achieves its finale with surprising alacrity, and out you rush, unreasonably satisfied and unaccountably eager to be snared again.

For somehow you have caught the spirit of the place. You tingle with it from crown to heel. To slip dimes and quarters through silly ticket windows, to swelter in stuffy amusement pens, to cancel every canon of conventionality, every rubric of discretion, to court perils, discomforts, and mellow swindles—such is your symphony. You spy on your soul and laughingly exclaim, "Lawkamassy on us, this is none of I!" Theoretically an institution for the vulgar herd, the park is preeminently a delight for the cultivated, since the *profanum vulgus* remains involved in the embarrassment of possessing no personalities in particular to slough off.

Emotions, however, they have—though of a primitive sort, responding only to extreme excitations. Or so, at least, you conclude from the emotional stimuli here provided; but perhaps, as so frequently happens in picture-shows, literary competitions, and the architectural exploits of a parvenu street, each phenomenon assumes exaggerated virulence by reason merely of desperation, hoping against hope to outdo the rest. On the other hand, the popular response seems to justify the managerial philosophy, which asserts that the people crave three things only—a chance to wonder, a chance to shudder, and a chance to be scared out of their wits.

"That most fascinating expression upon a child's face," cries Professor G. Stanley Hall—"that most fascinating and beautiful expression, the expression of wonder!" Children thrive in the park; at fifty they're children still. Once they paid "five pins, crooked ones not taken," to peep through a hole in a paper box; now they pay real money for Eleusinian delights. The word "mystic," printed in huge letters on the bill-boards, draws its scores of thousands, who burn to purchase pigs in pokes. And if, having entered the "mystic" gate, the middle-aged child should come upon illusions yet more mystical, he would be as elated as was Moses Primrose when he had sold his horse for a pair of shagreen spectacles.

To get the maximum of wonder out of the illusion, you mustn't be too rational, since at bottom the marvel isn't that the eye can sometimes be fooled, but that the eye can so rarely be fooled. When, at the age of four, you thought your railway train had started, and discovered that, instead, the train next to yours had been moving in the opposite direction, you crowed with glee; you felt that something most extraordinary had been taking place inside you, and you valued yourself more highly on account of it.

To be gulled, to know you are gulled, and to know that the people who gull you know they're gulling you—ah! the bliss! Here at the park a mimic railway carriage, with biograph pictures at its farther end, takes you spinning along the funicular "up Mt. Vesuvius"; likewise a make-believe airship transports you to realms beyond the stars, since a descending panorama connotes an ascending beholder; still subtler mysteries of optics permit your fellow mortals to be innocuously burned alive before your eyes, or turned into skeletons, or waited upon by spooks. But for illusions *par excellence* commend me to yonder fat and sleepy pythoness, who sits within the Temple of Palmistry and between yawns deludes the eye of faith. There is something magnificent about those yawns. As when the wire-dancer goes blindfold, they attest sublime self-confidence; also a conviction, majestic in its immovability, that whoso has paid a half-dollar for a hoax will find grace to swallow it.

Let us not be censorious; the palmist's case verges less closely upon deceit than upon romantic fiction. You consent to illusion, just as when you opened *The Prisoner of Zenda*. If, however, instead of surrendering yourself to Mr. Anthony Hope, you had chosen a book by George Gissing and detected flaws in its realism, vast disgruntlement would result. And so it does when you cross the threshold of Fair Japan, that "revelation and perfect, unabridged realization of the Kingdom of the Mikado and the Chrysanthemum." Later, though, you find it a very agreeable psychological lark, since the people are obviously undismayed by American girls in Japanese costumes, or by wisteria reproduced in paper, or by shabby little pools bordered with Portland cement; and as for vermillion gateways and the crudest and most inartistic of decorations, not the jiu-jitsu performance itself gets a serener acceptance as "the real thing." Well, Cimabue's Madonna was a pretty sad counterfeit of womanhood, though his contemporaries carried it in triumph through Florence; and they of the amusement park still tarry within the archaic era of aesthetic development.

In Beautiful Orient, on the contrary, you see the anachronism turned literally end for end. Thanks to Mr. Frank Carpenter and Mr. William Eleroy Curtis—newspaper heralds of the American invasion—the spectators think the Levant a sort of incommensurable Bowery, where racial customs already give way before an overwhelming tide of occidentalism. The Princess Zuleika (née Flannery) trips forth in a second-hand costume that once lent decorous adornment to a vaudeville soubrette, and you trace her theory of the dance less to Cairo or Stamboul than to Broadway. So be it! If we must have an American invasion, we must put up with the result. Nevertheless, some would fain have proof that "East is East," as "West is West," and that "never the twain shall meet." Such take comfort in camels, in wondrous narghiles, in jugglers and sword-swallowers, in whirling dervishes and musicians from Tangier. They cherish at least a faint hope that the Turkish Theatre will reflect oriental viciousness with something approaching fidelity. But fidelity, which thrives none too well in the Levant itself, fares ill indeed in a make-believe Levant; and if you will put yourself in the manager's place, you will see that there remains no necessity for fair play. A show as old as his, long advertised by its loving friends, is bound to draw. Says Tom to Jerry, "Gee! This is what Bill seen in Chicago!" Emerging—deeply grieved, but in excellent ethical repair—they horribly arraign poor Bill. Not so the average visitant, who would rather quaff his orientalism in tincture than in essence.

Yet, when our pleasurers aspire to craze their souls with vicarious terror, they insist upon "the real thing." How sweet that moment when a man—preferably a woman, ideally a young and comely woman—struts among lions, or drops from a balloon, or vaults through space in an inverted automobile. Barbarism? Yes, but whereas the Coliseum gloated upon the spectacle of death, these modern Romans glory in the escape from death. Light and cruel were the mob in Caesar's day, serious and cruel are these—unconsciously serious, unconsciously cruel. They don't comprehend that their hunger for shudders forces the management to gratify it, or it is they who have put another's life in jeopardy. Neither do they comprehend the far from trivial source of their enjoyment. Flaming sympathies, wild upsurgings of desire, and mad jubilance—when the dread crisis has passed—give the spectator a panoramic view of his own soul. Incapable, commonly, of introspection, he has experienced an interval of dazzling, astounding self-revelation. Out of his littleness, he rises to momentary greatness—feels himself terribly, almost epically, alive.

Still there's no denying that beneath these nobler passions lurks something morbid—morbid or (more precisely) primitive. Blind instinct leads thousands of men to congregate before the prison when a criminal is to be executed; they see nothing, hear nothing, nor do they expect to. Ah! but when somebody gets under the fender of a trolley car, the same blind instinct brings the same seekers after shudders; yet, once there, they lift the car bodily, rescue the sufferer, and exhibit civilized mercy almost simultaneously with prehistoric savagery! Nor will you particularly revere the more delicate individuals who pass by, with averted faces, too tender-hearted to witness pain. However vile the horror-thirst, its ulterior purpose (if you sanction that degree of teleology) is beneficent. The more shame, then, that it should be played with, here at the amusement park, where men and women see life imperiled without lifting a finger to prevent it, or even desiring to! The more amazing that these are the very men and women who, so brief a while ago, were cheerfully paying money to visit, and thus support, the infant incubators, whose sole object is the saving of endangered lives!

Self-contradiction—forgive it without disdain, in those undisciplined minds and hearts; it is a rather common failing with the best of us, and we have here to do with by no means the best or wisest. How easily they are deceived! They imagine they are witnessing a carnival of heroism—the performer goes so smilingly to his task; they overlook the necessity, circumstantial or temperamental, that has driven him to adopt such an atrocious calling. Besides, they're bad judges of danger. They think the young lion-tamer in especial peril, whereas it is usually the seasoned one who comes to grief. And they delight in the brandishing of whips—"Dauntless fellow, he even dares strike them!" Well, I once rubbed elbows with Mr. James J. Corbett, but not for worlds would I have ventured to punch him.

With equal innocence, the crowds deduce valor in the bronco-busters at the Wild West Show and Indian Congress, whereas few of our fellow-countrymen enjoy a more secure existence. The danger isn't in the breaking of a wild horse after you know how, it is in trying to break one when you're green. To applaud the courage of acquired skill becomes a mere ex post facto procedure. For "the real thing" the audience should transport itself westward to Wolfville and backward to 1890.

Yonder, at "Fire and Flames," the same guileless lack of discernment. Half a million dollars invested in tinder-boxes necessitates expensive fire-fighting apparatus and a large squad of firemen, and the park makes the people pay for them. Seated in a huge grandstand, you look out upon a tenement street, which swarms with such improvident Thespians as have laid by no money for the summer. As guttersnipes, factory girls, policemen, pawnbrokers, Chinese laundrymen, newsboys, and roisterers, they enact a travesty upon the life of the quarter, and what with fights, ambulance calls, robberies, arrests, and the clangor of patrol wagons, they do it full justice. But See! a wisp of smoke curls upward from Cohen's pawnshop! Then flames, and more flames. The alarm rings out, shouts rend the air, and in a moment the Department, with two steamers, a hose cart, a chemical, and a hook-and-ladder truck, comes charging through the throng, and attacks the conflagration, which has spread to adjoining buildings, at whose windows some forty women stand screaming. Up go the ladders, out spread the life nets. Girls leap headlong and are caught in safety. Others the firemen carry shrieking down their ladders. And all this, remember, amid clouds of smoke and frequent explosions. But the spectators—missing the point, as usual—forget that those who climb and those who leap have had long training either as firemen or acrobats, and that the only people really in mortal danger are the unfortunate Thespians. How they dodge the rushing engines, that Providence which watches over inebriates, babes, and play-actors alone knows.

Suppose, now, that instead of watching others coquet with Death, you should toy with her yourself. With infinite ingenuity, the amusement park affords you opportunity. Tempt any one of a dozen thanatopses, and you will derive an emotional reaction that shames literature, the drama, and the dare-devil exhibition as well. Note the ascending scale. The ballad-singer tells you about the imperiled hero, the actor impersonates the imperiled hero, the hired dare-devil *is* the imperiled hero. This passage from romance to realism, from realism to reality, can only go a step further. Its final achievement makes *you* the imperiled hero. Hitherto, by the exercise of sympathy, through imagination, you "put yourself in the place of" that wretched sight; sweeter were it to change places with him outright. Thus, by substituting the subjective for the objective, the acme of thrill would result. And, bless you, it shall!

Moreover it does—from the moment you first front the terror-breeding mechanical Torquemada. The bright face of danger, challenging the eternal juvenile within you, seems—exactly as in years gone by—to be taunting, "Fraidycat! you dassn't!" Eagerly you retort, "Yes, I dass!" Ah! but *do* you dass?" An army officer, they say, once suspected that his courage was dwindling, and set his mind at rest on that head by going up in an airship. By an analogous recourse to empiricism, you buy your ticket and suffer yourself to be packed into the abhorred vehicle, which will soon go leaping, flying, or diving till you're sure of your grit. If you only knew it, though, the act of supreme audacity has already been performed. What follows is the mere secondary heroism which Jackies display in an naval engagement. It takes nerve to enlist in the navy; a fellow could back out, even after entering the recruiting office. It doesn't take nerve to fight; a fellow can't possibly run away. And this, just now, is your status. However, you resolve to cut as brilliant a figure as may be before your own conscience, and you summon up that sham valor which consists in thinking it isn't afraid when it shakes in its boots. A rumble, a tug—you're off! A sharp pang of fear; then relief. "Not so bad after all!" you exclaim. A moment later you revel in a perfect delirium of speed, bumps, yanks, vaults, and sickening descents. You utter the cry of a tiny boy, "Scare me again! Scare me—scare me worse!" When finally you make your escape—gasping, panting, and bewildered to find yourself still alive—you flatter yourself that you could brave the very doors of Dis, you who only yesterday quivered like an aspen while discharging the cook!

Cook! Say not "Cook!" you have reverted to that cookless era when men hunted the mastodon. It isn't enough to describe the "chutes," for instance, as an apotheosis of the banister, or as the cellar door *in excelsis*. The passion that gets its satisfaction from these varied deathtraps takes you back to the troglodyte, perhaps even to the ape. Your simian ancestors, swinging from tree-top to tree-top, had much your sensation. They of the Neolithic Age sought it in the chase and in battle. A small boy gets it when a kind and thoughtful citizen turns him upside down. And you yourself, by a personal application of Darwinism, find it here and pronounce it glorious. Said an enthusiast to Mr. Charles Belmont Davis, "Easily the best sensation at the Island is the scenic railway with a wooden beam that looks as if it was going to hit you on the head. It's great!" Seneca was right: "The most happy ought to wish for death."

Nevertheless they don't. They want only a brush with it. For a brush with death makes life unutterably precious. We never love it so dearly or feel it so keenly as when it seems to be slipping from us. That is why people climb Matterhorns, drive motors at breakneck speed, and take pleasure rides in submarines. And even the most adventurous select a reliable guide, scrutinize every shaft and bolt of the chassis, and seek reasonable hope that the submarine will come again. Besides, they welcome the hair's-breadth escape only when they have chosen it freely—a circumstance that explains the anomaly noted by Mr. Mark Sullivan when he declared, "If a man suffered in a trolley car what ten thousand New Yorkers pay ten cents to have done to them at Coney Island, he would go to a hospital for a month, call himself a nervous wreck for the rest of his days, and sue the trolley company for $20,000 damages."

Apart from their sensationalism, these ready-made thanatopses charm also by their mystery. "I wonder how it feels?" muses the neophyte. Pray don't insist that imagination should suffice, for in the case of emotional reactions induced by mechanical deviltries or untried shake-ups of whatever sort, there's a world of unexpectedness. How does it feel to drive an automobile a hundred miles an hour? Mr. Barney Oldfield reports that "you are conscious only of a desire to go faster." How does it feel to be up in a balloon? Mr. Roy Knabenshue tells me the sensation is one of sweet repose. How does it feel to be shipwrecked? Mr. Winthrop Packard, thrice a castaway, says your first emotion savors wholly of disgust; you have confided yourself to a supposedly respectable, right-minded, businesslike ship, and now she plays you false.

What wonder, then, if *a priori* judgment flies wide of the mark regarding what a mortal goes through when he shoots the chutes. I had said it was like riding on the stone that somebody sends skipping across a mill-pond. I had not foreseen that the aquatic comedy would serve only as the epilogue to a gloria of speed, a downward rush that tossed all creation up to meet me; nor had I imagined that when the boat took water I should suffer a sting of regret at the anti-climax. Or what more transparent in its intentions that the "sceenic" railway—"sceenic" because it now and then dives through tunnels enlivened with representations of Venice, the Klondike, and Araby the Blest? Nevertheless, it deceives you by presenting its terrific "thank-you-ma'ams," so to speak, beam on, whereas you don't ride a railway in side elevation—you ride in lengthwise, and thus get its bumps and dips foreshortened. They rise like palisades, fall away like canyons. Moreover, lest familiarity breed contempt, the worst come last.

Surprised by chutes and funiculars, you are yet more surprised by "flying airships." Imagine a gigantic steel Maypole with steel rods dangling from its top instead of ribbons, and little roofed gondolas at their lower ends instead of dancers. The central mast rotates, the rods fly out by centrifugal force, and your tiny craft not only revolves, ever faster, ever taking a wider orbit, and ever soaring higher, but at the same time tips inward toward the centre, like a skater rounding a curve. This you call a rather wanton and extravagant complication of afflictions, concluding that any man with hardihood and sanity to survive them should receive both the sabre of the general staff and the white ermine of the judiciary. When the barker assures you his victims "feel only a refreshing coolness," you remind him that Dr. Guillotine said the same of his. Then, at the cost of drastic self-abnegation, you try it, when lo! you experience no more disquietude than a bird on the wing or the stars in their courses. The laws of physics uphold you, seem almost to caress you. You are silent, yes, and happy; while beneath you the world reels and swells and topples to and fro like mid-ocean billows, since every successive moment gives you a new scale of perspective. This, which you had in no wise foreseen, is what chiefly amuses you.

Behold now the bugaboo shows—Hell Gate and the Foolish House. Veiling or half-veiling their interior shudders and shocks, they spur the impulse for exploration, an impulse compounded of inquisitiveness, bravado, and the thirst for incident. As you watch the little shallops thread the whirlpool within the Hell Gate grotto, and see them sucked down at its vortex, you yearn to know what destiny awaits them. Also what torments rend their occupants. With certain highly Dantesque forebodings, you embark. Slowly, grimly, your circling boat drifts nearer that atrocious abyss. Sardonic jokes, from adventurers in craft ahead of you would purchase deliverance at a cost of half your lands. At last, it is but a single coil of the spiral that separates you from the drop to Avernus! Zounds, what a suspense! Then a rush, a sinking of the heart, a sound of grinding wood, and a plunge down a twisted cataract into chaos and resounding night. With your whole soul you combat fear, even transform it into joy. "Hail, horrors! Hail, infernal world!" And now you laugh. Light comes, and with it red devils amid flames, volcanoes spitting fire, gorgeous grottos all dripping with stalactites, and—very soothing to the eschatological emotions—icebergs and polar bears! Gradually you retrace the spiral, traversing canals built just under those of the preliminary whirlpool, and finally come out upon a little quay, rich in varied grotesqueries.

If half-veiled scares attract so powerfully, were it still not shrewder to veil them totally? Roar, "My attorney will call upon you!" and I squirm; mutter darkly, "I'll not say what I intended for thee," and I quake. Hence the charm of the Foolish House. It is vague and mysterious—without, a blend of the awesome and the comic; within, well, let's see! Darkness, a winding passage—innocuous enough, but wait! Next moment a frolicsome tornado has all but knocked you senseless. The floor wallows and shakes. Horrifying bumps confront your feet. What with tempests and earthquakes and night and labyrinthine confusion and stumbling-blocks combined, you wish yourself dead. Then relief! A crystal maze, humorous but not alarming. A row of concave and convex mirrors, showing you yourself as Humpty Dumpty, or as that gracefully attenuated celebrity, Jack the Beanstalk. Five minutes of laughter. After that, you bravely run the gauntlet of supplementary distresses, and when you emerge it is with a shining countenance as of the newly initiated by the "joiners."

Once free of its terrors, you begin to revere the psychological acumen that arranged them. One might fancy that a bugaboo show ought to be made as harrowing as possible. Not so. The crowd wants only enough hazing to shock the nerves agreeably; give it more and it bolts. That is why the mirrors and the crystal maze were introduced—a palliative like that employed by a dramatist when he weaves funny incidents into a "me-child, me-child" melodrama.

Such, then, are the more conspicuous joys—of wonder, of vicarious terror, and the first-hand hair's-breadth 'scape—vouchsafed by the amusement park. Others, still unmentioned, abound, beyond the wildest surmises of the higher mathematics. Who shall number the beatific Moxie stands, the popcorn and peanut stalls, the rapturous candy-mills; who shall compute the tintype galleries, bamboo slides, penny vaudevilles, sand-bumps, graphophones, merry-go-round, strength-testing devices, nickel-in-the-slot machines, Japanese "gambling" games, rifle-ranges, and establishments where "you get your money back if I fail to guess your weight within three pounds?" But chiefly there remain the contrivances for the better promotion of romance—the ball-room, Love's Journey, and the gay camaraderie of the board walk.

Then young folks arrive in couples? Yes and no. Many come singly—each lad with an as yet unidentified pompadour in his heart, each lass cherishing a shy anticipation. But how, you ask, shall those youthful strangers be made acquainted? Leave that to them. In the ballroom any well-seeming youngster may invite any girl to dance—an arrangement long since sanctioned by that maelstrom of proletarian jollity, the "social," where tickets ("gents 35 cents, ladies 25") connote partners and more partners and more partners, till everybody knows everybody else. Moreover, if you study the People's Column in a penny newspaper, you will see how puzzling to the masses is our custom of letting one another alone until introduced. "Introductions," writes Johnnie Blue, "are a fad that is greatly overdone."

The little shop girl shares his convictions. Nor need we waste shudders on her behalf; keen and knowing, ever on the defensive, she discourages such advantages as perplex her—whether in the ballroom, or, a shade less decorously, upon the board walk. Especially she distrusts cavaliers not of her own station. I have heard of a venturesome aristocrat who, seeing a handsome young woman, hastened to present himself; whereupon the fair one exclaimed, "Say, ain't you the galley article? Go *sell* your papers!"

And look not too harshly upon certain other somewhat disconcerting marvels of deportment. Arms, it is true, encircle waists, and half the allurement of the Foolish House inheres in its inky, winding passages. The proprietor of a Coney Island maze unblushingly announces, "The men like it because it gives them a chance to hug the girls, the girls like it because it gives them a chance to get hugged." Viewed vertically, from the altitude of personal dignity, such license takes a coloring by no means pleasant. Viewed horizontally, it becomes a mere convention. To the popular mind the caress means no more than the mildly affectionate phrases with which we begin and end our letters.

But what went ye out for to see? Youthful gaucherie repressed in an amusement park? Say, rather, youthful gaucherie granted full freedom, and neither more no less uncouth here than elsewhere. The park was not founded for the culture of decorum; it was founded for the culture of wild hilarity, in which mission it brilliantly and gloriously succeeds. It is the gayer too, by reason of its moral cleanness. Its laundered diversions attract a laundered constituency; and if it refuses to sell liquor (some parks do refuse), it expunges those hints of wrong-doing, which for all their bravado never fail to depress; and although its little shams and booby-traps need ethical tinkering here and there, they usually give the gullible their money's worth; a permanent amusement park can't afford out-and-out swindles. Still I sometimes fear it's an economic nuisance. Adding up your expenditures, you perceive that an evening's frolic has cost as much as a ticket for "Lohengrin," or two for "Candida," or three for Herr Rubeneck's instructive lecture; it has cost the young gentleman in the erroneous neckwear a sum that would have liquidated a week's board; and yet both you and he have enjoyed the sense of monetary frivolity which is the heart and soul of a holiday. Down with Dismal Science! Let us assert our superiority to cash—and swallow the consequence!

Nevertheless, I cannot escape the pathetic humor of this whole tumultuous situation. What more ludicrous and what more sad than the spectacle of vast hordes of people rushing to the oceanside, to escape the city's din and crowds and nervous strain, and, once within sight and sound of the waves, courting worse din, denser crowds, and an infinitely more devastating nervous strain inside an inclosure whence the ocean cannot possibly be seen? Is it thus they seek rest by a madly exaggerated homeopathy? Is it thus they cure Babylon, not with more Babylon, but with Babel gone daft? We Anglo-Saxons have scandalized the seaside long ere this, building our miniature London at Brighton, our miniature Bowery at Coney Island; we have spoiled our holidays from of old, hiding behind newspapers on coastwise steamboats amid entrancing scenery, talking Wall Street on the Grand Canal, transplanting high fashion to the very forest; yet not till of late have we achieved so frantic a travesty upon recreation (which ought to re-create) as in the tom-tom foolery of an amusement park.

Mr. Guy Wetmore Carryl, contemplating his marvels, exclaimed, "Never tell me again that Americans are a nervous people!" They are, though, and yonder amazing institution proves it. Manhattanitis, with its numerous congeners, isn't merely a disease, it's an obsession. It doesn't ask relief, it only asks aggravation. The sole treatment that it welcomes is the counter-irritant—powerful, drastic, and like in kind to itself. Of all the shrewd observations noted down in the now very considerable literature of this subject, the shrewdest, I judge, is the one that calls the amusement park "an artificial distraction for an artificial life."

WAGON SHOW TRANSPORTATION. MASS MOTORIZATION DID NOT OCCUR UNTIL WORLD WAR I.

VI.

THE TRAVELING CIRCUS

    The history of the American circus began at Philadelphia in the 1790s when John Bill Ricketts brought to this country his English-styled equestrian circus, consisting of various feats and stunts of comic and acrobatic horsemanship and performances of pantomimic spectacle, which combined the ring and the stage into a unified presentation. This mixture of circus and drama, of horse and actor, was never fully successful. Unable to compete with the more varied programs of the permanent theatres, and fulfilling a wanderlust inherent in equestrian entertainers, the circus took to the newly improved roadways of nineteenth-century America; and, under its familiar roof of canvas, annexed features of the menagerie, museum, and variety stage, thereby developing a format of performance and operation that has continued to the present.

    The circus is an institution of surprising longevity. Its entertainment program has changed very little in the past one hundred years. Its promotional gimmickry has been flamboyantly perverse. Its exploitation of caged or otherwise confined animals has been callous. Its petty swindling of its patrons is legendary. Its managerial greed has led to brutal, competitive wars of self-destruction. Yet, the blare, the pomp, the daring, the tinsel and glitter—yes, even the smell—of the ring spectacle has gulled us all into childish fantasy; and we return again and again to satisfy some, perhaps inexplicable, longing that is peculiar and particular within each of us.

22. CIRCUS

KNICKERBOCKER, JANUARY, 1839

Unrivalled attraction! grand entree! feats of the ring! ground and lofty tumbling! still vaulting by the whole company!

I know of some villages, which are happy in an unusual seclusion, whose situation protects them from the intrusion of the world. So surrounded are they by hills, and so embosomed in forests, so "remote from cities," and from public highways, that the heart of Zimmerman might envy their solitude. The most violent tempests in the political world can hardly affect them. They are like mountains whose summits are basking in the sunbeams, while their base is uprooted by the storm. "The wind and the hurricane rage in the distance; the destruction is beyond their horizon of peace."

Thither, by the eternal impediments of nature, no post-routes or rail-ways can ever come, to work out their magical changes; no manufactories stun with their clatter, or darken the atmosphere with smoke. The spirit of utility, which is abroad in the country, which levels to the earth so many monuments of affection, and forbids anything to stand as it is, cannot come *here*. There are few changes except the ever-recurring ones of nature and mortality. The aspect of to-day remains the same to-morrow; and the solitary spire which pierces the blue skies now, will fifty years hence look down upon the peaceful abodes of men "whose fathers worshipped in this mountain."

The primeval silence of these places remains almost unbroken; scarcely is echo awakened among the rocks. Their situation is not marked upon the maps, and their existence is a secret to the world. Perhaps a few quiet gentlemen come there in the summer, to sail on the clear lakes, or drop their lines for the golden-speckled trout. But they are wily fishermen; and when

The melancholy days return, the saddest of the year

and they go back to the marts of commerce, careful are they not to reveal the pleasant spots where they laid in wait for the "scaly people."

One might suppose that the current of life ran along almost too sleepily, and that the inhabitants of such places would be ready to die with weariness and disgust. But let it be remembered, that they do not live in idleness, nor are their sickly natures fed with excitement, as a food. The have sports and pastimes in abundance, and incidents which the bustling world would deem unworthy of notice are continually occurring, to relieve them from monotony, and to create a spicy variety of life. Sometimes a pedlar comes along, and is a welcome visitor. He opens doors without knocking, and enters with the familiarity of a friend. His variegated wares are spread out; brass buttons, and tortoise-shell combs, and suspenders, and ear-rings, and jewelry of pure gold. The house-wives find it to their advantage to purchase his salves and essences, and his o-*pod*-eldoc, as he terms it, which is a "sartin cure for the rhumatiz."

Ever and anon, there is a show of dancing puppets, and a barrel-organ turned by some worn-out soldier, whose simple airs a fat, rosy-faced woman accompanies, while in a very sweet voice, but a raw accent, she sings, rolling her dark, supplicating eyes to the windows:

> *I'd be a butterfly, born in a bow'r,*
> *Where roses and lilies and violets meet,*
> *Roving for ever from flower to flower,*
> *Kissing all things that is pretty, a-n-d sweet.*
> *I'd never languish for wealth or for power,*
> *I'd never sigh to see slaves at my feet.*

And not in vain does she spend her melody. For soon her eyes are refreshed by a pattering shower of silver coin, which honest boys collect from the earth, and place in her hands, while some kind-hearted spirit crowns the whole with a goblet of sparkling water. She inhales the draught, more delicious than wine of the old vintage, and passes on to the next cottage, leaving a God's blessing, sweet to the rustic ear as the lately-expired music. A few moments elapse, and her distant voice is again heard; for having detected from a window a golden-haired, beautiful girl, peeping from behind the jalousies of the honeysuckle, she sings of the "minstrel's return," or of a youth now far, far away, but whom at midsummer the propitious fates will restore to the embrace of his mistress. And again, in a song not excelled for a simplicity which touches the heart, she declares the enduring attachments of home:

> *Midst pleasures and palaces though I may roam,*
> *Be it ever so humble, there's no place like home.*

I charge all persons, and especially husbandmen, that they reward most generously these only relics of the troubadours. Many a weary mile do they walk, the messengers of music. Small is the boon which they ask or desire, and entirely unequal to their deserts. Treat them kindly, treat them tenderly, and they will repay you ten-fold; neglect them, and the doric muse has perished.

There are few wandering fortune-tellers in the country, nor are our villages rendered animate by the scene of a gipsey encampment. Let those arrant poachers remain in England; their absence is certainly to be regretted, on the score of the picturesque. Yet we cannot accord with the solemn exclamation of the nursery song:

> *Lo! mother Shipton and her cat*
> *Quite full of conjuration;*
> *And if more conjurers could be found,*
> *'T were better for the nation.*

A travelling caravan is an integral portion of the great institute in the metropolis. When the summer comes, it is broken up into parts, which are dispersed in every section of the country, that the imprisoned beasts may have the benefit of pure air. These consist, for the most part, of a lion, a tiger, a black bear, a camel, a wild cat, a hyena, some torpid snakes, coiled up in a box, and in a separate apartment a panorama, and a man who "sings Jim Crow." This latter is the most noxious beast of the whole clan. Besides these, a great number of monkeys, apes, and ring-tailed baboons are shut up in a community. These be capital fellows, full of spirits, which go the whole length of their ropes, and are better worth seeing, the spectators themselves being judges, than all the tigers, zebras, and hump-back camels, put together. Among themselves, they are "hale fellows," chattering and grinning, jibing, and cracking their jokes, as if in some forest of Africa, save when a by-stander rolls in an "apple of discord," or a cake, and then the big ones flog the small ones unmercifully; and herein consists the kernel of the joke. A Shetland pony goes round and round in a circle, surmounted by a jocko in scarlet uniform, who proves himself an indomitable horseman. He leaps on and off, handles the reins with address, and cracks his whip like a Jehu. Sometimes a small African elephant is made to kneel down, and receive a tower on his shoulders. Those of the company who desire to ride, are requested to step forward, "ladies first, gentleman after-*wards*." After a deal of hesitation, a servant-maid gathers courage, and simpering and dimpling, ambles into the arena. Her the showman politely assists to ascend. Another follows, and another, until all the seats are taken up. Then the beast moves around once around, with his slow and heavy tramp, the *ladies* descend from their airy height, and are able to go home and say that they have "ridden on the elephant." Last of all, a negro is encouraged to mount the animal's bare back, and broadly grinning, is looking down upon the crowd below, when the latter, being privy to a joke, gives a violent shrug, and hurls him, as from a terrific precipice, to the ground.

The menagerie is a very popular entertainment, unexceptionable on the score of morals, and visited by the "most straitest sects" of the people. Do you see that tall, thin, straight, bony, green-spectacled man, who pries curiously into all the cages, and shuts up like a jack-knife when he bends? That is Mr. Simpson. He is a judge of these things, and has a collection at home; an ostrich's egg, a stuffed partridge, and some bugs in a bottle of spirits. He is followed by the lady superior of the female seminary, and a score of pupils, that they may lose none of his valuable remarks.

"Aha!" quoth he. "Here we have the lion, most properly denominated the king of the beasts. He is a native of Africa, fierce in his might and terrible in his strength. Mark his flowing mane, his majestic port, his flaming eyes—his—his—his—*tail*. When he roars, heaven shakes, earth quakes, and hell trembles. Here, keeper, please be so good as to make this lion roar."

"Oh! no, no, no!" shriek a dozen voices, hysterically. "Don't let him roar!—don't let him roar!"

"Well, well, as you please," quoth Mr. Simpson, good-humoredly winking at madam.

"Here is the Jackal, who provides food for the lion; a miserable sycophant and panderer for a king. Mark his mean aspect, and dirty appearance. He is emblematic of man. Alas! there *are* jackals in the world; jackals literary and jackals political."

It is a season of still deeper excitement, in such a retired country village, when once a year, after several days' heralding, a train of great red wagons is seen approaching, marked in large letters, CIRCUS, 1, 2, 3, 4, and so on. This arrival has been talked of, and produces an immediate bustle and sensation. Fifty boys breaking loose from school, rush immediately to the street, and in treble tones cry "Circus!" The ploughman lets his plough stand in the middle of the field, and leans over the fence. The blacksmith withdraws his brawny arm from the anvil, and stands in the door of his smithy. A man in the act of shaving, comes out with his face lathered, and a towel under his chin. The old woman who was washing in the porch, takes her dripping and smoking fingers from the suds, peers over her spectacles, opens her mouth, and utters an ejaculation. The milkmaid leaves her pail to be kicked over by the cow. A wise-looking clerk puts his head out of the window, with a pen stuck in his ear. A cat on the eaves of a house likewise looks down. The mother runs to call Johnny, who is playing in the yard, quick-quick-quick! before the procession moves by. He is too late. Ba-a-a-a! An invalid in bed leaps up, thinks he feels better, and shall be "abundantly able to go."

Meantime the calvacade halts before the inn. The crowd closes in at once, to fest their eyes on the luggage, and see the company unpack. The spirited horses, perspiring with the long journey, stamp impatiently on the ground. The *corps* are a little out of patience, and annoyed by the crowd. A child gets under the horses' heels, and is dragged out by the hair of his head, unhurt. What rough-spoken, ill-looking fellows are the equestrians! How strangely will they be metamorphosed in a few hours—bright, dazzling, tricked out in gay attire, full of beautiful spangles! They are not themselves now; they are acting the difficult parts of everyday men. At night they will fall readily into their own characters, clowns, harlequins, and the most amusing fools in the world.

May I be there to see!

Rapidly the intelligence of their arrival spreads into the adjacent country. The whole community is on the *qui vive*. There are uneasiness, anticipation, excitement. The village belles lay out their trinkets, ornaments, and brightest calicoes, to adorn the boxes; the plough-boy scrapes his pence together, desperately determined on a standing in the pit. A discussion waxes warm among the graver part of the community, about the lawfulness of these amusements. Some of the young are troubled with doubts. The old people hesitate, demur, and at last give their consent. They have been young once themselves—such opportunities do not occur everyday. Indeed, it would be very difficult for anyone to demur, after reading the "bill of fare," a great blanket sheet, full of wood cuts and pictures; horses on the full run, and men bent into all possible shapes and contortions. "Unrivalled Attraction! Grand entrée. Four-and-twenty Arabian horses. Celebrated equestrian Mr. Burke. Feats in the ring. Grand leap. Cups and ball. The entertainments to conclude with the laughable farce of Billy Button, or the Hunted Tailor." As the hired man reads over this tempting bill, or failing to read, interprets the hieroglyphics, his mouth waters. "I *must go!*"—and he adds, resolutely clenching his teeth, "I *will go!*"

In the course of the day the equestrians have wrought industriously, and raised their white pavilion. It stands out on the green, in beautiful proportions, erected suddenly, as if by magic. A flag floats over its summit, on whose ample folds is inscribed "Circus." All things are ready for the evening's sport, and a death-like silence reigns over the village.

Who is he that walketh pensively in yonder green, beneath the shadow of the trees, with head bowed down, as if in thought, and plucking a leaf to pieces? It is the amiable minister of the parish. He is sore grieved in spirit. Hitherto has he led his flock without contradiction, conducting them safely through thorny places, and shielding them from the inclemency of the storm. And now forsooth the very devil has come to take them by force of arms. From his heart he regrets it. He has prayed over it, and wept over it, and slept over it, and dreamed of it. He has summoned a conclave of the principal men, remonstrated with the authorities of the town, and held up the whole thing in the length and breadth of its enormity. But the perverse men will heed none of his counsels or reproofs. He preached a sermon on the Sunday previous, in which he alarmed the young, and denounced in the most terrible terms all who should hold communion with Belial. He shed tears over the disregard of his reckless auditors. But there is mixed up with genuine grief a little vexation, because he cannot have his own way. If they will heed none of his counsel, if they will persist in their own downward course, he can but depart from them; he can but shake off the dust of his feet, and leave them to perish in their misdoings.

It is very hard to draw the line accurately betwixt virtue and vice, and it may be safer to err on the side of right. Yet there is a time for everything. We cannot always be serious. The mind must have its carnival. We must crack the nuts of folly. To become a fool once a year, is a mark of wisdom; to be perpetual fool is beyond endurance. The gradual accumulation of spirits in the dullest person, will at length reach a height when it demands an exit.

Qua data porta ruit

What signifies it, whether it be let off in a round explosion, or hiss away at intervals, like steam. Talk not of mingling the useful with sweet. We sometimes require folly without mixture—pure, unalloyed, unmitigated and concentrated folly. It is good to be attacked, to be sick, and to die with agonies of laughter. The storm of the passions purifies the atmosphere of the temper. With how much keener zest do we return to substantial pleasures, even as the sick man awakens to the deliciousness of health! Govern then your own conduct by the most rigid maxims, but beware how you denounce too bitterly, or condemn too terribly, unless yourselves are immaculate. Consistency is a most precious jewel. If you deem it a credit to abstain from trifles, indulging unreservedly in what is infinitely worse—if you cherish envy, or pride, or jealousy in the heart—if you sully by detraction the fair name of your neighbor, whom you are commanded to love as yourself—then certainly you "strain at a knat and swallow a camel." To do these things, and without compunction, may be esteemed a more palpable dereliction, than to laugh at the antics of a tumbler or a clown. The voiceless eloquence of a good example persuades the young to virtue, but the harsher precepts of a rigorous code, will be more apt to compel them to a vagabond life.

The sun is just resting on the borders of the horizon, and making the summer evening lonely, when the whole equestrian *corps*, a signal being given, sally forth and wind through the grass-skirted lanes of the village. A band of music goes before, drawn in a chariot by four dappled horses. The notes of the bugle floating exquisitely on the tranquil air, fill the rustic bosom with enthusiasm. The equestrians follow in gorgeous, spangled dresses, the clown standing up on one leg, with a straw in his mouth, and giving a foretaste of those facetious inanities which he will exhibit at even. Just at dusk, they return to the pavilion. A motley crowd rushes hurriedly through the streets. The minister of the parish looks out from his window, and weeps. He is a good man, and God will shelter his little flock from harm. The scrupulous and the wavering are now decided. Those who but yesterday said, crabbedly, that they had "no time, nor money nother, for such wild doings," bustle off, "just to see what's going on." Many persons of approved gravity attend, who "suld have known better." To the negro population, the occasion is a heyday and holiday. The Pompeys are there, and the Catos are there, and the noble lineage of the Caesars. Thus all the population are collected beneath the great tent. No; there are a few unhappy boys without, who peep hopelessly through the crevices of the awning, but whom the door-keeper will soon discover, and send harshly away. Just at this juncture, the gentleman who lives in the white cottage by the hill-side, and who has acted for a long time past in a very remarkable manner, having little intercourse with the neighbors, declining to answer questions, or to have his affairs inquired into, (he is either crazy or in love) passes by that way, and thrusting his hand in his pocket, presents the lads a shilling each. Smiles and gratitude reward him.

The area of the enclosure is divided into the ring, pit, and boxes. A circular wooden frame-work depends in the centre, containing a great many tarnished lamps, and magniloquently called a chandelier. "Splendid!" whispers the crowd. Let us inspect the company a few minutes, before the performance commence. The circular seats are crowded to the very roof. Behold there the bloom and the flower of the country—the daughters of stout yeomen, brought hither by their beaux to view this rare spectacle. Did ever a tent, since the days of Cleopatra, contain such feminine charms? Was ever the circle of Old Drury studded with such brilliant gems? Those are no fictitious roses which compose that head-dress, and it is the livelier tinge of the unrouged cheek which makes those roses blush. Let me direct your attention to that sweet girl opposite, just under the eaves of the pavilion, seven seats to the right of that ill-assorted patch. *Simplex munditiis*! How simple her adornment! A single pale flower is in her jet-black hair, and her eyes were too dark, did not the softest lashes attemper their luster. Alas! "consumption, like a worm in the bud, feeds on her damask cheek!" And yet she knows it not. Lighthearted, she frequents the place of merriment, and mingles sportively in the dance. But she will pass away as doth a leaf, in autumn, or with milder breath of spring. Her companions will lament her, and they will pluck the garland of the May-queen to pieces, to scatter upon the grave.

These thoughts are sadly out of place, but grim death will be thrusting his visage everywhere, and there are goblins in every masquerade. But there is nothing spectral in the looks of Helen—. She is seventeen, and very beautiful, and wild as a roe. Health sparkles in her eye, and riots in the rich bloom of her cheeks. She has more suitors than Penelope, but in two words her character may be told. She is CO-QUETTE. We might sit gazing in that quarter for ever, for it is very hard to withdraw one's eyes from the fair. They are sure to come back again, the truants; yet for the present, let us turn them to the rougher sex. Behold that man of gigantic stature, near the entrance of the tent. He lately emigrated from Connecticut, and stands seven feet two inches in his shoes. He wears a cerulean blue coat, buttoned up to his nose, and a tall, steeple-loafed hat. *Sic itur ad astra*. To see him entering the village, in this plight, driving a team of jack-asses before a square box of a wagon, and sitting bolt-upright on a load of pumpkins, you would be apt to call, in dialect of his own people, "an almighty lengthy creatur." When he walks through the aisle of the church on Sunday, he overtops the tallest man in the congregation, by a whole head. He will be a conspicuous mark here. See if the clown does not take his cognizance of him, before the play is done.

There stands a dandy, his legs apart, and forming with the ground an isosceles triangle. He wears straps a yard long, his breeches being that much too short, and a very vulgar broach in his false bosom. His guard chain dangles in festoons about his vest, and a brass chain is terminated in a great ornament in the region of his knees. Mark his confused look. He thinks everyone is gazing at him. "How will you swop watches, onsight onseen?".

There is a jolly butcher, and there a farmer, of ruddy complexion and cheerful aspect, whip in hand, covered with dust, who has ridden hard, after mowing all day in the meadow, to bring his wife and daughters to the circus. He is not afraid to contribute of his substance to the wants of the needy, nor to the amusement of his family, of whom he is justly proud. Next to him sits an old man, holding a beautiful little boy, four years old, upon his knee, answering all his fears. Look at the idiot boy, grinning luridly upon the scene, with lolling tongue and watery mouth wide open, and white, unmeaning eyes. Look at that old man, with neck bent unmoveably upon his breast, and so he has lived for many, many years—a pitiable object. There is another unfortunate, as thin as grim death, who is the victim of a tape-worm. He can yet laugh, and shake his lean sides. Thus wise men and fools are mingled in this epitome of a world. Let us turn to a more promising specimen of human nature; that fat, gouty old gentlemen, so comfortably provided for; wild Harry he was called, in his youth. He quivers like a jelly, and one peal of hearty laughter, which he appears upon the verge of, will shake him into dissolution. He resembles that remarkable delineation of "Tam O'Shanter," struck from the free-stone into very life, by Thom, the self-taught artist. I hope the clown won't look at him. Have mercy, I pray thee, dear Mr. Harlequin! Indulge your facetious personalities upon the lean ones, who have enough room to expand in, and who can afford to split their sides a-laughing. But cast none of your ill-timed fooleries in that quarter. I doubt if he will hold together as it is, but if you throw at him a joke direct, Wild Harry is a dead man!

Are there any in the whole area who will experience more genuine satisfaction, than the descendants of Ham? They are huddled together in one corner, dark, cloud-like, a distinct people. How will smiles and pleasantry be diffused over their features, like light bursting from the darkness! How will the whites of those eyes be uprolled in extacy, those even teeth glisten like ivory, and laughter break forth from the bottom of their souls, every laugh worth a dollar! There, there!—listen to that shout! An unfortunate cur, who has strayed inside by accident, has got his toes severely trampled upon, and lamentably yelping, and running the gauntlet, is kicked out of doors. It is high time that the performances commenced. "Music! music!" shout the crowd; and the orchestra without more ado plays a national air. Another piece is performed, and the tramping of horses is heard without.

Do you remember the feelings which possessed you, so charmingly described in one of the essays of Elia, when, a child, you were taken for the *first time* to the theatre; when the green curtain was drawn, and the tardy musicians crept one by one from some subterranean place into the orchestra, and at last the overture was over, and the bell rang, and the risen foot-lights burst upon the scene of enchantment? Such feelings of intense anticipation pervade the rural audience. For now all things are ready, the passage is cleared, and silence reigns within the pavilion. The horses are coming! "Heavens! look at that white-haired, cat-eyed boy, on the very edge of the ring! He will certainly be run over."

Leave him alone, leave him alone. He will take care of himself, I warrant you. Nought is never in danger. Tramp, tramp, tramp! There they come. Observe the grand entree, by four-and-twenty Arabian horses, while the rustic mother claps her infant to her breast, scared by these terrible sports. At the first irruption of the cavalcade, the audience are bewildered with the general splendor of the scene. The horses, beautifully marked and caparisoned, are obedient to the slightest will of the rider, and yet by their proud looks and haughty bearing, seem conscious of their lineage; while the equestrians vie with each other in rich costume, and their plumes dropping softly over their painted faces, make them as bright as Lucifer, in the eyes of the crowd. They ride gracefully, displaying to advantage their elastic forms, swollen into full proportion by exercise and training. As soon as the audience is sufficiently recovered to particularize the different members of the troop, they are attracted by the grotesque behaviour of the clown, who has got upon his horse the wrong way, and sits preposterously facing the tail. In this manner he slips on and off, encouraged with immense laughter. Next the remarks go round, and everyone praises to his neighbor the remarkable lightness and agility of a juvenile equestrian. He has not yet completed his eleventh summer, and not a horseman in the troop can vie with him in daring. The ladies who adorn the dress circle, regard him with smiles and approbation. *O! pulchrum puerum!* What a fair boy! How his ringlets flutter over his brow, in beautiful dishevelment, fanned by the wanton breeze. They could almost pluck him from his flying steed, and arrest his course with kisses. So light and agile is he, that he appears not human, but, as he flies round the ring with a daring rapidity, and his snow-white trowsers and gemmed vest mingle their colors, and become indistinct, he seems like an apple-blossom floating on the air. But look! look! What the devil is that fellow at, disrobing himself? He has kicked himself out of his pantaloons, and thrown away his coat, his horse flying all the while. "Angels and ministers of grace defend us!" he is plucking off his very—shirt! Nay, nay, do not so be alarmed, nor turn away your heads, ye fair ones, timidly blushing. Look again, and behold a metamorphosis more wonderful than any in Ovid; for lo! he pursues his swift career in the flowing robes of a woman! And now the pony is to perform a no less wonderful exploit, and leap through a balloon on fire. But why should I enumerate all the feats if this wild crew? What with riding, leaping, vaulting, and the most astonishing pirouettes, the first part of the diversions is enacted in a charming style. Who can say that he is not satisfied thus far, or has not got the worth of his money? Not that jolly butcher, not that farmer, not that sedentary schoolman, who has materially assisted his digestion by laughing. "There is no medicine so good as the genuine ha! ha!"

To me, who am a genuine lover of human nature, and who sit curtained round in a stage-box, as it were, unnoticed by every one, and noticing every one, there is chuckling delight in looking, not upon the actors of the scene, but on the motley crowd, and listening to such speeches as are naturally drawn from the occasion.

"I'll tell you *one* thing, and that ain't *two*," remarks a spectator to his neighbor. "That boy is wonderful, but if the clown isn't the old one, he is a nigh kin to him."

"That's a fact."

"He can twist himself wrong side out, he can."

"Ay, ay, you're right there, and he can tie himself into a bow knot."

"These fellows," says another, "haven't got no bones into their bodies; they are made of Ingen rubber."

"Bill," remarks the ostler to his bare-footed companion, usually yclept Villiam Viggins, a very bad boy, "fine sort of life, eh, Bill? What say to try fortunes with 'em? Jeffries, the head man, gin me a fair offer this mornin' to go along with him, and see a little for the world, what I've always had a great hankerin' for, and the great folks of the world, and sight of things that I and you never dreamed of, and won't never dream of, if we stay here from now to never. I say, Bill, I've a might great notion of it, and should be glad of you for your company. You are prudenter than I be, by a good sight; contrariwise I am a better bruiser than you be, though I say it. We should pull together han'somely, and make our fortunes. It's a-high time, Bill that we should 'stablish a ch'racter. But what takes my eye, these circus-actors live like gentlemen. They crack their jokes, they do, drink their wine, and live on the fat o' the land. Why can't we do the same, Bill? I can't see what's to pervent it. There's no two ways about it, and if it is not all true, just what I tell you, then you name's not Villiam Viggins. And then it must be mighty agreeable to be dressed in such fine clothes, and to ride on such flashy horses, and have nothin' to do but to be looked at, and to be laughed at, and to go a-larkin' and travellin', and seein' all the world, and to be admired at by all the girls in the country. I say Bill, the notion takes you, you dog; I see it does. And now come let's go out, and have a glass o' beer, and a long nine betwixt us, and talk the matter over a little, afore the entertainments begin ag'in.

"In the country where I was fetched up," said the son of Anak, "no such doings as these is permitted. Two years ago, come next May, a company of circus-actors crossed over the Sound, and come to Bozrah. They sot themselves down, but didn't stay long, I guess, before they were attackted by the town-officers, and sent packing. They pulled up stakes, and took away their duds, and never come back, as I know on. For the people sot their faces like a flint agin 'em. Some few was for letting them act, but Deacon Giles opposed the motion, and carried his p'int, and on the Sabbath followin' stopped a load of hay on full drive through the town of Bozrah."

In such conversation and exchange of sentiments, the interval "between the acts" is wiled away. The second part of the diversions is a fescennine dialogue, made up of alternate strokes of rude raillery, interspersed with songs and merriment, affording as keen a relish as the best Attic salt.

De gustibus non disputandum

Last of all, comes BILLY BUTTON, OR THE HUNTED TAILOR. I forget the plot of this piece, exactly, which is yearly enacted with much acceptation in every considerable village in the country. There are some very good points about it, that never amiss to a rural audience, as when the perverse pony shakes off the cabbaging tailor from his back, not allowing him around the ring. And now the entertainments are about to conclude, let us indulge a wish that the ladies who have been seated near the crevices in the awning, may not catch their death a-cold, and that no evil whatever may result from the occasion. The clown bounces into the arena with a bow; doffs his harlequin aspect, and assumes the serious air of an everyday man. "Ladies and gentlemen, the entertainments of the evening are concluded. We thank you for your polite attendance." In a twinkling the canvas is rent down over your heads, the lights are extinguished, and while the equestrians are already preparing to depart to the next village, the motley assemblage moves homeward through the dark night, yelping like savages.

23. LIVING IN THE COUNTRY

PUTNAM'S MAGAZINE, APRIL, 1855

...There is one institution, which, in a child's eye point of view, possesses a majesty and beauty in the country altogether unappreciable in a large city. I allude to the *Menagerie*! For weeks, juvenile curiosity has been stimulated by pictorial representations at the Depôt and Post-Office. There is the likeness of the man who goes into the cage with the wild beasts, holding out two immense lions at arms' length. There is the giraffe with his neck reaching above a lofty palm tree, and the boa constrictor with a yawning tiger in his convoluted embrace. If you observe the countenances of the small fry collected in front of a bill of this description in the rural districts, you will see in each and all, a remarkable enlargement of the eye, expressive of wonder.

Conjecture, expectation, and surmise,

are children's bedfellows, and the infantile pulse reaches fever heat long before the arrival of the elephant. At last he comes, the "Aleph"... of the procession! swinging his long cartilaginous shillelah in solemn concord with the music. Then follow wagons bearing the savage animals in boxes with red panels; then a pair of cloven-footed camels; then other wagons all mystery and red panels; then pie-bald horses and ponies, and then the rear guard of the caravan drags its slow length along. "My dear," said Mrs. Sparrowgrass, "we must take the children and go the menagerie." This seemed a reasonable request, and of course we went. When we approached the big tent we heard the music of wind instruments, the sound of a gong, and the roaring of lions. This divided our juvenile party at once, one half wanted to go in, and the other half wanted to keep out; Mrs. Sparrowgrass joined the seceders, and in consequence, we separated at the entrance of the canvas edifice. When we got in we heard that the lion tamer had finished his performances, and that the elephant had been around, but there was a great deal of sport going on in the ring—the monkey was riding on his pony. At this announcement the young ones were immensely excited, and tried to get a peep at it, but, although I held them up at arms' length, they could see neither monkey or pony. Then I tried to work a passage for them to the front, but the ring being invested with a border of country people thirteen deep, this was out of the question. So I concluded to wait until the crowd dispersed, and to keep the young Sparrowgrasses in good humor, I held them up and let them read the signs on the top of the cages. "ROYAL BENGAL TIGER," "BLACK LION FROM NUBIA," "YELLOW ASIATIC LION," "THE GNU," "WHITE POLAR BEAR," &c., &c., &c. By and by the clapping of hands announced the close of the performance, and the dense mass of people became detached, so we made our way through the crowd towards the elephant. All of a sudden, we saw a general rush towards us, and we heard somebody say that, "something had broke loose!" Not being of an inquisitive turn of mind, I did not ask what it was, but at once retired under a wagon load of pelicans, and put the young Sparrowgrasses through a door which I made in the side of the tent with my pruning knife. The people poured out of the big door and from under the edges of the tent, but they had not run far before they stopped and proceeded to make inquiries. Some said it was the polar bear, whereupon several respectable looking men suddenly climbed over a fence; others said it was a monkey, at which all the boys set up a shout. The intrepid conduct of the cash-taker had much to do with restoring confidence. He stood there, at the entrance of the tent, smoking a cigar with imperturbable firmness. So we all concluded to go back again and see the rest of the show. When we got to the door we found the entrance fee was twenty-five cents. We represented that we had been in before. "That may be," replied the cash-taker, "but we don't sell season tickets at our establishments."

Finding the discussion was likely to be violent upon this point, I retired, with some suspicion of having been swindled. When I got home, Mrs. S. asked me "if I had seen the elephant?" I told her the whole story. "Well," said she, "that's just the way I thought it would be. I'm glad I did not go in."

24. CIRCUS DAY

by Eugene Wood
MCCLURE'S MAGAZINE, SEPTEMBER, 1905

I.

Only the other day, the man, that in all this country knows better than anybody else how a circus should be advertised, said (with some sadness, I do believe) that it didn't pay any longer to put up show-bills; the money was better invested in newspaper advertising.

"It doesn't pay." Ah me! How the commercial spirit of the age plays whaley with the romance of existence! You shall not look long upon the show-bill now that there is no money to be had from it. "Youth's sweet-scented manuscript" is about to close, but ere it does, let us turn back a little to the pages illuminated by the glowing colors of the circus poster.

Saturday afternoon when we went by the engine-house, its brick wall fluttered with the rags and tatters of "Esther, the Beautiful Queen," and the lecture on "The Republic: Will it Endure?" (Gee! But *that* was exciting!) Sunday morning, after Sabbath-school, there was a sudden quickening among the boys. We stopped nibbling on the edges of the lesson leaf and followed the crowd in scuttling haste. Miraculously over-night the shabby wall had blossomed into thralling splendor. What was Daniel in the Lions' Den compared to Herr Alexander in the Same? Not as the prophet is pictured, in the farthest corner of the lions, and manifestly saying to himself: "If only I was out of this!" But with his head right smack dab *in* the lions mouth. Right *in* it. Yes. sir!

"S'posin'!" we gasped, all goggle-eyed, "jist s'posin' that there lion was to shut his mouth!—Ga-ash!"

The Golden Text? It faded before the lemon-and-scarlet glories of the Golden Chariot. Drawn by sixteen dappled steeds, each with his neck arching like a fish-hook and reined with fancy scalloped reins, it occupied the center of the foreground. The band rode in it, far more fortunate than our local band whose best was Charley Wells's depot 'bus. And nobler than all his fellows was the bass-drummer. He had a canopy over him, a carved and golden canopy, on whose top revolved a clown's head with its tongue stuck out. On each quarter of this rococo shallop a golden circus-girl in short skirt gaily skipped rope with a nubia or fascinator or whatever it is the women call the thing they wrap around their heads in cold weather when they hang out the clothes. There were big pieces of looking glass let into the sides of the band-wagon, and every decorator knows that when you put looking-glass on a thing it is impossible to fix it so that it will be any finer.

Winding back and forth across the picture was the long train of tableau-cars and animal cages, diminishing with distance until away, 'way up in the upper left-hand corner the hindmost van was all immersed in the blue-and-yellow haze just this side of out-of-sight. That with our own eyes we should behold the glories here set forth we knew right well. Cruel Fortune might cheat us of the raptures to be had inside the tents, but the street-parade was ours, for it was free.

It seems to me that we did not linger so long before these pictures, not before those of the rare and costly animals, which, if we but knew it, were the main reason why we were permitted to go (if we did get to go). To look at these animals is improving to the mind, and since we could not go alone, an older person had to accompany us, and—and—I trust I make myself clear. But we did not want to improve our minds if it was a possible thing to avoid it. The pictures of these animals were in the joggerfy book anyhow, though not in colors, unless we had a box of paints. There can be no doubt that the show-bill pictures of the menagerie were in colors. I seem to recollect that Mr. Galbraith, who kept the dry-goods store across the street from the engine-house was very much exercised in his mind about the way one of these pictures was printed. It was the counterfeit presentment of the Hi-po-pot-a-mus, or Bohemoth of Holy Writ. His objection to the Hip—you know—was not because its open countenance was so fearsome, but because it was so red. Six feet by two of flaming crimson across the street in the afternoon sun made it necessary for him to take the goods to the back window of the store to show the customers. He didn't like it a bit.

No. Neither before the large and expensive pictures of the street-parade, nor the large and expensive wild beasts did we linger. The swarm was thickest, and the jabbering loudest, the "O-o-h's," the "M! Look's," the "Geeminently's" shrillest, in front of where the deeds of high emprise were set forth. Men with their fists clinched on their breasts, and their neatly slippered toes touching the backs of their heads, crashed through paper-covered hoops beneath which horses madly coursed; they flew through the air with the greatest of ease, the daring young men on the flying trapeze, or they posed in living pyramids.

And as the sons of men assembled themselves together, Satan came also, the spirit I, that evermore denies.

"A-a-ah!" sneers his embodiment in one whose crackling voice cannot make up its mind whether to be bass or treble, "A-aah, to the show they down't do hay-uf what they is in the pitchers."

A chilling silence follows. A cold uneasiness strikes into all the listeners. We are all made wretched by destructive criticism. Let us alone in our ideals. Let us alone, can't you?

"Now—now," pursues the crackle-voiced Mephisto, pointing to where Japanese jugglers defy the law of gravitation and other experiences of daily life, "now, they cain't walk up no ladder made out o' reel sharp swords."

"They can so walk up it," stoutly declares one boy. Hurrah! A champion to the rescue! The others edge closer to him. They like him.

"Nah, they cain't. How kin they? They'd cut their feet all to pieces."

"They kin so. I seen 'em do it. The time I went with Uncle George I seen a man, a Japanee. —Yes, sharp. Cut paper with 'em. —A-a-ah, I did so. I guess I know what I seen an' what I didn't."

The little boys breathe easier, but fearing another onslaught, make all haste to call attention to the most fascinating one of all, the picture of a little boy standing on top of his daddy's head. And, as if that weren't enough, his daddy is standing up on a horse and the horse is going around the ring lickety-split. And, as if these circumstances weren't sufficiently trying, that little show-boy is standing on only one foot. The other is stuck up in the air like five minutes to six, and he has hold of his toe with his hand. I'll bet you can't do that just as you are on the ground, let alone on your daddy's head, and him on a horse that's going like sixty. Now you just try it once. Just try it. —A-a-ah! Told you you couldn't.

Now, how the show-actors can do that looks very wonderful to you. It really is very simple. I'll tell you about it. All show-actors are born double-jointed.

You have only two hip-joints. They have four. And it's the same all over with them. Where you have only one joint, they have two. So, you see, the wonder isn't that they can bend themselves every which way, but how they can keep from doubling up like a footrule.

And another thing. Every day they rub themselves all over with snake-oil. Snakes are all limber and supple, and it stands to reason that if you take and try out their oil, which is their express essence, and then rub that into your skin, it will make you supple and limber, too. I should think gartersnakes would do all right, if you could catch enough of them, but they're so awfully scarce. Fish-worms won't do. I tried 'em. There's no grease in 'em at all. They just dry up.

And I suppose you know the reason why they stay on the horse's back. They have rosin on their feet. Did you ever stand up on a horse's back? I did. It was out to grandpap's, on old Tib....No, not very long. I didn't have any rosin on my feet. I was going to put some on, but my Uncle Jimmy said: "Hey! What you got there?" I told him. "Well," he says, "you jist mosey right into the house and put that back in the fiddle-box where you got it. Go on, now. And if I catch you foolin' with my things again, I'll....Well, I don't know what I will do to you." So I put it back. Anyhow, I don't think rosin would have helped me stay on a second longer, because old Tib, with an intelligence you wouldn't have suspected in her, walked through the wagon-shed and calmly scraped me off her back.

And did you ever try to walk the tightrope? You take the clothes-line and stretch it in the grape-arbor—better not make it too high at first—and then you take the clothes-prop for a balance-pole and go right ahead—er—as far as you can. The real reason why you fall off so is that you don't have chalk on your shoes. Got to have lots of chalk. Then after you get used to the rope wabbling so all-fired fast, you can do it like mice. And, while I'm about it, I might as well tell you that if you ever expect to amount to a hill of beans as a trapeze performer you must have clear-starch with oil of cloves in it to rub on your hands. Finest thing in the world. My mother wouldn't let me have any. She said she couldn't have me messing around that way. I blame her as much as anybody that I am not now a competent performer on the trapeze.

I don't know that I had better go into details about the state of mind boys are in from the time the bills were first put up until after the circus had actually departed. I don't mean the boys that get to go to everything that comes along, and that have pennies to spend for candy, and all like that, whenever they ask for it. I mean the regular, proper, natural boys, that used to be "back home," boys whose daddies tormented them with: "Well, we'll see—" that's so exasperating!—or, "I wish you wouldn't tease, when you know we can't spare the money just at present." A perfectly foolish answer, that last. They had money to fritter away at the grocery, and the butcher-shop, and the dry-goods store, but when it came to a necessity of life, such as going to the circus, they let on they couldn't afford it. A likely story.

"Only jist this little bit of once. Aw, now, please. Please, cain't I go? Aw now, I think you might. Aw now, woncha? Aw, paw. I ain't been to a reelly show for ever so long. Aw, the Scripture pammerammer, that don't count. Aw, paw. Please cain't I go? Aw please!" And so forth and so on, with much more of the same sort. No. I can't go into details. It's too terrible.

Even those of us whose daddies said plainly and positively: "Now, I can't let you go. No, Willie. That's the end of it. You can't go." Even those, I say, hoped against hope. It simply could not be that what the human heart so ardently longed for should be denied by a loving father. This same conviction applies to other things, even when we are grown up. It is against nature and the constituted scheme of things that we cannot have what we want so badly. We boys lay there in the shade and pulled the long stalks of grass and nibbled off the sweet, yellow ends, as we dramatized miracles that *could* happen just as well as not, if they only *would*, consarn 'em! For instance, you might be going along the street not thinking of anything but how much you wanted to go to the circus, and how sorry you were because you hadn't the money and your daddy wouldn't give you any, and first thing you'd know, you'd stub your toe or something, and you'd look down and there'd be a half-a-dollar that somebody had lost—Gee! If it would only be that way! But we knew it wouldn't, because only the other Sunday, Brother Longenecker had said: "The age of miracles is past." So we had to give up all hopes. Oh, it's terrible. Just terrible!

But some of the boys lay there in the grass with their hands under their heads, looking up at the sky, and making little white spots come in and out on the corners of their jaws, they had their teeth set so hard, and were chewing so fiercely. You could almost hear their minds creak, scheming, scheming. I suppose there were ways for boys to make money in those times, but they always fizzled out when you came to try them, to say nothing of the way they broke into your day. Why, you had scarcely any time to play in. You'd go 'round to some neighbor's house with a magazine, and you'd say: "Good-afternoon, Mrs. Slaymaker. Do you want to subscribe for this?" Just the way you had studied out you would say. And she'd take it, and go sit down with it, and read it clear through while you played with the dog, and then when she got all through with it, and had read all the advertisements, she'd hand it back to you and say: No, she didn't believe she would. They had so many books and papers now that she didn't get a chance hardly to read in any of them, let alone taking any new ones. Were you getting many new subscribers? Just commenced, eh? Well, she wished you all the luck in the world. How was your ma? That's good. Did she hear from your Uncle John's folks since they moved out to Kansas?

I have heard that there were boys who, under the dire necessity of going to the circus, got together enough rags, old iron, and bottles to make up the price, sold 'em, collected the money, and went. I don't believe it. I don't believe it. We all had, hidden under the back-porch, our treasure-heap of rusty gates, cracked firepots, broken griddles, and lid-lifters, tub-hoops and pokers, but I do not believe that any human boy ever collected fifty cents' worth. I want you to understand that fifty cents is a whole lot of money, particularly when it is laid out in scrap-iron. Only the tin wagon takes rags, and they pay in tinware, and that's no good to a boy that wants to go to the circus. And as for bottles—well, sir, you wash out a whole, whole lot of bottles, a whole big lot of 'em, a wash-basket full, and tote 'em down to Mr. Case's drug and bookstore, as much as ever you and your brother can wag, and see what he gives you. It's simply scandalous. You have no idea of how mean and stingy a man can be until you try to sell him old bottles. And the cold-hearted way in which he will throw back ink-bottles that you worked so hard to clean, and the ones that have reading blown into the glass—Oh, it's enough to set you against business transactions all your life long. There's something about bargain and sale that's mean and censorious, finding this fault and finding that fault, and paying just as little as ever they can. It gets on one's nerves. It really does.

The boys that made the little white spots come on the corners of their jaws as they lay there in the grass, scheming, scheming, scheming, planned rags, and bottles, and scrap-iron, and more also. Sometimes it was a plan so much bigger that if they had kept it to themselves, like the darkey's cow, they would have "all swole up and died."

"Sst! Come here once. Tell you sumpum. Now don't you go and blab it out, now will you? Hope to die? Well....Now, no kiddin'. Cross your heart? Well....Ah, you will, too. I know you. You go and tattle everything you hear. Well....Cheese it! Here comes somebody. Make out we're talkin' about sumpum else. *Ah, he did, did he? What for, I wonder?* (Say sumpum, can't ye?)...Why'n't ye say sumpum when he was goin' by? Now he'll suspicion sumpum's up, and nose around till he....Aw, they ain't no use tellin' you anything....Well....Put your head over so's I can whisper....Sure I am....Well, I could learn, couldn't I? Now don't you tell a living soul, will you? If anybody asts you, you tell 'em you don't anything at all about it. Say why'n't you come along? I promised *you* the last time....That's jist your mother callin' you. Let on you don't hear her. Aw, stay.... Aw, you don't either have to go. Say. Less you and me get up early, and go see the circus come in town, will you? I will, if you will. All right. Remember now. Don't you tell anybody what I told you. *You* know."

II.

If a fellow just only *could* run off with a circus! Wouldn't it be great? No more splitting kindling and carrying in coal; no more: "Hurry up, now, or you'll be late for school"; no more poking along in a hum-drum existence, never going any place or seeing anything, but the glad, free, untrammeled life, the life of a circus-boy, standing up on top of somebody's head (you could pretend he was your daddy. Who'd ever know the difference?) and your leg stuck up like five minutes to six, and him standing on top of a horse—and the horse going around the ring, and the ringmaster cracking his whip—aw, say! How about it?

Maybe the show-people would take you, even if you didn't have two joints to common folks' one, and hadn't had early advantages in the way of plenty of snakes to try the grease out of. And then...and then....Travel all around, and be in a new town every day! And see things! The waterworks, and Main Street, and the Soldiers' Monument, and the Second Presbyterian Church. All the sights there are to see in a strange place. And then when the show came back to your own hometown next year, people would wonder whose was that slim and gracile figure in the green silk tights and spangled breech-clout that capered so nimbly on the bounding courser's back, that switched the natty switch and shrilly called out: "Hep! Hep!" They'd screw up their eyes to look hard, and they'd say: "Yes sir. It is. It's him. It's Willie Bigelow. Well, of all things!" And they'd clap their hands, and be so proud of you. And they'd wonder how it was that they could have been so blind to your many merits when they had you with them. They'd feel sorry that they ever said you were a "regular little imp, if ever there was one," and that you had the Old Boy in you as big as a horse. They'd feel ashamed of themselves, so they would. And they'd come and apologize to you for the way they had acted, and you'd say: "Oh, that's all right. Forgive and forget"....And they'd miss you at home, too. Your daddy would wish he hadn't whaled you the way he did, just for nothing at all....And your mother, too, *she'd* be sorry for they way *she* acted to you, tormenting the life and soul out of you, sending you on errands just when you got a man in the king row, and making you wash your feet in a bucket before you went to bed, instead of being satisfied to let you pump on them, as any reasonable mother would. She'll think about that when you're gone. It'll be lonesome then, with nobody to bang the doors, and upset the cream-pitcher on the clean table-cloth, and fall over backward in the rocking-chair, and break a rocker off. Your daddy will sigh and say: "I wonder where Willie is tonight. Poor boy, I sometimes fear I was too harsh with him." And your mother will try to keep back her tears, but she can't and first thing she knows she'll burst out crying, and...and...and old Maje will go around the house looking for you, and whining because he can't find his little playmate....It will seem as if you were dead—dead to them, and...Smf! Smf! (Confound that orchestra leader anyhow! How many times have I got to tell him that this is the music-cue for "Where is My Wandering Boy To-night?")

We were all going to get up early enough to see the show come in at the depot. Very few of us did it. Somehow we couldn't seem to wake up. Here and there a hardy spirit compasses the feat. I don't think anybody ever does it more than once.

All the town is asleep when this boy slips out of his front gate and snicks the latch behind him softly. It is very still, so still that though he is more than a mile away from the railroad he can hear Johnny Mara, the night yardmaster, bawl out: "Run them three empties over on Number Four track!" the short exhaust of the obedient pony-engine, and the succeeding crash of the cars as they bump against their fellows. It is very still, scarey still. The gas-lamp flaring and flickering among the green maples at the corner has a strange look to him. His footfalls on the sidewalk sound so loud he takes the soft middle of the dusty road. He fears someone pursuing him and his bosom contracts with fear, as he stands to see who it is. Although he hardly knows the boy bound on the same errand as his, he takes him to his heart, as a chosen friend. They are kin.

On the freight-house platform they find other boys. Some of them have waited up all night so as not to miss it. They are from across the tracks. They have all the fun, those fellows do. They can swear and chew tobacco, and play hooky from school and have a good time. They get to go barefoot before anybody else, and nobody tells them it will thin their blood to go in swimming so much. Yes, and they can fight, too. They'd sooner fight than eat. Our boys, conscious of inferiority, keep to themselves. The boys from across the tracks, show off all the bad words they can think of. One of them has a mouth-harp which he plays upon, now and then opening his hands hollowed around the instrument. Patsy Cubbins dances to the music, which is a thing even more reckless and daredevil than swearing. Patsy's going with a "troupe" some day. Or else, he's going to get a job firing on an engine. He isn't right sure which he wants to do the most.

Now and then a brakeman goes by swinging his lantern. The boys would like to ask him what time it is, but for one thing they're too bashful. Being a brakeman is almost as good as going with a "troupe" or a circus. You get to go to places that way, too, Marysville, and Mechanicsburg, and Harrod's—that is, if you're on the local freight, and then you lay over in Cincinnati. Some ways it's better than firing, and some ways it isn't so good. And then there is another reason why they don't ask the brakeman what time it is. He'd say it was "forty-five" or maybe "fifty-three," and never tell what hour.

"Say! Do you know it's cold? You wouldn't think it would be so cold in the summer-time."

The maple-trees, from being formless blobs, insensibly begin to look like lacework. Presently the heavens and the earth are bathed in liquid blue that casts a spell so potent on the soul of him that sees it that he yearns for something he knows not what, except that it is utterly beyond him, as far beyond him as what he means to be will be from what he shall attain to. One dreams of romance and renown, of all that should be and is not. And as he dreams the birds awaken. In the East there comes a greenish tinge. Far up the track there is a sullen roar, and then the husky diapason of an engine whistle. The roar strengthens and strengthens.

It is the circus train!

Under the witchcraft of the dreaming blue, each boy had a firm and stubborn purpose. Over and over again he rehearsed how he would go up to the man that runs the show, and say: "Please, mister, can I go with you?" And the man would say, "Yes." (As easy as that.) But the purpose wavered as he saw the roustabouts come tumbling out, all frowsy and unwashed, rubbing the sleep out of their eyes, cross and savage. And the man whose word they jump to obey, he...he's kind of discouraging. It's all business with him. They may plead with their eyes; he never sees them. If he does, he tells them where to get to out of that, and how quick he wants it done, in language that makes the boldest efforts of the boys from across the tracks seem puny in comparison. The boys divide into two parties. One follows the buggy of the boss canvasman to Vandeman's lots where the stand is made. They will witness the spectacle of the raising of the tents, but they will also be near the man that runs the show, and if all goes well it may be he will like your looks and saunter up to you and say: "Well, bub, and how would you like to travel with us?" You don't know. Things not half so strange as that *have* happened. And if you were right there at the time....

The other party lingers awhile looking up wistfully at the unresponsive windows of the sleeping cars, behind which are the happy circus-actors. Perhaps the show-boy that stands up on top of his daddy's head will look out. If he should raise the window and smile at you, and get to talking with you maybe he would introduce you to his pa, and tell him that you would like to got with the show, and his pa would be a nice sort of a man, and he's say: "Why, yes. I guess we can fix that all right." And there you'd be.

Or if it didn't come out like that, why maybe, the boy would be another "Little Arthur, the Boy Circus-rider," like it told about in *The Ladies' Repository*. It seems there was a man, and one day he went by where there was a circus, and in a quiet, secluded, vine-clad nook only a few steps from the main tent, he heard somebody sigh, oh, so sadly and so pitifully! Come to find out, it was Little Arthur, the Boy Circus-rider. He had large, sensitive, violet eyes, and a wealth of clustering ringlets, and he was very, very unhappy. So the man took from his pocket a Bible that he happened to have with him, and he read from it to Little Arthur, which cheered him up right away, because up to that moment he had only heard of the Bible. (Think of that!) And that night at the show, what do you s'pose? Little Arthur fell off the horse and hurt himself. And this man was at the show and he went back in the dressing-room, and held Little Arthur's hand. And the clown was crying, and the actors were crying, for they all loved Little Arthur in their rude, untutored way. And Little Arthur opened his large, sensitive, violet eyes, and saw the man, and said off the text that the man taught him that afternoon. And then he died. It was a sad story, but it made you wish it had been you that happened to have a Bible in your pocket as you passed the secluded, vine-clad nook only a few paces from the main tent, and had heard Little Arthur sigh so pitifully. It was those sensitive eyes we looked for in the sleeping-car windows, and all in vain. I think I saw the wealth of clustering ringlets, or at least the makings of it. I am almost positive I saw curl-papers as the curtain was drawn aside a moment.

But whether a boy stands gazing at the sleepers, or runs over to the lots, there is something pathetic about it, something almost terrible. It is the death of an ideal. I can't conceive of a boy coming down to the depot to see the circus train come in another time. Hitherto, the show has been to him the *ne plus ultra* of romance. It comes in the night from 'way off yonder; it goes in the night to 'way off yonder. It is all splendor, all deeds of high emprise. It stands to reason then, that the closer you get to it, the closer you get to pure romance. And it isn't that way at all.

What gravels a boy the most of all is to have to do the same old thing over and over again, day after day, week in, week out. He cannot blind himself to the fact, once he has seen the circus come in, that everything is marked and numbered; that all is system, and that everything is done to-day exactly as it was done yesterday, and as it will be done tomorrow.

"What town is this?" he hears a man inquire of another.

"Blest if I know. What's the odds what town it is?"

Didn't know what town it was! *Didn't care!*

The keen morning air or something makes a fellow mighty unromantic, too. Perhaps it was the thin blue woodsmoke from the field-stoves, and the smell of the hot coffee and the victuals the waiters are carrying about, some to the tent where the bare tables are for the canvasmen, some to the table covered with a red and white tablecloth as befits performers. These have no rosy cheeks. Their lithe limbs are not richly decked with silken tights. Insensibly the upper lip curls. They're not so much. They're only folks. That's all, just folks.

But when ideals die, great truths are born. To such a boy at such a moment there comes the firm conviction which increasing years can only emphasize: Home is but a poor prosaic place, but Home—Ah, my brother, think on this— Home is where Breakfast is.

"Hay! Wait for me, you fellows! Hay! Hold on a minute. Well, ain't I a-comin' jis' 's fast 's ever I kin? What's your rush?"

It is the exceptional boy who has this experience. The normal one preserves the delicate bloom of romance, by never seeing the show until it makes its Grand Triumphal Entree in a Pageant of Unparalleled Magnificence far Surpassing the Pomp and Splendor of Oriental Potentates.

The hitching-posts are full of whinnering country horses, and people are in town you woundn't think existed if you hadn't seen their pictures in *Puck* and *Judge*, people from over by Muchinippi, and out Noodletoozy way, big, red-necked men with the long loping step that comes from walking on the plowed ground. Following them are lanky women with their front teeth gone, and their figures bowed by drudgery, dragging wide-eyed children whose uncouth finery betrays the "country jake," even if the freckles and the sun-bleached hair could keep the secret.

From the far-off fastnesses where there are still log-cabins chinked with mud, they have ventured to see the show come into town, and when they have seen that, they will retire again beyond our ken. How every sense is numbed and stunned by the magnificence and splendor of the painted and gilded wagons as they rumble past, the driver rolling and pitching in his seat, as he handles the ribbons of eight horses all at once!

The allegorical tableau-car solemnly waggles past, Europe and Asia and Africa and Australia brilliant in grease-paint and gorgeous cheese-cloth robes. And can you guess who the fat lady up on the very tip-top of all is, upon the tip-top where the wobble is the worst? Our own Columbia! It must be fine to ride around that way all dressed up in a flag. But a sourer lot of faces you never saw in your life. No. I am wrong. For downright melancholy and despondency you must wait till the funny old clown comes along in his little bit of a buggy drawn by a little bit of a donkey.

"And, oh, looky! Here comes the elephants, just the same as in the joggerfy books. And see the men walking beside them. They come from the place the elephants do. See, they have on the clothes they wear in that country. Don't they look proud? Who wouldn't be proud to get to walk with an elephant? And if you ever do anything to an elephant to make him mad, he'll always remember it and some day he'll get even with you. One time there was a man, and he gave an elephant a chew of tobacco, and—O-o-ooh! See that man in the cage with the lions! Don't it just make the cold chills run over you? I wouldn't be there for a million dollars, would you, ma?

"What they laughing at down the street? Ma, make Lizzie get down; she's right in my way. I don't want to see it pretty soon. I want to see it *naow!* Oh, ain't it funny? See the old clowns playing on horns! Ain't it too killing? Aw, look at them ponies. I woosht I had one. Johnny Pym has got a goat he can hitch up. What was that, pa? What was that went 'Oo-OOoomh!'"

"Whoa, Nell, whoa there! Steady, gal, stead-ay! Ho, there! Ho! Whoa— whoa-*hup*! Whaddy y' about? Fool horse. Whoa...whoa...so, gal, so-o-o. Lion, I guess, or a tagger, or sumpum or other."

And talk about music. You thought the band was grand. You just wait. Don't you hear it down the street? It'll be along in a minute now....There it is. That's the cally-ope. That's what the show-bills call: "The Steam Car of the Muses."...Mm—well, I don't know but it is just a leetle off the pitch, especially towards the end of a note, but you must remember that you can't haul a very big boiler on a wagon, and the whistles let out an awful lot of steam. It's pretty hard to keep the pressure even. But it's loud. That's the main thing. And the man that plays on it—no, not that fellow in the overalls with a wad of greasy waste in his hand. He's only the engineer. I mean the artist, the man that plays on the keys. Well, he knows what the people want. He has his fingers on the public pulse. Does he give them a Bach fugue, or Guillmant's "Grant Coeur?" 'Deed, he doesn't. He goes right to the heart, with "Patrick's Day in the Morning," and "The Carnival of Venice," and "Home, Sweet Home," and "Oh Where, Oh Where has my Little Dog Gone?" He knows his business. A shade off the key, perhaps, but my! Ain't it grand? So loud and nice!

"Well, that's all of it....Why, child, I can't make it any longer than it is.... What do you want me to drive round into the other street for? You've seen all there is to see. Got all your trading done, mother? Well, then I expect we'd better put for home. Now, Eddy, I told you 'No' once, and that's the end of it. Hush up now! Look here, sir! Do you want me to take and 'tend to you right before everybody? Well, I will now, if I hear another whimper out o' ye. Ck-ck-ck! Git ep there, Nelly."

Some day, when we get big, and have whole, whole lots of money we're going to the circus every time it comes to town, to the real circus, the one you have to pay to get into. For if merely the street parade is so magnificent, what must the show itself be?

III.

How people can sit at the table on circus day and stuff, and stuff the way they do is more than I can understand. You'd think they hadn't any more chances to eat than they had to go to the show. And they can find more things to do before they get started! And then, after the house is all locked up and everything, they've got to back after a handkerchief! What does anybody want with a handkerchief at a circus?

It's exasperating enough to have to choose between going in the afternoon and not going at all. Why, sure, it's finer at night. Lots finer. You know that kind of a light the peanut-roaster man has got down by the post-office. Burns that kind of stuff they use to take out grease-spots. Ye-ah. Gasoline. Well, at the circus at night, they don't have just one light like that, but bunches and bunches of them on the tent-poles. No, silly! Of course not. Of course they don't set the tent afire.

But say! What if they did, eh? The place would be all full of people, laughing at the country jake that comes out to ride the trick-mule, and you'd happen to look up and see where the canvas was ju-u-ust beginning to blaze, and you'd jump up and holler: "Fire! Fire!" as loud as ever you could because you saw it first, and you'd point to the place? Excitement? Well, I guess yes. The people would all run every which way, and fall all over themselves, and the women would squeal—And do you know what I'd do? I'd just let myself down between the bed-slat benches, and drop to the ground, and lift up the canvas and there I'd be all safe. And after I was all safe, then I'd go back and rescue folks.—We-ell, I s'pose I'd *have* to rescue a girl. It seems they always do that. But it would be nice, I think, to rescue some real man. He'd say; "My noble preserver! How can I sufficiently reward you?" and take out his pocketbook. And I'd say" "Take back your proffered gold," and make like I was pushing it away, "take back your proffered gold. I did my duty." And then I'd forget all about it. And one day, after I'd forgotten all about it, the man would die, and will me a million dollars, or a thousand. I don't know. Enough to make me rich.

And say! Wouldn't the animals get excited when they saw the show was afire? They'd just roar and roar, and upset the cages, and maybe they'd get loose. O-o-o-Oh! How about that? If there was a lion come at me, I'd climb a tree. What would you do? Ah, your pa's shot-gun nothing! Why, you crazy, that would only infuriate him the more. What you want to do is to take an express rifle, like Doo Challoo did, and aim right for his heart. An express rifle is what you send off and get, and they ship it to you by express.

So you see what a fellow misses by having to go to the show in the afternoon, like the girls and the babies. The boys from across the tracks get to go at night. They have all the fun. When they go they don't have to poke along, and poke along, and keep hold of hands so as not to get lost.—Aw, hurry up, can't you? Don't you hear the band playing? It'll be all over before we get there.

But finally the lots are reached, and there are the tents, with all kinds of flags snapping from the center-poles and the guy-ropes. And there are the sideshows. Alas! You never thought of the side-shows when you asked if you could go. And now it's too late. It must be fine in the side-shows. I never got to go to one. I didn't have the money. But if the big painted banners, bulging in and out, as the wind plays with them, are anything to go by, it must be something grand to see the Fat Lady, and the Circassian Beauty, whose frizzled head will just about fit a bushel basket, and the Armless Wonder. They say he can take a pair of scissors with his toes and cut your picture out of paper just elegant.

Oh, and something else you miss by going in the afternoon. At night you can sneak around at the back, and when nobody is looking you can just lift up the canvas and go right in for nothing. —Why, what's wrong about that? Ah, you're too particular. —And if the canvasman catches you, you can commence to cry and say you had only forty cents, and you wanted to see the circus so bad, and he'll take it and let you in, and you can have ten cents, don't you see, to spend for lemonade, red lemonade, you understand, and peanuts, the littlest bags, and the "on-riest" peanuts that ever were.

As far as I can see, the animal part of the show is just the same as it always was. The people that take you to the show always pretend to be interested in them, but it's my belief they stop and look only to tease you. Away, 'way back in ancient times, there used to be a man that took the folks around and told them what was in each cage, and where it came from, and how much it cost, and what useful purpose it served in the wise economy of nature, and all about it. That was before my time. But I can recollect something they had that they don't have any more. I can remember when Mr. Barnum first brought his show to our town. It didn't take much teasing to get to go to that, because in those days Mr. Barnum was a "bigger man than old Grant." *The Life of P.T. Barnum, Written by Himself* was on everybody's marble-topped center-table, just the same as *The History of the Great Rebellion.* You show some elderly person from out of town the church across the street from the Astor House, and say: "That's St. Paul's Chapel. General Montgomery's monument is in the chancel window. George Washington went to church there the day he was inaugurated president," and your friend will say: "M-hm." But you tell him right across Broadway is where Barnum's Museum used to be, and he'll brighten right up and remember all about how Barnum strung a flag across St. Paul's steeple and what a fuss the vestry made. That's something he knows about. That's part of the history of our country.

Well, when Mr. Barnum first came to our town, all around one tent were vans full of the very identical "Moral Waxworks" that we had read about, and had given up all hopes of ever seeing because New York was so far away. There was the "Dying Zouave." Oh, that was a beauty! The *Advance Courier* said that "the crimson torrent of his heart's blood spouted in rhythmic jets as the tide of life ebbed silently away," but I guess by the time they got to our town they must have run out of pokeberry juice, for the "crimson torrent" didn't spout at all. But his bosom heaved every so often, and he rolled up his eyes something grand! I liked it, but my mother said it was horrid. That's the way with women. They don't like anything that anyone else does. There's no pleasing them. And she thought the "Drunkard's Family" was "kind o' low." It wasn't either. It was fine, and taught a great moral lesson. I told her so, but she said it was low, just the same. She thought the "Temperance Family" was nice, but it wasn't anywhere near as good as the "Drunkard's Family." Why, let me tell you. The "Drunkard's Wife" was in a ragged calico dress, and her eye was all black and blue, where he had hit her the week before. And the "Drunkard" had hold of a black quart bottle, and his nose was all red, and he wore a plug hat that was even rustier and more caved in than Elder Drown's, if such a thing were possible. And there was—But I can't begin to tell you of all the fine things Mr. Barnum had that year, but never had again.

Another thing Mr. Barnum had that year that never appeared again. It may be that after that time the Funny Old Clown did crack a joke, but I never heard him. The one that Mr. Barnum had got off the most comical thing you ever heard. I'll never forget it the longest day I live. Laugh? Why, I nearly took a conniption over it. It seems the clown got to crying about something. —Now what was it made him cry? Let me see now. —Ain't it queer I can't remember that? Fudge! —Well, never mind now. It will come to me in a minute.

I feel kind of sorry for the poor little young ones that grow up and never know what a clown is like. Oh, yes, they have them to-day, after a fashion. They stub their toes and fall down the same as ever, but there is a whole mob of them and you can't take the interest in them that you could in the one, the only, the inimitable clown there used to be, a character of such importance that he got his name on the bills. He was a mighty man in those days. The ring-master was a kind of stuck-up fellow, very important in his own estimation, but he didn't have a spark of humor. Not a spark. And he'd be swelling around there, all so grand, and the clown, just to take him down a peg or two, would ask him a conundrum. And do you think he would ever guess one? Never. Not a one. And when the clown would tell him what the answer was, he'd be so vexed at himself that he'd try to take it out on the poor clown, and cut at him with his large whip. But Mr. Clown was just as spry in his shoes as he was under the hat, and he'd hop up on the ring-side out of the way, and squall out: "A-a-a-ah! Never touched me!" We had that for a byword. Oh, you'd die laughing at the comical remarks he'd make. And he'd be so quick about it. The ring-master would say something, and before you'd think, the clown would make a joke out of it. —I wish I could think what it was he said that was so funny the time he started crying. Seems to me it was something about his little brother. —Well, no matter.

Yes, sir, there are heads of families to-day, I'll bet you, that have grown up without ever having heard a clown sing a comic song, and ask the audience to join the chorus. And if you say to such people: "Here we are again, Mr. Merryman," or "Bring on another horse," or "What will the little lady have now? The banners, my lord?" They look at you so funny. They don't know what you mean, and they don't know whether to get huffy or not. Well, I suppose that it had to be that the Funny Old Clown with all his songs, and quips, and conundrums, and comical remarks should disappear. Perhaps he "didn't pay."

I can't see that the rest of the show has changed so very much. Perhaps the trapeze performances are more marvelous and breath-suspending than they used to be. But they were so far and far beyond what we could dream of then, and to go still farther as little impresses us as to be told that people live even farther off than Idaho. The trapeze performers are up-to-date in one respect. The fellow that comes down with his arms folded, one leg stuck out and the other twined around the big rope, revolving slowly, slowly—well, the band plays the intermezzo from "Cavalleria Rusticana" nowadays when he does that. It used to play: "O Thou Sweet Spirit, Hear my Prayer!" But the lady in the riding-habit still smiles as if it hurt her when her horse walks on its hind legs; the bareback rider does the very same fancy steps as the horse goes round the ring in a rocking-chair lope; the attendants still slant the hurdles almost flat for the horse to jump; they still snake the banners under the rider's feet as he gives a little hop up, and they still bang him on the head with the paper-covered hoop to....Hold on a minute. Now....Now....That story the clown told that was so funny, that had something to do with those hoops. I wish I could think of it. It would make you laugh, I know.

People try to lay the blame of the modern circus's failure to interest them on the three rings. They say so many things to watch at once keeps them from being interested in any one act. They can't give it the attention it deserves. But I'll tell you what's wrong: There isn't any Funny Old Clown, a particular one, to give it human interest. It is all too splendid, too magnificent, too far beyond us. We want to hear somebody talk foolish and human once in a while.

They pretend that the tent was too big for the clown to be heard, but I take notice it wasn't too big for the fellow to get up and declaim: "The puffawmance ees not yait hawf ovah. The jaintlemanly agents will now pawss around the ring with tickets faw the concert." I used to hate that man. When he said the performance was not yet half over, he lied like a dog, consarn his picture! He knew it, and we knew it, and we knew that there were only a few more acts to come. We wanted the show to go on and on, and always to be just as exciting as at the very first, and it wouldn't! We had got to the point where we couldn't be interested in anything any more. We were as little ones unable to prop their eyelids open and yet quarrelling with bed. We were surfeited, but not satisfied. We sat there and pouted because there wasn't any more, and yet we couldn't but yawn at the act before us. We were mad at ourselves, and mad at everybody else. We clambered down the rattling bed-slat seats, sour and sullen. We didn't want to look at the animals; we didn't want to do this, and we didn't want to do that. We whined and snarled, and wriggled and shook ourselves with temper, and we got a good hard slap, side of the head, right before everbody, and then we yelled as if we were being killed alive.

"Now, mister, if I ever take you any place again, you'll know it. I'd be ashamed of myself, if I was you. Hush up! Hush up, I tell you. Now you mark. You're never going to the show again. Do you hear me? *Never.* I mean it. You're never going again."

But at eventide there was light. After supper, after a little rest and a good deal of food, while chopping the kindling for morning (it's wonderful how useful employ tends to induce a cheerful view of life) out of her dazzling treasure-heap of jewels, Memory took up one after another a glowing recollection and viewed it with delight. The evening performance, the one all lighted with bunches and bunches of lights, was a-preparing and in the gentle breeze the far-off music waved as if it had been a flag. A harsh and rumbling noise as of heavy timbers falling tore through the tissue of sweet sounds. The horses in the barn next door screamed in their stalls to hear it. Ages and ages ago on distant windswept plains their ancestors had harkened to that hunting-cry, and summoned up their valor and their speed. It still thrilled in the blood of these patient slaves of man, though countless generations of them had never even so much as seen a lion.

"And is that all the difference, pa, that the lion roars at night and the ostrich in the daytime?"

Out on the back porch in the deepening dusk we sat, with eyes relaxed and dreaming, and watched the stars that powdered the dark sky. Before our inward vision passed in review the day of splendor and renown. We sighed, at last, but it was the happy sigh of him who has full dined. Ambition was digesting. In our turn, when we grew up, we too were to do the deeds of high emprise. We were to be somebody.

(I never heard of anybody sitting up to see the show depart. And yet it seems to me that would be the best time to run off with it.)

The next day we visited the lots. It was no dream. See the litter that mussed up the place. We were all there. None had heard the man that runs the show say genially: "Yes, I think we can arrange to take you with us." Here was the ring; here the tent-pole holes, and here a scrap of paper torn from a hoop the bareback rider leaped through. —Oh, I know now what I as going to tell you that the clown said. The comicalest thing!

He picked up one of these hoops and began to sniffle.

So the ring-master asked him what he was crying about.

"I—I—was thinking of my mother. Smf! My good old mother!"

Well, you know that'll make anybody serious, so the ring-master asked him what made him think of his mother.

"This." And he held up the paper-covered hoop.

The ring-master couldn't see how that put the clown in mind of his mother. He was awful dumb, that man.

"It looks just like the pancakes she used to make for us."

Well, sir, we just hollared and laughed at that. After we had quieted down a little, the ring-master says: "As big as that?"

"Bigger," says the clown. "Why, she used to make 'em so big we used 'em for bed-clothes."

"Indeed?" (Just like that. He took it all in, just as if it was so.)

"Oh, my, yes! I mind one time I was sleeping with my little brother, and I waked up just as *cold*—Brrr! But I was cold."

"But how could that be, sir? You just said you had pancakes for bed-clothes."

"Yes, but my little brother got hungry in the night and et up all the cover."

Laugh? Why they screamed. Me? I though I'd just about go up. But the ring-master never cracked a smile. He didn't see the joke at all.

Good-by, old clown, friend of our childhood, good-by, good-by forever! And you, our other friend, the street parade, must you go, too? And you, the gorgeous show-bills, must you tread the path toward the sundown? Good-by! Good-by! And in that dreary land where you are going, the Kingdom of the Ausgespielt, it may comfort you to recollect the young hearts you have made happy in the days that were but nevermore can be again.

WILLIAM L. SLOUT

25. ON THE ROAD WITH THE "BIG SHOW"

by Charles Theodore Murray
COSMOPOLITAN, JUNE, 1900

There is a wonderful fascination in modern circus life, for those employed in it as well as for those who see only its romantic side. Its hardships have been greatly lessened since the special trains and schedule time have eliminated the lumbering and uncertain caravans that worked laboriously from town to town; but this change has been attended by a proportionate elimination of the romance.

Ask the boy who has sat up all night by the country roadside in front of the old farm-gate to see the circus-wagons go by in the darkness. He is a pretty old boy now, but not all these succeeding years crowded with events have effaced the memory of that picture or of that sweet, awful thrill of youthful joy. There were first the faraway sounds of grinding of wheels and creaking of axles, long before anything came in view. Then the indistinct outline of the big cages became visible in faint silhouette above the stake-and-ridered fences. Slowly, sluggishly, nearer and nearer—the panting of the great horses, the restless footfalls that have the sound of claws, the low moan that is half a whine from the wild beasts pacing the cages, the heavy lumbering tread of the elephant yet out of sight but distinctive above the clattering hoofs of ring horses and ponies—and then the shadows became realities, the phantom circus became a tangible "gigantic aggregation" to the boyish eyes. It was preceded by the manager's buggy and two to three light, covered vehicles containing performers, and the big band-wagon. Then came the cages, with their somnolent drivers perched high in front, the long pole-wagons and the ring-horses carefully blanketed, while the great elephant brought up the rear in stately majesty. The managers slept against each other, the performers dozed and nodded in their conveyance, the bandsmen were dead to the world, the cage-drivers merely held the reins and let the horses follow the preceding team at their own sweet will. Not a human sound broke the stillness of the night—only the wheels, the painting of the horses, the restless tread of clawed feet, the heavy step and sighing breath of the weary elephant.

Not a human face could be seen—only the dark outlines of muffled forms, wiggling, wavering pitching this way and that with the uncertain irregularity of the oldtime country road. Then, phantom-like again, the train slowly disappeared into the darkness whence it had sprung, and its unseen and awe-stricken young worshiper stole silently back to bed by way of the bedroom window. He knew the bandwagon was laden with heavy brass and sheepskin music, though he had heard it not; he knew the cages were richly ornamented with gold, though he had seen it not. In his dreams he saw everything clearly. He reviewed the whole street parade—took in the entire show. And the next day he walked four miles to town and back again to sit as closely to the ring as possible, where the horse ridden by the beautiful lady in spangles could throw dirt all over him.

But that was a long time ago and the boy is getting old. The romance of the road is dead to him—the circus of to-day is a pleasure to him chiefly through its revival of tender boyhood memories. And you could never make him believe that the boy of to-day ever sees the three special trains of cars with the royal outfit of the modern circus with half the interest that was attached to that phantom caravan silently grinding along the country road.

It is true that the boy of the present lives in another world from the first happy day when the bill-posters appear in town to glorify waste places with pictures of magnificence and wonder. He, too, is keen for the coming of the "aggregation." Wakened by some boyish freemasonry, he escapes in the early morning by the window and a convenient roof, and betakes himself to the railroad yard, there to sit shivering on the top of a sidetracked freight-car, straining eager eyes down the track. It may be his fortune to see the trains coming in—see the sleepy men rise out of impossible beds—see the canny elephant descend, and the great wagons, deftly guided, swing to the ground and roll away. More likely, after an hour's waiting, he learns that the circus is long since in and unloaded. He runs to the show-grounds—to find already the rings laid out, the poles up, and the canvas rising on creaking tackle.

It is true that the excitements of circus-day still appeal to the boy as does nothing else in his experience. The holiday look of town; the seething country-folk along the curbs; the calls of lemonade, pop-corn and balloon merchants; at last the approach of the first bandwagon, with clamorous hints from adown the street or rival musicians behind; the impressive passing of horsemen, ladies, chariots, marvelous beasts of desert and jungle; and finally the delicious joy of the calliope's shriek—still the American boy's experience comprehends all this. Still the big tent erects its stately dome; still before the side-show the great banners wave, inviting with compelling charm the ingenuous youth to mysterious joys. But to the old boy the elder days were better.

How does this change affect the circus people? More than it affects the old boy. First, and broadly, the railroad has civilized the circus man. If the modern circus has eliminated the romantic features of show life, it has also extracted the moral poison. The circus business was formerly a "low-down" calling, as was still earlier the theatrical business. Those who engaged in it were fakirs and humbugs and worked any sort of scheme and placarded the dead walls to skin the public. It was recognized as necessary to deceive. A circus company, as a genuine, honest organization doing a legitimate business, and contracting and meeting obligations like any other business association, was unheard of, unknown.

The company was organized on the principle that included not only the deception and plunder of the public, but combined self-defense when the outraged public resented the imposition. There was always a readiness to resort to brute force, and the celerity with which the road show could move from one jurisdiction to another practically exempted it from legal restraint. The showman was not only an unscrupulous but a turbulent fellow, generally speaking, apt to "clean out" country towns by way of brass "knucks" as well as by cards and dice and the nimble pea. Performers were merely athletic rowdies. Canvasmen were but hired thugs permitted to do pretty much as they pleased. No attempt on the part of managers seems to have been made to control their employees. The men were quartered in hotels in the town and were free to indulge in all sorts of dissipation betweentimes. These conditions had not only a highly immoral influence among circus life—they made physical excellence among circus athletes extremely rare.

It is to emphasize this influence of moral upon physical culture, that I draw this comparison between the old and the new. First came the moral reform that followed the new conditions of circus life, when physical excellence quickly rose and spread through the acrobatic world. The great railroad show did the business by rendering former conditions impossible. Simultaneously with the discovery by circus proprietors that the business world would yield greater and more certain returns by being conducted on an honest commercial basis, their employees found that greater physical excellence could be attained and higher salaries earned by leading sober and moral lives. Whether they voluntarily came to that conclusion or were forced into it by the new conditions, is immaterial so far as their unquestioned benefit is concerned—they have arrived.

The great railway show, therefore, not only revolutionized the form of the circus business. It made it respectable. The circus manager in time discovered that the best results in life are obtained by a reasonable observance of the cardinal virtues. He does not consider the matter from a religious point of view, but purely from that of business. Rum-drinking, card-playing, and lewd conduct of any kind, are, if persisted in, sure to meet dismissal halfway. Further, a liberal premium is place on good conduct, a certain amount of cash being set aside as a gift to every employee who remains through the season under the conditions named.

There is one incidental feature of the modern railway show that has a salutary effect as regards discipline and the substantial welfare of circus employees. This feature is the traveling restaurant. The tremendous size of the three-ring circus drives it to the suburbs for a tenting field. The number of men employed, and their pressing duties, require that they should be fed and lodged on the spot. As for the lodging, there are the sleeping-cars close at hand. Hotels are superfluous. They could not be used even if there were sufficient room and kitchen accommodations for five hundred or six hundred people, since the railroad trains pull out for the next town immediately after the night performance. This sleeping-car-tent life separates the showman from the attractions and vices of the town, gives him pure air, good food, and drink free from intoxicants, and saves him money. The feeding of all these people is let out by contract, and the caterer must provide wholesome food approved by the owner of the show. The proprietor of one of our best-known shows himself ate at least once, and sometimes twice or three times, a day at the same table with his people, to see that they got what should be given to them. He had a special car lying near at hand, with a degree of domestic comfort rarely provided for other magnates, including a first-class cook, but he preferred to sit among his captains and lieutenants under the tent, with a circus-board for a seat and his feet in the grass. When that grass is wet, or instead of grass it happens to be mud, straw and chaff are liberally used—sometimes cinders. The wages of the canvasmen and the stablemen, hostlers, grooms, et cetera, are made to include meals. The performers and petty officials, heads of departments, et cetera, purchase tickets out of which meals are punched as they get them. The ticket class sit in certain seats, the heads of departments at one table, the performers at another, petty officials or sub-bosses at another, though all are served with the same food from the same kitchen. The seats are the traditional circus board seat that has a tendency to fly up unexpectedly at either end and meet you halfway in the middle. Behind the outside rows along the canvas are short ropes with running nooses that form convenient hat- and coat-racks where nails would be impossible. The kitchen is the first thing unloaded from the cars, and is set up and agoing at once. The fresh meat and bread, et cetera, contracted for in advance, are delivered on the spot at the same time, and breakfast is soon under way. An immense wagon range, sheltered from the wind, is operated from a footboard, while two or three great caldrons for coffee and for hot water are placed picturesquely over open campfires. The butcher, protected from the sun by canvas overhead, falls to cutting up the carcasses of beef, mutton and pork, which in chops and steaks are gaily tossed up to the cooks on the range. A long bench bears washbasins, and big towels begin clean the first ablution, on the part of many, for the day. *[sic]* In the meantime the restaurant-tent has been spread and a score of waiters in white aprons start a lively clatter of dishes and spoons in preparation for breakfast. Across-lots from the cars come scattering groups, and men and women performers singly and in pairs.

Under the loud cries of the bosses, the stake-men are driving home the long iron-bound tent-pins, the heavy sledges following each other like pattering rain drops, and so closely one upon the other that the stake never seems to stop moving, but to crawl down into the reluctant earth to escape the powerful blows. Other gangs are spreading the big canvases where the lot surveyor has indicated each tent belongs by little flagged iron pins. Still others are unloading cages and animals; parade stuff is being rubbed up and got ready; the vast herds of horses and elephants, camels, zebras, and other led animals of the menagerie, are being provided with a comfortable meal.

Every gang has its particular morning task and not until that job is completed can they get breakfast. When it has been done, each man of that gang is handed his meal-ticket by the sub-boss and the gang goes to the basins and "grub." The performers go straight across the fields through the circus debris from their sleeper to the restaurant, guided by the ascending smoke.

This morning scene is most inspiring.

To the layman it is the particular hour of the whole circus day. The air, the morning sunshine, the rush of feet, the shouting of orders, the neighing of horses, the clack of boards, the sharp appetite—ah! how it sends the blood quickening through the veins! And in all of this seeming chaos and confusion inextricable, the great tents rise as by fairy magic, and from the ten acres of canvas the flags and banners are broken out to the breeze and flutter and snap as if they were sentient things and partook of the general hilarity. I say it seems chaotic and altogether unreasonable, yet it is the systematic perfection of system in which all things are made to come together at a given moment and in proper order. It is only a perfectly trained, though a quite noisily working, human machine.

And the usual score of small boys who are paid in admission-tickets for unloading from the wagons the seats for the arena and carrying this material to its proper place, can make more noise than do half a thousand brawny circus men. I wonder if the old boys has as much to say in the long-ago?

The morning parade is set for nine o'clock on the road. The wagons and chariots are uncovered and wiped down till the gilding shows up like real gold. Grooms are on the jump getting the horses in trim, and everybody, male and female, is being rapidly arrayed in uniform. These four hundred horses have been watered, groomed and fed, and woe to the unhappy stableman who has left a tarnish on the glossy coat of one of the superb animals of the ring.

The elephants are the first animals unloaded, and by this time have consumed a few tons of hay, which takes the edge off their appetite. The band appears on the sward in full regalia, while the performers begin to emerge from the dressing-rooms in gorgeous equestrian costume. At a signal from the equestrian director, all take to the saddle. Meanwhile, though it is but half-past eight, nearly every driver is in place. Nine o'clock means nine o'clock in a big circus—the man or woman who is five minutes late will find a hole in his or her salary at the next payday. Things move by clockwork. On the minute, the gay calvacade begins to unwind from the apparent tangle and to debouch upon the crowded town. Until one has ridden in the street parade, one has really never seen the circus.

Upon returning from the morning parade, there is very little time to rest before luncheon. This time is usually occupied by the women mending their costumes, or embroidering, or getting ready their trunks for the afternoon performance. The male performers lounge in their dressing-room, which is separated from that of the opposite sex by a high canvas partition, write letters, or investigate the condition of the ground where they are to work later. They are on the lookout for stones, bits of glass, et cetera, often found in these outlying lots, and which mean sprains or cuts and a premature close of season. Luncheon soon follows parade, and the afternoon performance quickly succeeds luncheon. There is just about time to make due preparation for the ring. When the afternoon performance is over, there is another brief interval of rest, when dinner is announced. An hour later and preparation begins for the night performance. During this preparation each trunk is carefully made ready for the baggage-wagon—only the last costume needs to be placed therein and everything is ready for the road again. Within ten minutes the big top comes down and the performers scramble for the cars. The rule is for the trains to pull out as soon as loaded—there is no certainty of the hour. So there is no loafing about the town. It is straight to train, and as there are no conveniences for sitting in these circus sleepers, it means to bed.

When the performers have long retired, the work of loading the trains goes rapidly on, special care being exerted not to disquiet the animals. The elephants are always handled with the utmost caution, owing to the uncertainty and power of the tremendous beasts and their liability to sudden fright. There is nothing in such a case but the counter-irritant of cold steel.

Now note the routine of the circus performer—early rising, early breakfast, morning parade, luncheon, afternoon performance, two hours' rest, dinner, night performance, to bed. The same thing day in and day out right through the season. No dissipation, no recreation, no amusement, no society—save the rest of Sunday and the society of fellow-performers.

If it happens to be in a big city, he may indulge in a hotel or restaurant dinner on Sunday afternoon, but he does so rarely, preferring to write letters on the top of his trunk in the dressing-room or doze away the hours stretched in some shady place on the greensward.

As for the canvasman force, Sunday is cleaning-up and rubbing-down day. The hundreds of poles are gone over with fresh paint every Sunday and a multitude of other details come in as extra on that day. These require a good round half-day's work. As for the animal men, stable hands, grooms, et cetera, they have the same round of duty as required of them during the week. The railroad men get practically a day off between Sunday morning and Monday night.

There is practically no ring practice on the road. This portion of the performer's work is supposed to have been completed before starting out. Rehearsals close with the Madison Square Garden season. They are quite impossible on the route.

The ring-rider is practising in his ring-barn all winter, while the circus manager is studying the maps and statistics of the country and laying off the circus field for the coming campaign. All ring-leaders do not own their own ring-barns, in which case they must hire one or use that provided at the show's winter quarters.

There one may see singular sights. A young woman floating through the air by a rope affixed to a surcingle at the middle of the back is to a charming sight, but it is right funny. This rope is attached to a pulley on a swinging crane above and has an able-bodied man at the other end of it. An acting ringmaster cracks his whip and keeps the steady old ring-horse jogging while the woman tries her business. When she falls, the man at the other end of the rope throws his weight on it and eases her ladyship to the ground. This eliminates the question of accident and leaves the mind and muscle of the rider free to accomplish the desired act. The male ring-rider practises in the same way.

The trapeze artists and acrobats generally practise all winter more or less at some gymnasium, wherever they may happen to live. On the road they find two performances a day as much as physical culture can stand. And as they must ride in the daily parade, there are no hours or opportunities for drill, even if desirable. The modern circus performers, male and female, are as a class sober, industrious, and moral of private life. In all that goes to make up the decent and intelligent qualities of men and women they are the equals of the men and women of the theatrical profession. In fact, there are less scandal and more goodness of heart observable in circus life than in the theatrical world.

It is a wearing life, and the hard faces must be correctly attributed to the constant presence of the element of personal danger in the mind, and not, as is commonly done, to a life of irregularity. Most people now recognize the "bicycle face," so called from the drawn, hard expression the countenance takes after the bicycle habit becomes fixed. It comes of the same cause as the "circus face." The dangers of the ring are never met from performance to performance except with anxiety and something like dread; and it is not until the work of the day is over that the ring-rider, the charioteer and the trapeze artist can breathe freely and lie down in the narrow berth on the car feeling thankful that the limbs are whole and that the blood continues to circulate throughout a sound body. A few years of this wearing anxiety of mind and women and men take on the hard-set "circus face." Even young children used in the "carrying act" in the ring soon acquire this face, and it marks the pretty young woman performer even more emphatically than those who have no pretensions to beauty. The total absence of some sort of distraction that will take the mind from the dangerous act and break up that face into smiles occasionally, would probably lessen the severity of the "circus face," but only the final act really cures it.

To the onlooking crowds all is easy, smooth-moving and delightful. But to achieve it all, how much has been necessary, what pains have been spent, what perils daily encountered!

VII.
VAUDEVILLE

The "acts" or "turns" of the vaudeville stage are centuries old; they have existed since ancient man developed creative communication. The music and dance in religious ceremonies, the pantomimic story-telling at social celebrations, and the demonstrations of physical accomplishment for athletic competitions are precursory expressions of presentational amusements. Outstanding musicians, dancers, actors, athletes, etc., because of their distinct abilities, were separated from the group for solo exhibitions. As such, they became "acts."

But modern vaudeville is clearly an American institution, formed for a society that wanted, and perhaps needed, unadulterated entertainment. The scrubby variety halls and concert saloons of the nineteenth century, where cheap beverages were dispensed to a raucous and unseemly audience, were stepping stones for a new mode of variety performance. They led from the Bowery to upper Broadway, from ignominity to respectability, from a scattering of shambled rooms to gaudy elegance, from impoverished independent ownerships to expensive corporative chain operations. Enterprise and salesmanship gave vaudeville an American character. Careful packaging for the largest possible audience was a mark for success. Entertainment was watered down to appeal to the widest denomination of morality and taste. And although many of the "acts" were highly entertaining, and many of the performers were uniquely talented, vaudeville, as an American institution, enjoyed less than fifty years of glorified duration, until, weakened by its own watered formula and the greed of its entrepreneurs, it fell before the onslaught of a modern age.

26. SKETCHES OF THE PEOPLE WHO OPPOSE OUR SUNDAY LAWS

HARPER'S WEEKLY, OCTOBER 8, 15, 1859

I. A SUNDAY EVENING SACRED CONCERT

One recent Sunday evening, as I was walking alone on the undignified side of Broadway, rain began to fall with violence. The circumstances were disagreeable. Novelty of raiment is not such a matter of course with me that I can calmly witness watery injury to the first bloom of my broadcloth. Externally, I was new that evening. When I left home I had fancied myself tolerably radiant and glossy. I took some thought of the morrow, and gazed anxiously around in search of shelter.

Light streamed from a door-way just before me. A bulky poster, splashed all over with notes of admiration, invited entrance and promised entertainment. The rain and an inconquerable instinct impelled me inward. As I passed the threshold a small lad thrust a programme upon me, from which I learned that two sacred concerts, in immediate succession, were to take place, and that the price of admission to both would be thirteen cents.

I distinctly remember asking, in a tone of quiet facetiousness, as I handed over the requisite amount, what course was usually adopted by persons whose musical desires might be limited to a single concert a night? I also remember that the answer betrayed unevenness of temper on the part of the dispenser of tickets. From that moment I remained discreetly silent.

A long and narrow passage, dimly lighted, led to the concert-room. When I entered I thought it wise to assume the careless air of a habitual visitor. As a natural consequence, I exposed myself to ridicule by plunging down two or three unexpected steps near the door-way. Some rude men laughed, and I shrunk, abashed, into a convenient arm-chair.

It was an apartment of odd proportions—too large to be called a chamber, and too small to be called a hall. It had a very attenuated appearance, owing to the great excess of its length over its breadth. It was filled with men and boys, of generally loose deportment, odors of spirituous nature, and smoke. On the whole, the idea of sanctity did not seem to oppressively prevail, nor did the audience appear to be deeply impressed with the seriousness of the occasion. On the contrary, they were talkative, not to say turbulent. Some of them had evidently attained the uppermost ecstasy of imbibition. I noticed a universal tendency toward cocktails, so far as the surrounding adults were concerned; while the minors, as a rule, gave themselves up to a steady flow of lager beer. Cigars circulated freely, irrespective of age.

At one end of the room a stage was erected, and displayed a rural scene of peculiar qualities. There were sunflowers blossoming from trees with green trunks and blue leaves. There was a river which rose any where and flowed no where, and which was inhabited by one duck. There was a horse with a clump of bushes growing out of his back—apparently without incommoding him in the smallest degree, for he stood on two legs and sniffed the air proudly. Over the middle of the stage was painted, in gilded letters, the word "Excelsior," which was sufficiently appropriate, ample opportunity appearing on all sides for the carrying out of that ambitious sentiment. Down below stretched a row of weary foot-lights, principally used by the audience at large for the ignition of cigars. The other decorations of the room were pictures, abundantly disposed about, and not distinguished by reticence of design, and elaborate placards announcing future benefits of the favorites of the establishment.

Through pools redolent of tobacco, and among the intricacies of the loungers' legs, four or five young girls, bewildering in their amplitude of crinoline, threaded their brisk way. Their duty was to respond to bibulous calls, and to absorb as much small change as came within their reach. Occasionally they playfully varied the monotony of their occupation by innocent familiarities with congenial spirits among the audience. A gentleman who sat beside me had his hair twisted into complicated forms, and was otherwise manipulated several times during the evening by these sprightly damsels. It seemed to afford him extreme satisfaction, for on each repetition he invited his gentle tormentress to come down to the store next day and select for herself a new dress at his expense.

There was one young girl who carried around bouquets, vaguely hoping that, in the enthusiasm of inebriety, some liberal-minded patron of the arts might purchase a few, and fling them upon the stage; whence, of course, they would be immediately returned to her, to be again put through the same profitable process as soon as possible. This floral speculatress beamed with an approach to beauty which would have made her an object of interest had it not been for an incessant internal irritation of the nose, which demanded constant attention at the end of her finger. Pardon the relation of the nasal fact; I put it as delicately as I can.

Gathering together some fragments of conversation near at hand, I learned that the first concert of the evening was over, and that the second was about to begin. Not to be taken by surprise, I examined the programme. It was a pleasant document. The list of impending performers, in glorified big type, was calculated to excite anticipation. It was a cosmopolitan array. France, Germany, Italy, Ireland, and the land of the free and the home of the brave, were all represented. There was Miss Julia Jenkins, "the American *prima donna*," who led the list. Other names followed, variously swathed in swelling adjectives. There was Miss Fanny Farmer, "the queen of song;" and Miss Lizzie Schwöze, "the fascinating danseuse;" her sister Matilda, "the youthful prodigy;" Mademoiselle Leonora, "the Sylph of the South;" Signor Richards, "operatic vocalist;" and others lost to memory. The order of entertainment involved a singular succession of sacred exercises, among which Ethiopian jigs and feats of juggling were prominent.

A bell tinkled, and the orchestra appeared. It consisted of a piano-forte and a violin. Another tinkle, and the concert opened.

The overture was a horn pipe.

The opening chorus was a jig for voices.

Then the "operatic vocalist" discoursed of the reallums of love beyond the sky. His appearance was stern and his manner intense. His general effect, particularly as regarding costume, was thrilling. There were stripes like snakes running all down the legs of his trowsers and up his coat-collar. He was given to gesticulation, and was encored for his energy. A gentleman who followed him, having studied the causes of the "operatic vocalist's" success, essayed imitation, but failed, by reason of having only one arm, which brought jeers upon him.

The "Sylph of the South" floated in through the foggy atmosphere, and was welcomed with personal and highly-colored compliments. She bore with her the American flag on a sharp stick, which she stuck into the middle of the stage, and ambulated around it. She curtsied to it, and she folded it in her arms, and wreathed herself sinuously all over it. The she skipped away a little distance, and pointed her toe at it. Then she suddenly lost sight of it, and gave symptoms of distress, and ran eagerly about, looking in obscure corners for it, shaking her head dismally the while. Finally she discovered it by the luckiest accident in the world, grasped it with delight, turned around five times, and ran off. It was quite a poem. The audience instantly drank up all its liquor, in order to pound an encore on the tables with the empty tumblers. Then the "Sylph of the South" did it all over again.

She was not personally alluring. She was shaggy as to hair, and physically deficient. Her stockings did flap like loose masts on a breezeless day. Her dancing, it struck me, was not provocative of delirium, but she was the "Sylph of the South," and she was honored.

A young man gave illustrations of the styles of Messrs. Forrest, Kean, Macready, and Anderson, and revealed the fact that nature, had, in the matter of voice and manner, endowed those imminent persons with precise similarity. Here the audience was critical and rebellious. The small boys first cackled, then exploded.

"Ain't he vocifurious?" said one.
"Give him some gin to get his voice up!" said another.
"Wake me up when he goes!" said a third.
"Ah, now, do soak up!" said a fourth.

Thus persecuted, the young man exerted himself, spoke feelingly to the "most noble Decembers of Rome"—looking at the small boys all the time—and entreated them not to "draw their daggers from their scaffolds." It was, however, unavailing, and the young man was obliged to retire, crushed.

The proceedings of the sacred concert were then suspended until an old gentleman who had succumbed to sundry cocktails could be got out. As his friends eliminated him, he called for a lamp-post, by which to keep himself erect, and grew very angry because it was not brought to him at once. In the excitement of this operation the stage-door was opened, and the "Sylph of the South" and the "queen of song" were seen sitting on stools, disheveled, their minds intent upon a mug of porter.

The concert then went on, with services more or less—generally less—sacred. The "American *prima donna*" sang. The "youthful prodigy" did some light fantastic, accompanying herself with castanets. A man with a black face exuded the "Essence of Old Virginny." Bangos twanged in dulcet tones. A light-handed professor tossed balls in the air, and balanced carving-knives on the end of his nose. And the crowd grew more tumultuous, more indulgent of their appetites, more fugacious, until it seemed as if a touch of Bedlam had set in.

Yet there was one relief—one jewel in the dung-hill—one flower wasting its sweetness.

The "American *prima donna*" could not sing a bit. Her tones came tumbling out promiscuous, disjointed. But such tones! Her voice sometimes rose towering "above the smoke and stir of that dull spot," and carried the soul with it as it soared. It was a marvel, and, more than all, a marvel to find it there. There, to be sure, it will fade and decay, and none shall know of it. To think that so bright a light should be hidden, as it is and ever will be! Ah! Miss Julia Jenkins, if fortune had been kinder you might have won a fame!

The concert and the clamor progressed together. Smoke gathered and settled about in almost impenetrable clouds. The hum of voices deadened the performances. The calls for liquid luxuries multiplied.

A woman entered and passed among the throng, laughing boisterously. Her face was flushed, her eye misty but not with emotion, her step insecure. By the men she was greeted with loud cordiality; the waiting-women, whose sense of decency was shocked, turned backs upon her. At this she flashed with wrath, and a scene was threatened. It was determined by some that she was an intruder; others, chivalrously inspired by potations, disputed this position. An argument ensued. The discussion waxed warm, and all present were drawn within its vortex. I concluded that I might with propriety withdraw.

The stars shone as I stepped into Broadway again. I might now saunter spotless.

Having experienced a sacred concert, I confess to some curiosity to know what a secular one would be, under the same management.

II. Sunday Evening in a Beer Garden

Along the sidewalks of the Bowery move multitudes of idlers. The crowd is oppressive, for it is Sunday night; and Germany, knowing no home delights, pours itself forth in social revelry. Mingle for a moment with the throng, and you can not easily extricate yourself. You are drawn irresistibly with its slow but unceasing current. Attempt to disentangle yourself, you are grievously jolted and jammed. Provoked to wrath, you plunge violently forward, and are stranded on a cellar door, or wrecked among the cobble-stones. Notwithstanding a sense of injury, you take, perhaps, a cheerful view of things, and endeavor to yield graciously to the inevitable vicissitudes of a Sunday evening ramble in the Bowery.

From shop windows partially illuminated a feeble light is cast around. As the throng passes you see that the German element predominates. The faces are much the same, heavy and stolid. The lethargic spirit of lager beer seems to have settled upon them. You are convinced that the only liveliness they know is that of hops. The dull regular murmur of voices is seldom broken, except when feminine shrillness indicates the crushing of a crinoline, or bewails the fracture of a bonnet. Beyond these there are few tokens of animation.

Toward 8 o'clock the tide reaches it height, and begins to drain off into the reservoirs on every side. These are the Beer Gardens—some large, some small, some rich, some rude, but all abundantly provided with the sweet restoring fluid, and with numberless appliances for mental relaxation and the free circulation of current coin.

You join the crowd again, and are straightway borne through a spacious door-way into a well-lighted passage, upon the walls of which you read the odd announcement—"Positively no liquors sold here on Sunday," which strikes you as laying it on with a thickness you would hardly have expected. A little farther on you are admonished that this the "Volk's Garten," and that you are to pay twelve cents for the double privilege of entrance and a double glass of beer after you get in. You receive your ticket and proceed.

Why, this is a show, indeed!

It is a large circular hall, the floor dotted with tables and benches, and all thickly filled—the benches with men, women, and children, the tables with various articles intended to afford internal comfort. A gallery, likewise occupied, is above. The seats are generally so arranged as to command fair view of the little stage erected at the rear, upon which a massive fräulein, scantily skirted, is bobbing vigorously to the music of a small orchestra close by. The music, which is good, does not atone for the dancing, which is vaccine. Over the theatre, which is a mere box, is stationed a brazen band, ready melodiously to blow the instant the performance beneath shall terminate. There, it is over; the fräulein squirms a parting salute and retires, while the solemn strains of the Champagne galop echo from above, and cover her retreat.

The "Volk's Garten" has claims to artistic consideration. The walls are decorated with luxurious landscapes, drawn from any number of quarters from the globe. The ceiling is scattered all over with figures of dancing women of every nationality. A rosy Santa Claus, with unbounded stomach, presides jubilantly from the arch of the theatre. There is a dashing balloon suspended by a rope from the centre of the "Garten," which every now and then descends to the ground in all the glory of gold foil and red stripes and waving banners glistening in the gaslight, for no ostensible purpose, after accomplishing which it forthwith rises again. But the artistic taste is more directly cultivated than by displays of gaudy coloring and twisted female forms. There are little doors everywhere leading off to more distinguished exhibitions. At one of these two small boys in Turkish jackets, and with pasteboard flower-pots on their heads, unlike cherabim continually do cry, "Now gentleman is your chance to see the most wonderful exhibition in the world—only ten cents; step right in, nothing you ever saw like it," and so forth. You are impelled by curiosity, and seize a programme. Mysterious announcements of "optic plastics" appear. Closer examination shows you that it is, after all, a lottery, to receive the prizes of which each purchaser of a ticket will have a chance. Of course there is no resisting this, and your ten cents are unhesitatingly bestowed. You glance at the exhibition, and find a collection of stereoscopes, prominent among which is the Emperor Napoleon from a German point of view, as large as life and twice as blood-thirsty, and with a particular sharpness to the waxed ends of his mustache. After this you will be very likely to turn your attention elsewhere.

Against the wall are little stalls erected in convenient spaces. In one stands a courteous gentleman, who offers you dice, and points to a placard which tells you that you may throw for twenty-five cents, and that every throw wins, but fails to entice you, as you have observed that the winnings are apt to be of a cumbersome character, like huge vases, or camp-stools, or deal tables, which you would find difficulty in carrying about with you for any length of time. In another stall, a complicated machine similar to a roulette table both in purpose and appearance, is operated, no doubt with industry and skill. In another, confectionery is sold; in another, flowers—that is to say, flowers would be, only nobody buys.

Open doors lead to scenes of more active occupation—to the billiard-room, to the bowling-alley, to the shooting-gallery, where two shots for three cents are permitted, with guns from which the bullets are propelled by strong springs instead of powder, and to the oyster-room, whither corpulent Herren repair, after much absorption of beer, to try testaceous experiments to the extent of two or three dozen. You fancy you see a sort of humorous twinkle in the eyes of those who eat, as if touched with mirth at the idea of introducing the unsuspecting bivalves to a fluid so different from that in which they have been reared, and you picture in your mind the probable astonishment of the oysters themselves upon their immersion in the bubbling beer.

But the crowd swells, individually and collectively, so that your progress is impeded. You ooze out from it, and by a lucky chance catch a vacant seat just left by a stout citizen, who, distended by many draughts, seeks to restore his faculties by locomotion. Beside you, now, sits a placid mother, quaffing the produce of the brewery, while an infant in her arms essays natural nourishment from a less artificial source. Other children rest their tired little heads upon her shoulder and that of the father. They have been well pleased all along, but by nine o'clock their capacity is exhausted. Opposite are some rugged fellows, who, after intense and prolonged study of the wine placards on the walls, call for their favorite schoppins, and give the whole of their minds to them.

All around are men and women, variously attired and variously enjoying themselves. The supply of beer is prodigious. This beverage seems to satisfy the popular demand. Eccentric tastes there are, however, that seek a wider range of gratification. Here and there tall cylindrical vessels, containing a kind of white beer, to the amount of more than a quart, tower above the ordinary glasses like steeples above the city house-tops. You get a notion that anxious mothers hold their children closer when these draw near, inspired by a natural fear that the innocents may fall in and get drowned, and be thus unhappily brought to an untimely bier. Then there are schoppins of sparkling wine, which claim affectionate attention from a respectable minority. For the children there are ice-creams on hand, but seldom brought into requisition. Cakes and confectionery are made more frequent use of, and are considered not wholly unworthy of parental consideration.

You do not see much evidence of deep delight. There is little excitement of any kind. The nearest approach to it is furnished by a flushed young Teuton at an adjoining table, who is earnest in his devotion to a pretty American girl who sits next to him. There is vacancy in his face and fullness in his tongue. His English is not only broken—it is also mixed. He utters eloquent endearments to his sweet heart, who does not like to repel them, although she would prefer to listen under other circumstances. Occasionally he leaves off to take alternate puffs at his cigar and his beer; sometimes, moreover, losing distinction in his joys to that degree that he puffs out the beer and swallows the smoke. When his attention is in this way distracted, the young girl urges departure upon him, but he repudiates the proposal with scorn, and orders more beer.

People laugh at him, and he laughs too; and then asks the young woman in a stage whisper what the joke is. She seems hurt; and observing that she is troubled, he conceives the notion that someone has inflicted an annoyance upon her, and beseeches her to designate the offender, that he may "smash" him. She endeavors to remove the suspicion, but he is not to be convinced, and glares around, muttering vague allusions to his physical capabilities. By way of manifesting unconcern he subsequently turns his thoughts to the stage, where a portly man is singing bassly of the lady of his love, and asks the young woman which of the two vocalists she prefers. On second examination he says three. When the massive fräulein beforementioned glides into view again, he follows her sprightly movements not only with his eyes but with his whole head. At the next performance of the band, too, he nods out of time, and makes futile and very ludicrous attempts to whistle an obligato. Then he frowns, as if to signify that the band is going all wrong; and lifting his beer in the direction of his mouth, pours some of it down the side of his neck—after which he looks fiercer than ever.

Presently his eye rests upon a sign which "requests the audience not to stand on chairs and tables." He becomes intent. He ponders. He leans back and surveys the sign with increasing interest. A while he doubts; but pretty soon he appears to have come to a decision. He drops his hand upon the table and says, "Why not?" Then he illustrates the perverseness of human nature by determining to defy that sign. He declares that nothing shall prevent him from mounting both chair and table. The young girl's remonstrances avail nothing. He rises, by slow degrees, to his feet. He puts his foot many times through the air, and at length proceeds in planting it infirmly on the bench. He chuckles with a proud consciousness of daring and triumph, and then rolls down among a number of legs. Hereupon he is induced to withdraw; and his companion, crying noiselessly, follows in sorrow, not in anger.

It is past ten o'clock. The band discourses with undiminished energy; the smoke from hundreds of pipes and cigars is spreading; the beer continues its downward flow. Thus eyes, ears, and mouths are filled. The crowd expands each minute. It is a little confusing. You find, by inquiring, that the services are not intended to close before midnight, and you venture to believe that you have had enough. You spend some uncomfortable minutes working your way out. The knots of people everywhere obstruct you. In some places the knots are rather tight, but patience and persistence eventually bring you forth. You are in the Bowery again, and again in a resistless tide of humanity you permit yourself to float up town.

On the whole, you are not enamored of the Beer Garden.

SUNDAY EVENING IN A BEER GARDEN

WILLIAM L. SLOUT

27. THE ROOF-GARDENS OF NEW YORK

by Vance Thompson
COSMOPOLITAN, SEPTEMBER, 1899

It was ten years ago that a theatrical manager—happy man!—invented a new amusement. He was a little like Xerxes, who offered a great prize for the invention of a new pleasure—and won it himself. Up above the domes and Moorish towers of the New York Casino this manager built a garden. There were chairs and tables; there were swaying lanterns and spindling palm-trees; and notably, there was a little stage, where an orchestra played waltzes and where, now and then, shrill girls sang comic songs. The performance was not very artistic, and it had more than the due measure of dullness. The main thing was that there was a delightful sense of novelty in taking one's pleasure—even sadly—on a roof. Not since Babylon had there been gardens in the air. There was something uncanny and delicious in lolling in the upper air—far above the grinding tumult of the city, and its summer heat—and being sung to and danced at, even though it were by tenth-rate entertainers. The newness of the venture insured its success, for New Yorkers have a more than Athenian fondness for new things. Today there are a half-dozen roof-gardens in New York, and every summer night ten thousand people take their pleasure there. Of course, in a decade many things have come to pass. The mild little performances of the oldtime Casino have given way to huge spectacles and brilliant and accomplished vaudeville. The roof-gardens, too, have grown in size and luxury. But the germ of them all was in that first aërial concert—when the band played Waldteufel waltzes and a shrill girl sang a De Koven ballad.

In these days, when the inventors of such trivial matters as liquefied hydrogen and wireless telegraphy are being laureled, some conspicuous honor should be found for the inventor of this new pleasure—the roof-garden.

The second of these gardens was built on the roof of the Madison Square Garden, beneath the slim, gilt Diana. Orchestral concerts, with a slight infusion of vaudeville, were given. The first distinct advantage along the lines that the roof-garden entertainment has since followed, was made at Koster & Bial's. Little by little the "concert features"—to use the theatrical slang—were crowded out and the performance became pure vaudeville. It was not until four years ago, however, that the roof-gardens became popular and—this is quite as important—came to be looked upon as respectable. Almost everyone can remember when the American music-hall was considered not quite the proper thing. Adventurous visitors to London and Paris would go to the music-halls (with such a pretty air of daring!), but few of them had the courage to explore the irregular theatres of New York. There was never any especial reason why the "best people" should not have gone to Koster & Bial's or Hammerstein's; it was simply one of Mrs. Grundy's vague, but determined, prejudices. Of course, there was the tobacco-smoke, and that was unpleasant; and there was a Bohemian air about the beer-mugs; but the performances were usually perfectly respectable. The credit for removing this prejudice should be given to the roof-gardens. In the open air, under the stars, tobacco-smoke is no great evil; even the glasses of beer look less lawless. And Mrs. Grundy, having once inspected these horrid vaudeville performances, found in reality they were quite harmless, very merry and enjoyable. Moreover, this good lady's presence made them all the better. The art is better, the morals are better, and there is a decided improvement in good taste. And this I think should be accounted to Mrs. Grundy for a sort of righteousness.

I do not wish to idealize this flippant—Doctor Johnson would have called it fissiparous—form of entertainment. Its best quality is its honest gaiety. Clowns, tumblers, dancers, trained dogs, and jugglers of the white magic—here there is good honest mirth; and if the songs are silly, they make no pretense of being anything else; they do not aspire to be literature. In fact, the aim of the aërial is to give one careless, harmless mood in which

> From tavern to tavern
> One saunters along,
> With an armful of girl
> And a heartful of song.

And to attain this mood—it is Mr. Le Gallienne's—is profitable now and then, at all events. After all, it is an instrument of happiness.

The six great roof-gardens of New York differ only in kind. In some there is a greater pretense of magnificence. In others there is more homeliness. One and all are broad-arrowed, however, with a sort of well-bred Bohemianism. The elevator that carries you to the roof, lifts you out of your smug, citified habits of thought. Perhaps in summer the only "spectacle" for honest people is that of nature. But there is a good deal of nature on a roof-garden. The trees have a fine look of being absolutely real. It requires only a little imagination to take the palms seriously. And always there are the stars. The crowd, of which you are one, is gipsily inclined. Men and women go wandering about, or loll at the small tables. On the stage, of which you can catch a glimpse through the tree-tops, a big blonde woman in white satin is singing a "coon song." The audience is mildly pleased. Over the clink of the ice in the glasses and the clatter of the beer-mugs, you hear a little ripple of applause. The chanteuse beams her gratitude and bursts with astonishing vehemence into the chorus:

> I'm happy when I'm by ma baby's side,
> She's the onliest one in all dis world I idolize
> I know she loves me true;
> I loves ma baby, 'deed I do,
> I'm happy when I'm by ma baby's side.

The audience storms its approval and you—if you are a cynical person—feel a touch of compassion for this poor humanity which can be so easily amused. The old songs were better, you suggest? I am not quite sure of that. In the first place, only the best of the old songs have come down to us. When those of today are winnowed by the years, a great many really good popular songs may be found. And again, these negro lilts and ragtime ballads are both new and native, and contain—I like to think—the seeds of the American music that is to be someday. "Ma Rag-time Girl" is as original, in its way, as the Hungarian czardas, and may quite as well serve as the foundation of a new school of national music.

The curtain falls for a few moments; over in one corner, under the dwarf palms, is a band of Neapolitan troubadors; while they are playing, it is proper enough, and pleasant, to lean over the parapet of the roof and stare down at the city.

The streets are like cañons of brick and steel. Mile after mile they stretch away with pin-points of twinkling light. You can almost see the rivers of hot air, flowing to and fro. The noise of the city comes up to you harmonized, as it were, into one iron chord—the grim musical symbol of New York. It is nearly midnight, but the streets are thronged with little black figures of men and women sauntering. When a few thousand idlers flit away to mountain or sea-shore, it is fashionable to speak of the town as "empty." But the population of New York is the same day in and day out. The country sends as many as it takes. Summer-night audiences are very cosmopolitan. They do not have the exact look of New Yorkers. Few, with the exception of the waiters, wear evening clothes. There is a surburban air about these men in caps and straw hats and these girls in shirt-waists. And all these foreigners—otiose Germans from the far East side, Italians from Harlem and the lands nearby, the flotsam of the Broadway hotels—make up a very cosmopolitan audience. And to please them (there can be no other reason) the performance is quite as international. The curtain goes up—this time on three clowning sisters from a Berlin "Wintergarten"; they are followed by a Senegambian comedian, a Spanish dancer and an Italian contortionist. It is a spectacular lesson in geography. A tramp stumbles on the stage—grotesque in his rags. His elementary pleasantries, his grimaces and contortions, are very cheap; you know they are cheap; and yet when he draws a lighted match from his trousers pocket, you laugh consumedly. It is a test of your fitness for a roof-garden. Unless you can laugh at that ragged buffoon when he attempts to sit down where there is no chair, you are far too complicated and superior a person for the simple joys of roof-gardening. This is no place for subtlety. Wit and epigram wilt in hot weather. There were two Dutch comedians who held a long conversation after the manner of their kind.

"Undt why," asked the jolly one, "vas you alwayss say de same ting?"

"Because it alwayss ist de same ting," said the melancholy one, with subtle, far-seeing philosophy.

That is the sort of remark that one likes to take home and nibble at in the lonely hours, but the roof-garden audience did not "give it a hand"—to adopt the stage-phrase. What the audience really liked were the "dumb acts"—that is, the acrobats, the trained animals, the dancing and the pantomime. Now and then a patriotic song—the waving of flag and some impossible heroic rhyme for Funston—woke an unusual enthusiasm. A ballad of home and mother, sincere in spite of its maudlin tone, fitted the taste of the audience like a glove. But the clou of every performance was either a globe-balancer, a trained dog, a contortionist or the white Pierrot. It seems to me that it is a good sign that the facile and estival gayety of the roof-gardens should content itself with so little. Always it is a good sign when people amuse themselves simply. The good M. Renan was of this way of thinking. His chief ambition was to be able to derive esthetic satisfaction from the spectacle of a man balancing a plate on his nose.

The pantomime at the Aërial Magnolia Grove—the pompous and rather absurd name of the roof-garden on the New York Theater—was more in the nature of a ballet than it should have been. Still, it had the saving grace of simplicity. It was "after the ball." Within, the dancers are going to and fro, but Pierrot, white and gloomy, sits on the doorsteps, musing. This little figure in the grostesque blouse—with its oblong moon of a head and white, tragic mask of a face—is the oldest of all the theatrical effigies. It has come all the way from Greek tragedy. That floured face—it is a relic of the bronze mask of Orestes and the terra-cotta mask of Agamemnon. He mimed for Nero, this little white mute, translating into eloquent gestures the loves and heroisms of Rome; and here he sits in Broadway—ancient as the stars, modern as the garlands of electric lights—the eternal stage-type of humanity. The guests come joyously from the ball. They are whirling harlequins and columbines. Pierrot dances with them, for he is natural, merry and gay; and then when the dancers flutter away and the lights in the ball-room die out, he sinks down on the door-step again and covers his head—this white horror of a head!—with his sleeve. That is all. But to the serious-minded roof-gardener it is the "tragedy of man."

Pierrot passes—though without Pippa's fatuous optimism. A little man, all spangles and grace and mirth, comes rolling across the stage on a huge globe. It is difficult and you do not wish it impossible. An "eccentric" girl twists herself into a barrel and out again. She does it with the liveliest air of satisfaction. She smiles blithely, as one who would say, "There is no pleasure comparable with contorting oneself in a barrel!" The audience, indolently pleased, seems to agree with her. And it does look pleasant—if there does not come to you unbidden a picture of a dingy girl in a garret, laboriously learning how to twist herself into a barrel and out again.

And that little spangled man on the globe! Think of his months of absurd tottering—his falls and bruises—his empty grimaces, somewhere in a garret—before he was ripe for the floodlights. I dare say it is unthrifty to look at the wrong side of the canvas, but I never see one of these spangled things capering by the floodlights without seeing as well the hot garret, where he toiled and tumbled and did not smile. A performance—even a "dumb act"—is always a battle, waged against the public. There is something heroic in it, too—one against a thousand—and one's only weapon a balancing globe or a neglible plate to spin on one's nose. A battle of this sort has all the picturesque disparity of little David's duel.

There is a Japanese girl whose way of life is to mount, barefooted, a ladder the steps of which are Japanese swords. The interest of the act lies, of course, in the chance that she may make a false step—may linger a second too long on one of the sharp stairs—and cut her feet. Perhaps I have very little footlight courage; but to me this young woman comes with something of the wonder of a miracle. Almost any man might find it in him to go up San Juan hill. But to go up that ladder of swords! That, it seems to me, is a more desperate sort of courage.

I wonder how she was persuaded to mount that ladder the first time. Was it only ambition that urged her on?

The roof-gardens differ in kind and this is quite as true of the audiences. The American Roof-garden, for instance, has its own patrons. They come from what Mr. Hamlin Garland would call the "middle-west" of New York. There are certain adventurers from Broadway, who have discovered that through the yellow arches of this roof-garden there is to be had a wonderful view—the cliffs and crags of the iron city, the North river with its fleets, and the thin lights of the Jersey shore—but in the main the audience is made up of those who speak of Eighth avenue as "The Av'noo." They are distinctively—defiantly—"Noo Yorkers." The program humors their prejudices and cultivates their animosities. It is here, for instance, that you will hear the latest topical song. The actuality is shot as it flies. If Mr. Croker's horse wins a race; if some political warrior makes a speech; if there is a strike or an election, the swift song-maker has it down in immediate jingle. In fact, the American Roof-garden lives up to its name. It is conducted on the Aristophanic principle that "No country's mirth is better than our own." It is to this roof-garden that the inquiring foreigner should give his nights. As far as Hammerstein's is concerned, one might as well be at Ronacher's in Vienna or the Wintergarten in Berlin. There is nothing American about it, not even the name. Nor, in spite of its name, is it "Venetian." It is essentially cosmopolitan. Its audience has the peculiar

Broadway look. The men have a fashionable, well-bred look; you know them at once; they are the kind of men who are born at thirty-five with high collars and two ounces of brain. It is the idler type in which New York is growing richer day by day. The performance is broadly international. This chanteuse has trailed her life across a background of Europe and Wall street; a stout, riotous old woman, she sings, "coon" songs for the delight of faded Broadway idlers. It is pathetic or it is absurd, just as you please. But was it at Hammerstein's that I saw her? Perhaps it was at the New York, across the way. It makes no difference. These two roof-gardens are very much alike. Their appeal is to the cosmopolitan intelligence, to the international mind. The trained dogs of these roof-gardens obey orders in French and Italian. And this, I take it, is the climax of the urban.

The Casino, again, has its individual audience. It has, too, its own songs; its own Pierrot, winsome and French; its own peculiar kind of humor. The jokes that snap and flutter across the footlights are of the Broadway sort. In England there is the sort of entertainment that is known as Gaiety-Girlism. It is not easy to describe. It is not quite vaudeville, and it is not quite burlesque. While it abounds in literary parody and burlesques life with a fine ironic sense, it is never very far from the simple tom-foolery of the music-hall. The Casino naturalized this style of entertainment. It translated the Gaiety Girl into the Girl of New York. A little of this roguish wit—of this flamboyant "girlism"—has mounted to the roof-garden among the Moorish domes. Spending an evening there is like reading Brantôme—you feel as though you were walking through an avenue of swishing silken skirts.

Music still holds its own on the skyey esplanades of the Madison Square Garden Roof-garden—music joyously complicated with dancing pickaninnies. Throwing pennies at little darkies capering on the stage, is New York's latest dissipation. It is an amusement like any other. Indeed, it is preferable in its way to the melodies jangled out by sleigh-bells, and the tunes tortured from "musical ladders" and by "musical pavers." ("I have a reasonable good ear for music," said Nick Bottom, "let us have tongs and bones.")

Enfin, you may go wayfaring from roof-garden to roof-garden and find exactly what you please.

There is a confusion of amusement—Barthemy Fair and Drury Lane rolled into one. Almost everything that has ever amused mankind is tried once more up here between the street-lamps and the stars. You may see a descendant of the trick horse that diverted Doctor Johnson; the dwarfs that Fielding showed at Smithfield are still capering; as of old, there are dancing-girls and slim, unhappy contortionists; the old jokes still arrow across the footlights. As the melancholy Dutch comedian said, it always is the same thing.

A few years ago there was a theory—for which Mr. Howells contended—that out of all this music-hall confusion there was to come the American drama. It was assumed that the variety stage was the matrix of all that is new, native and original in the drama. "Ned" Harrigan's simple clowneries and dialect drolleries were proclaimed from the housetops. In them were discerned the germs of the long-expected American drama. Mr. Howells was not the only one who was cheated by this chimera. It seemed very plausible. Then the bubble burst. We discovered that Mr. Harrigan was not a new Aristophanes. We learned that no great drama has ever come up out of the variety halls. Over in London they made the same mistake and learned the same lesson. If we are to get a racial drama in this country, it will come—as it always has—from above and not from below; it will be the creation of the cultured, observing, cerebral man, and not of the painted girl or the stage tramp. The standard has been perceptibly raised. There is still a great deal of what must seem folly to the wise. And—though vulgarity is not always an unmitigated evil—there is an undue quantity of vulgarity. Yet on the whole, the roof-garden shows are innocent and merry. They appeal to the primitive sense of humor, and to a rather imperfectly developed artistic sense. The worse that can be said of them is that they grant too much to the Broadway idler, who is weak as flesh, "if not weaker"—like the wooden leg of the gentleman in "Martin Chuzzlewit." This aside, there is no great harm in them. And in these four-walled days it is a distinct advantage to be able to take one's pleasure under the stars.

28. THE VAUDEVILLE THEATRE

by Edwin Milton Royle
SCRIBNER'S MAGAZINE, OCTOBER, 1899

The Vaudeville Theatre is an American invention. There is nothing like it anywhere else in the world. It is neither the Café Chantant, the English music-hall, nor the German garden. What has been called by a variety of names, but has remained always and everywhere pretty much the same—reeky with smoke, damp with libations, gay with the informalities of the half-world—is now doing business with us under the patronage of the royal American family.

Having expurgated and rehabilitated the tawdry thing, the American invites in the family and neighbors, hands over to them beautiful theatres, lavishly decorated and appointed, nails up everywhere church and army regulations, and in the exuberance of his gayety passes around ice-water. He hasn't painted out the French name, but that is because he has been as usual, in a hurry. Fourteen years ago this may have been a dream in a Yankee's brain; now it is a part of us. The strictly professional world has been looking for the balloon to come down, for the fad to die out, for the impossible thing to stop, but year by year these theatres increase and multiply, till now they flourish the country over.

Sometimes the vaudeville theatre is an individual and independent enterprise; more often it belongs to a circuit. The patronage, expenses, and receipts are enormous. One circuit will speak for all. It has a theatre in New York, one in Philadelphia, one in Boston, and one in Providence, and they give no Sunday performances; and yet these four theatres entertain over 5,000,000 people every year, give employment of 350 attachés and to 3,500 actors. Four thousand people pass in and out of each one of these theatres daily. Ten thousand dollars are distributed each week in salaries to the actors and $3,500 to the attachés. Take one theatre for example, the house in Boston. It is open the year round and it costs $7,000 a week to keep it open, while its patrons will average 25,000 every week. On a holiday it will play to from ten to twelve thousand people. How is it possible?

A holiday to an American is a serious affair so the doors of the theatre are open and the performance begins when most people are eating breakfast; 9:30 A.M. is not too soon for the man who pursues pleasure with the same intensity he puts into business. There are no reserved seats, so one must come first to be first served. One may go in at 9:30 A.M. and stay until 10:30 at night. If he leaves his seat, though, the nearest standing Socialist drops into it and he must wait for a vacancy in order to sit down again.

Not over two percent of an audience remains longer than to see the performance through once, but there are persons who secrete campaign rations about them, and camp there from 9:30 A.M. to 10:30 P.M., thereby surviving all of the acts twice and most of them four or five times. The management calculate to sell out the house two and a half times on ordinary days and four times on holidays, and it is this system that makes such enormous receipts possible. Of course, I have taken the circuit which is representative of the vaudeville idea at its best, but it is not alone in its standards or success, and what I have said about the houses in New

York, Boston, and Philadelphia applies more or less to all the principal cities of the country, and in a less degree, of course, to the houses in the smaller cities.

Some of these theatres are never closed the year round. Some are content with three matinees a week in addition to their night performances. Others open their doors about noon and close them at 10:30 at night. These are called "continuous" houses. It is manifest, I think, that the vaudeville theatre is playing an important part in the amusement world and in our national life. Perhaps we should be grateful. At present it would seem that the moral tone of a theatre is in the inverse ratio of the price of admission. The higher the price, the lower the tone. It is certain that plays are tolerated and even acclaimed on the New York stage today which would have been removed with tongs half a dozen years ago.

On the eighteenth day of last April, the member of Parliament for Flintshire made a formal query in the House of Commons in relation to the drama, asking "if the Government will, in view of the depraving nature of several plays now on the stage, consider the advisability of controlling theatres by licenses." The honorable member appeared to think one censor in the person of the Lord Chamberlain not enough for the growing necessities of London. As we are no longer manufacturers but importers of plays, and largely by way of London, it is not strange that there should be some talk here of a legal censorship for our playhouses.

So far as the vaudeville theatres are concerned, one might as well ask for a censorship of a "family magazine." It would be a work of supererogation. The local manager of every vaudeville house is its censor, and he lives up to his position laboriously and, I may say, religiously. The bill changes usually from week to week. It is the solemn duty of this austere personage to sit through the first performance of every week and to let no guilty word or look escape. But this is precautionary only.

"You are to distinctly understand," say the first words of the contracts of a certain circuit, "that the manager conducts this house upon a high plane of respectability and moral cleanliness," etc.

But long before the performer has entered the dressing-rooms, he has been made acquainted with the following legend which everywhere adorns the walls:

NOTICE TO PERFORMERS

YOU ARE HEREBY WARNED THAT YOUR ACT MUST BE FREE FROM ALL VULGARITY AND SUGGESTIVENESS IN WORDS, ACTIONS, AND COSTUME, WHILE PLAYING IN ANY OF MR. ------'S HOUSES, AND ALL VULGAR, DOUBLE-MEANING AND PROFANE WORDS AND SONGS MUST BE CUT OUT OF YOUR ACT BEFORE THE FIRST PERFORMANCE. IF YOU ARE IN DOUBT AS TO WHAT IS RIGHT OR WRONG, SUBMIT IT TO THE RESIDENT MANAGER AT REHEARSAL.

SUCH WORDS AS LIAR, SLOB, SON-OF-A-GUN, DEVIL, SUCKER, DAMN, AND ALL OTHER WORDS UNFIT FOR THE EARS OF LADIES AND CHILDREN, ALSO ANY REFERENCE TO QUESTIONABLE STREETS, RESORTS, LOCALITIES, AND BARROOMS, ARE PROHIBITED UNDER FINE OF INSTANT DISCHARGE.

_____, GENERAL MANAGER

And this is not merely a literary effort on the part of the management; it is obligatory and final. When we have accepted as conclusive the time-honored theory that "You must give the public what it wants," and that it *wants* bilge-water in champagne glasses, we are confronted with the vaudeville theatre, no longer an experiment, but a comprehensive fact.

The funniest farce ever written could not be done at these houses if it had any of the ear-marks of the thing in vogue at many of our first-class theatres. Said a lady to me: "They [the vaudeville theatres] are the only theatres in New York where I should feel absolutely safe in taking a young girl without making preliminary inquiries. Though they may offend the taste, they never offend one's sense of decency." The vaudeville theatres may be said to have established the commercial value of decency. This is their corner-stone. They were conceived with the object of catering to ladies and children, and, strange to say, a large, if not larger, part of their audiences is always men.

What I have said does not describe all theatres which may have "fashionable vaudeville" over their doors. Godliness has proved so profitable that there be here, as elsewhere, wolves masquerading in woollens, but the houses I have described are well known. Nor have the stringent regulations of these theatres exiled the "song-and-dance man," who was wont to rely on risqué songs and suggestive jokes—they have only forced him to happier and saner efforts, and the result is not Calvinistic; on the contrary, nowhere are audiences jollier, quicker, and more intelligent, and the world of fashion is not absent from these theatres primarily designed for the wholesome middle classes.

I never for a moment suspected that these admirable regulations could be meant for me, or that indeed I was in need of rules and regulations, but my self-righteousness, as was meet, met with discipline. I had a line in my little farce to this effect: "I'll have the devil's own time explaining," etc. I had become so familiar with the devil that I was not even aware of his presence, but the management unmasked me and I received a polite request (which was a command) to cast out the devil. I finally got used to substituting the word "dickens." Later on, the local manager, a big handsome man, faultlessly attired, in person begged me "to soften the asperities." Need I add that this occurred in Boston? When I travel again I shall leave my asperities at home.

A friend of my was leaving a spacious vaudeville theatre, along with the audience, and was passing through the beautiful corridor, when one of the multitude of uniformed attachés handed him this printed notice:

GENTLEMEN WILL KINDLY AVOID CARRYING CIGARS OR CIGARETTES IN THEIR MOUTHS WHILE IN THE BUILDING, AND GREATLY OBLIGE
THE MANAGEMENT.

My friend was guilty of carrying in his hand an unlighted cigar.

How careful of the conduct of their patrons the management is may be noted from the following printed requests with which the employees are armed:

GENTLEMEN WILL KINDLY AVOID THE STAMPING OF FEET AND POUNDING OF CANES ON THE FLOOR, AND GREATLY OBLIGE THE MANAGEMENT. ALL APPLAUSE IS BEST SHOWN BY CLAPPING OF HANDS.
PLEASE DON'T TALK DURING ACTS, AS IT ANNOYS THOSE ABOUT YOU, AND PREVENTS A PERFECT HEARING OF THE ENTERTAINMENT.
THE MANAGEMENT.

Popular Amusements in Horse and Buggy America

When we were playing in Philadelphia, a young woman was singing with what is known as the "song sheet," at the same theatre with us. Her costume consisted of silk stockings, knee-breeches and a velvet coat—the regulation page's dress, decorous enough to the unsanctified eye; but one day the proprietor himself happened in unexpectedly (as is his wont) and the order quick and stern went forth that the young woman was not to appear again except in skirts—her street-clothes, if she had nothing else and street-clothes it came about.

These are the chronicles of what is known among the vaudeville fraternity as "The Sunday-school Circuit," and the proprietor of "The Sunday-school Circuit" is the inventor of vaudeville as we know it. This which makes for righteousness, as is usual, makes also for great and abiding cleanliness—physical as well as moral. I almost lost things in my Philadelphia dressing-room—it was cleaned so constantly. Paternal, austere perhaps, but clean, gloriously clean!

The character of the entertainment is always the same. There is a sameness about its infinite variety. No act or "turn" consumes much over thirty minutes. Everyone's taste is consulted, and if one objects to the perilous feats of the acrobats or jugglers he can read his programme or shut his eyes for a few moments and he will be compensated by some sweet bell-ringing or a sentimental or comic song, graceful or grotesque dancing, a one-act farce, trained animals, legerdemain, impersonations, clay modelling, the biograph pictures, or the stories of the comic monologuist. The most serious thing about the programme is that seriousness is barred, with some melancholy results. From the artist who balances a set of parlor furniture on his nose to the academic baboon, there is one concentrated, strenuous struggle for a laugh. No artist can afford to do without it. It hangs like a solemn and awful obligation over everything. Once in while an artist who juggles tubs on his feet is a comedian, but not always. It would seem as if a serious person would be a relief now and then. But so far the effort to introduce a serious note, even by dramatic artists, has been discouraged. I suspect the serious sketches have not been of superlative merit. Though this premium is put upon a laugh, everyone is aware of the difference between a man who rings a bell at forty paces with a rifle, and the man who smashes it with a club, and the loudest laugh is sometimes yoked with a timid salary. The man who said: "Let me get out of here or I'll lose my self-respect—I actually laughed," goes to the vaudeville theatres, too, and must be reckoned with.

So far as the character of the entertainment goes, vaudeville has the "open door." Whatever or whoever can interest an audience for thirty minutes or less, and has passed quarantine, is welcome. The conditions in regular theatres are not encouraging to progress. To produce a play or launch a star requires capital of from $10,000 upward. There is no welcome and no encouragement. The door is shut and locked. And even with capital, the conditions are all unfavorable to proof. But if you can sing or dance or amuse people in any way; if you think you can write a one-act play, the vaudeville theatre will give you a chance to prove it. One day of every week is devoted to these trials. If at this trial you interest a man who is looking for good material, he will put you in the bill for one performance, and give you a chance at an audience, which is much better. The result of this open-door attitude is a very interesting innovation in vaudeville which is more or less recent, but seems destined to last—the incursion of the dramatic artist into vaudeville.

The Managers of the vaudeville theatres are not emotional persons, and there were some strictly business reasons back of the actor's entrance into vaudeville. We do not live by bread alone, but by the saving graces of the art of advertising. It was quite impossible to accentuate sixteen or eighteen features of a bill. Some one name was needed to give it character and meaning at a glance. A name that had already become familiar was preferred. The actor's name was used to head the bill and expand the type and catch the eye, and hence arose the vaudeville term—"HEAD-LINER."

This word is not used in contracts, but it is established and understood, and carries with it well-recognized rights and privileges, such as being featured in the advertisements, use of the star dressing-room, and the favorite place on the bill; for it is not conducive to one's happiness or success to appear during the hours favored by the public for coming in or going out. The manager was not the loser, for many people who had never been inside a vaudeville theatre were attracted thither by the name of some well-known and favorite actor, and became permanent patrons of these houses.

At first the actor, who is sentimental rather than practical, was inclined to the belief that it was beneath his dignity to appear on the stage with "a lot of freaks," but he was tempted by salaries no one else could afford to pay (sometimes as high as $500 to $1,000 per week) and by the amount of attention afforded to the innovation by the newspapers. He was told that if he stepped from the sacred precincts of art, the door of the temple would be forever barred against him. The dignity of an artist is a serious thing, but the dignity of the dollar is also a serious thing. None of the dire suppositions happened. The door of the temple proved to be a swinging door, opening easily both ways, and the actor goes back and forth as there is a demand for him and as the dollar dictates. Indeed, the advertising secured by association with "a lot of freaks" oiled the door for the actor's return to the legitimate drama at an *increased salary*.

Manifestly, it has been a boon to the "legitimate" artist. To the actor who has starred; who has had the care of a large company, with its certain expenses and its uncertain receipts; who has, in addition, responsibility for his own performance and for the work of the individual members of his company and for the work of the company as a whole, vaudeville offers inducements not altogether measured in dollars and cents. He is rid not only of financial obligation, but of a thousand cares and details that twist and strain a nervous temperament. He hands over to the amiable manager the death of the widely mourned Mr. Smith, and prevalent social functions, Lent and the circus, private and public calamities, floods and railroad accidents, the blizzard of winter and the heat of summer, desolating drought and murderous rains, the crops, strikes and panics, wars and pestilences and opera. It is quite a bunch of thorns he hands over!

Time and terms are usually arranged by gents, who get five per cent of the actor's salary for their services. Time and terms arranged, the rest is easy. The actor provides himself and assistants and his play or vehicle. His income and outcome are fixed, and he knows at the start whether he is to be a capitalist at the end of the year; for he runs almost no risk of not getting his salary in the well-known circuits.

It is then incumbent on him to forward property and scene-plots, photographs and cast to the theater two weeks before he opens, and on arrival, he plays twenty to thirty minutes in the afternoon and the same at night. There his responsibility ends. It involves the trifling annoyance of dressing and making up twice a day. In and about New York the actor pays the railroad fares of himself and company, but when he goes West or South, the railroad fares (not including sleepers) are provided by the management.

The great circuit which covers the territory west of Chicago keeps an agent in New York and one in Chicago to facilitate the handling of their big interests. These gentlemen purchase tickets, arrange for sleepers, take care of baggage, and lubricate the wheels of progress from New York to San Francisco and back again.

The actor's only duty is to live up to the schedule made and provided....

...It cannot be denied that the vaudeville "turn" is an experience for the actor. The intense activity everywhere, orderly and systematic though it is, is confusing. The proximity to the "educated donkey," and some not so educated; the variegated and motley samples of all strange things in man and beast; the fact that the curtain never falls, and the huge machine never stops to take a breath until 10:30 at night; being associated after the style of criminals with a number, having your name or number shot into a slot in the proscenium arch to introduce you to your audience; the shortness of your reign, and the consequent necessity of capturing your audience on sight—all this, and some other things, make the first plunge unique in the actor's experience.

One comedian walks on and says, "Hello, audience!" and no further introduction is needed; for the audience is trained for the quick and sharp exigencies of the occasion, and neither slumbers nor sleeps.

One of the first things to surprise the actor in the "continuous" house is the absence of an orchestra. The orchestra's place is filled by pianists who labor industriously five hours a day each. As they practically live at the piano, their knowledge of current music and their adaptability and skill are often surprising, but they are the most universally abused men I have ever met. Everyone who comes off the stage Monday afternoon says of the pianist that he ruins their songs; he spoils their acts; he has sinister designs on their popularity, and he wishes to wreck their future. The pianist, on the other hand, says he doesn't mind his work—the five thumping, tyrannous hours—it is the excruciating agony of being compelled to sit through he effects of the imbecile beings on the stage. It is the point of view!

The Monday-afternoon bill is a tentative one, but thereafter one's position on the bill and the time of one's performance are fixed and mathematical for the remainder of the week. The principal artists appear only twice a day, once in the afternoon and once in the evening, but there is an undivided middle, composed of artists not so independent as some others; which "does three turns" a day (more on holidays), and forms what is picturesquely known as the "supper bill." The "supper bill" explains itself. It lasts from five o'clock, say, till eight or eight-thirty. Who the singular people are who do not eat, or who would rather see the undivided middle than eat, will always be a mystery to me. But if they were not in *esse*, and in the audience, the management would certainly never retain the "supper bill."

The man who arranges the programme has to have some of the qualities of a general. To fix eighteen or nineteen different acts into the exact time allotted, and so to arrange them that the performance shall never lapse or flag; to see that the "turns" which require only a front scene can be utilized to set the stage for the "turns" which require a full stage, requires judgment and training; but there is very little confusion even at the first performance, and none thereafter....

...It is manifest, I think, that vaudeville is very American. It touches us and our lives at many places. It appeals to the business man, tired and worn, who drops in for half an hour on his way home; to the person who has an hour or two before a train goes, or before a business appointment; to the woman who is weary of shopping; to the children who love animals and acrobats; to the man with his sweetheart or sister; to the individual who wants to be diverted but doesn't want to think or feel; to the American of all grades and kinds who wants a great deal for his money. The vaudeville theatre belongs to the era of the department store and short story. It may be a kind of lunch-counter art, but then art is so vague and lunch is so real.

And I think I may add that if anyone has anything exceptional in the way of art, the vaudeville door is not shut to that.

29. THE LIFE OF A VAUDEVILLE ARTISTE

by Norman Hapgood
COSMOPOLITAN, FEBRUARY, 1901

A famous American actress, now one of our most popular stars, was, a few years ago, in decided need of money. A vaudeville manager offered her eight thousand dollars to play eight weeks in his houses. She refused.

A famous American singer, for years one of the most popular attractions of light opera, last year went into vaudeville, and naturally was asked by the reporters how she liked it. "I don't mind," she said, in effect, "appearing between a cat circus and an aggregation of trained monkeys; since the animal artists are the best of their kind."

This was partly a difference between two individuals, but perhaps even more a change in the times. The lines between the legitimate and vaudeville have been shattered of late, owing mainly to that greatest of stimulants, money, but partly to improved surroundings in the vaudeville world, and to the introduction of the one-act play. The salaries paid to successful performers in music-halls and continuous houses are almost absurdly large compared with those paid most of our best-known stars and leading men and women. One woman was advertised by a circuit of continuous performance houses last year as receiving a larger salary than the President of the United States, and the statement was nearer the truth than are most theatrical announcements, in the making of which an abundant power to lie is a fundamental necessity. There was a report last season that Madame Modjeska intended to enter the continuous houses. She did not do it, but the possibility was taken seriously, and there was nothing absurd in it, as there would have been a few years earlier. It is coming to be something like the American tour of foreign actors, a respectable way of fattening a depleted bank account. Take the amount of money paid in a season to stars who are not dramatists or managers, and compare the average with the average of the salaries made by the leaders in vaudeville, and one of the charms of the inferior occupation would speedily become apparent. As "money talks," and as the managers of the vaudeville houses have proved that these big salaries pay them, as they could not pay "legitimate" managers, the flow of well-known actors from the dramatic stage to the continuous and music-hall stages is likely to increase. The drift the other way is less marked. The only cases, I think of at this minute are two, and the change probably meant a large pecuniary sacrifice in both cases. Yvette Guilbert has talked, off and on, for years, of making the change, just as opera singers, who can act, so often talk of going into drama, and so seldom do. The person who voluntarily goes from a big salary to a small one is, in the theatrical business, even more then elsewhere, a rarity.

It is often made a subject of comment that the morals of the stage have become more like those of ordinary respectable society. So they have, but the difference still remains wide between the average morals of the vaudeville or regular stage and those of wholesale grocers' wives, for instance. I notice that this is the truth usually exaggerated by pictures and cheap articles, and therefore presumably it is the fact in which the public is most interested. How the women on the vaudeville and the regular stage compare in this respect, it would not be easy to state with complete conviction. Thousands of chorus-girls are among the steadiest matrons in the world, talking at ballet rehearsals about how their daughters are getting on at school; and, on the other hand, thousands of chorus-girls are not. The subject might, perhaps, with fair safety, be summed up thus: the women in vaudeville differ more even than those on the regular stage.

A large part of the actresses on the regular stage are neither one thing nor the other. They are perfectly respectable and yet they lack all the best elements of domestic life. Their work absorbs them to such an extent that nothing else exists. They get what one who knows them well calls "actressitis." Nothing brings a real response of interest out of them but what touches their particular professional affairs. In the theater every night from seven to twelve, perhaps, or an hour less, and two afternoons a week, and rehearsing besides, they are exposed to this complete absorption in their work and limitation to one set of ideas, as women who work only an hour in the afternoon and an hour in the evening are not. Moreover, the vaudeville actress, usually doing her turn alone, does not, like her regular sister, have the daily chat with the company, in which each talks about her own affairs or those of her companions, who return the favor.

This is a salient element in the life of a vaudeville actress—the comparative lightness and freedom of her work. Not for her the sacrifices necessary in the existence of any woman, not of super-human strength, who wises to do powerful and progressive work in the drama. Take almost any one from among our best actresses and you will find her life one of almost pathetic abnegation and concentration. She goes to bed after the play—no late suppers for her. She gets up pretty late, and takes a rest every afternoon. She rides, walks, takes massage, uses all the devices of common sense to be in condition for her best efforts and to keep her youth. Especially at the first hints that youth is going does she cling to its preservers, of which the first is sleep. Your vaudeville "artiste" leads a far less enthralled life. For her there is none of the long, steady, serious labor, calling upon every faculty, in the development of her art. Her stock in trade is likely to be a little trick, incapable of much development, and not calling for any great study, or accumulation of energy, or for the best mental and physical state. It may be a piquant way of singing or dancing, or of delivering soft or ambiguous words, and even in the continuous it usually takes a few minutes work every day. Add the time needed for making up and getting to and from the theater, and you have a pretty leisurely existence left. In London a vaudeville performer frequently appears at two theaters in the same evening, but that does not hold here. This large amount of leisure is spent by vaudeville actresses according to their nature, in leading either a more human or a "gayer," a more dissipated and irregular, life than do the women of the ordinary stage.

The market does much to mold the artist, in any line, and our vaudeville friend faces an audience much less particular than those which support our fashionable theaters. The histrionic temperament above all other responds to what is desired of it, and the woman on the vaudeville stage feels little or none of that demand for "refinement" which is on the increase in the theaters. There are cases where this is part of her stock in trade, but they are very rare. Usually she sees before her one or two species of audience, roughly speaking. If it is a continuous house, or a house with two performances every day, in the shopping district, the audience may be extremely respectable, but it will not be subtle, and it will be satisfied without the most delicate shades of art, so that it is generally believed that, even in the very best vaudeville house we have, an actor going from the legitimate stage soon uses broader effects in response to the tastes of the spectators. There are two continuous houses on a certain street in New York, within a block of each other. A knowledge of the tone of the two would be enough to suggest the differences in the lives of the various "artistes" in the same general world, both artistically and professionally. Sometimes the same person will appear at both places, but in the main the personnel is unlike, the superiority of the performance in tone and ability at one house corresponding to the superior quality of the patrons. The same contrast holds between the most respectable "continuous" and the ordinary music-hall, which has its exhibitions in the evening and is supported as largely by "sporty" men as the other is by the steady bourgeoisie. Naturally, the "artiste" whose business it is to please the taste of sporty men leads, a good proportion of the time, a life of ordinary gaiety and frivolity, but there are always exceptions, and plenty of them, and among the women of the vaudeville stage who are sound and even domestic in habits are some whose popularity with the chief pleasure-seekers of the music-halls is greatest.

The vaudeville performer, however thoroughly an artist, is not likely to be sought out by "society," as the presentable actress now is. I have happened to know but of one woman in that line whose acquaintance was at all widely sought by people who are supposed to constitute "society." There is, indeed, a quite ignorant hostility, among those women who rule the social destinies of the world, to anybody associated in their minds with music-halls. They imagine a vaudeville lady as appearing, dressed in little, in a hall filled with tobacco, casting immodest winks at not wholly ideal men, and they, therefore, however desirous of procuring specimens for their drawing-rooms, draw the line against the whole vaudeville world. "I am pretty liberal, but I couldn't do that," said a social leader, telling about staying away from a lunch because one of these music-hall ornaments was to be there. "But you gave a dinner for Miss ------," said I, naming a person inferior in education, talent, taste and personal associations. "I know it," said the pillar of society, "but I have to draw the line somewhere, you know." The life of a vaudeville actress is a life apart, only less in degree than the life of a regular actress was even less than a hundred years ago.

She is vagabond, also, through the needs of her profession, though not necessarily a "rogue and vagabond," in the words of the Elizabethan legal description. She rushes about the country and the world, sometimes playing a long engagement, but usually staying only a week in a place. Her accommodations in the theater have been until lately very bad. They must be visited to be appreciated, for pictures give a somewhat too rosy suggestion of these quarters. The usual dressing-room for such an actress is small, dark, drafty, cold or hot, and ugly, and this is true even where it would hardly be expected; as it is true, also, that the vaudeville theaters are usually dirty and uncomfortable, "behind," to a highly unpleasant degree. At most of them, the performers stand about as they please in groups, and chat, or watch what is happening on the stage. Along these lines a change has been made lately, by one manager, which is of real importance to the profession and will be likely to spread. This man, owner of a circuit of houses, has introduced regulations as strict as those which prevail in the best theaters. Everything is scrupulously clean and well ordered, the dressing-rooms are neat, large and pleasant, and the performers are forced to stay in them until their turn is called, instead of gossiping about the wings. Moreover, there is a set of rules which throws light on the lives and habits of some professionals, who are strictly forbidden the use of profanity and slang in the theater—not in this vague generalization only, but in a list of the offensive words, some of which are little more than inelegant. Now, just as an actor will take less money in the legitimate than in the vaudeville, so this manager, having made his continuous houses handsomer, healthier and more comfortable than those of his rivals, can secure the best talent for less money than his rivals, and they will soon find it a good policy to follow his lead. He is able, for instance, to get an "artiste" for six hundred dollars a week who could readily get eight hundred from other managers. The men of superior business ability who now control so many theaters do some harm, but they also do the kind of good a business man is particularly fitted for, and the same kind of practical insight has begun the reformation of the vaudeville business. One element which this growing strictness tends to take away from the life behind the scenes is the "chappy"—the young man, namely, who hangs about such places and such women—and who is made unwelcome under the new régime, where he was unmolested before.

One special hardship that frequently belongs to the vaudeville player's life is the unbrokenness of the work, there being the same demand in summer that there is in winter, so that she may go on, if she needs the money, every week in the year, twice every day, even appearing in what are politely called "sacred concerts" on Sunday. One has to be pretty callous not to feel doing the same little act some six hundred times a year. Many a vaudeville actor, sick of this meaningless iteration, sighs for an opportunity in the "legitimate;" and, on the other hand, I have heard one of the most successful actors of our stage swear that if he could earn his living by two little turns a day, and get rid of the deadly long nights and afternoons in one part, he would not hesitate a minute—but he probably would. Of course, the great majority of vaudeville players have no opportunity to decide which stage they will appear on. They usually lack talent sufficient for success in the drama and those who could hold prominent place in the regular theater are the exceptions....

...Taking the word "artiste" not in its French sense, but as it is used in the theater business in America, as being of feminine gender, and also taking it as denoting a certain grade of work, I have left out of account a mass of women whose performances go under the name of vaudeville. A city like New York, for instance, contains hundreds of saloons, or little show-houses with saloons connected, where vaudeville is given, at which no admission-fee at all is charged, and in which the expense of the show is paid for by the increased sale of drinks. Naturally, the existence of these performers contains little glamour. Even taking the vaudeville actress at the top, the amount of glamour in her life is greatly exaggerated, as is the brilliancy of any successful actor's life, in the public imagination. It exists, of course. Many more men will fall in love with a woman on the stage than would with the same woman in private life. On the stage, she has a pedestal, a setting, that brings her out and enhances her power of attraction, probably more even than social prominence or money. A rich woman can pass for clever, handsome or fascinating on much less wit, beauty or charm than a poor one; and a girl who stands on a public stage every night, made up, dressed up, the focus of the light and of the attention of hundreds, will inevitably receive more personal attention afterward than she would in any other way. In the street, in the cars, in restaurants, on steamers, there are always people who know her by sight, and seek an opportunity to make her acquaintance, and when they do know her, they think her more interesting than she really is. As Voltaire said, it is unsatisfactory to be hanged in private; we all wish to be noticed by our fellow creatures; and a pretty girl in the chorus will always be the center of a much greater amount of interest than a large-souled and deep-minded woman of equal beauty quietly treading the paths of ordinary life.

INDEX

Aërial Magnolia Grove, 187
Agassiz, Prof., 19, 30
Agricultural Building, 109
"The Agricultural Fair," 13, 67-91
"The Alabama State Fair," 76-77
Albany County, 47
Albany Road, 34, 75
American Roof Garden, 188
American Social Science Association, 16
"American Society," 13
"Americans at Play," 21-23
Amish, 82
Amusement Parks, 117-143
"The Amusement Park," 133-143
"Amusements for the Poor," 16-20
Animal shows—SEE ALSO: Menageries, 131, 157-170
Apple bee, 13
Aquarama, 127
Army-Navy equipment, 103
Art Hall, 100, 102-103
"Asphodal," 119
"At the Fair," 112-116
Athletics (baseball team), 11
Atlantic City, 12
Atlantic Monthly, 99-105, 133-143
Atlantics (baseball team), 11
Automobiling, 65
Axel, Madame, 118
Baden-Baden, 53
Ballet, 120-121
Baltimore, 12, 37, 126
Barn-dance, 13
Barnum, P. T., 134, 167
Barrel-organ, 147
Baseball, 11-12
Bathing, 13, 45-46, 56-57, 59, 61-63
Bathing-machines, 57
"The Belle's Strategem," 121
Beer gardens, 123, 181-184
Bertin, Mlle., 120
Bethnal Green Museum, 18
Bicycling, 10
Billiards, 66, 123, 182

"Billy Button, or the Hunted Taylor," 154
Block Island, 61
Blondin—SEE ALSO: Gravelet, Blondin, 119-120
Boating, 126
Booth, Edwin, 52
Boston, 12-13, 15-16, 20, 75, 99, 192
Bostwick, Mrs., 120
Bourse, 68
Bowery, 71, 137, 143, 177, 181
Bowling, 123, 182
Brasch, Miss, 96
Brighton, 49-50, 57, 68, 75, 129, 143
Brighton Beach Hotel, 129
Brillant, Paul, 120
Broadway, 177, 181, 187-189
Brooklyn, 10, 18
Buffalo, 93
Buggy-driving, 10
"Building of the Ship," 17
Bunyan, John, 24
Butler, Anne, 96
Byron, George Gordon, 37
Cactus, 109
Calliope, 165, 172
Calve, Mlle., 121
Cambridge, 75
Camp-meeting, 58
Canada, 102, 127
Canal Street, 107
Cape Charles, 37
Cape Cod, 15
Cape Henry, 37
Cape May, 12
Carpenter, Frank, 137
Carryl, Guy Wetmore, 143
Casino at Narragansett, 61, 63-66
"Catarina, Queen of the Bandits," 121
Cattle drover, 69
"Cattle-Fair Day in New England," 68-75

Centennial Exhibition, 93, 99-105, 111
Central Park, 10
Century Magazine, 21-31, 106-116
Chamberlin's club-house, 53
Chantilly, 53
Charlottesville, 51
Chesapeake Bay, 37
Chiarini (tight-rope specialist), 125
Chicago, 11, 28, 50-51, 78, 90, 93, 112-116, 195
Chippendale, Mr., 118
"Christianity and Popular Amusements," 24-31
"Chutes," 141
Cimabue, 137
Cincinnati, 11, 162
Cincinnati Art School, 102
Circus, 58, 145-176
"Circus," 146-154
"Circus Day," 157-170
Clam-bake, 58
Clancarty, Countess, 96
Cliff Walk, 65
Clowns, 167-169
Colombian Exhibition, 93, 112-116
"The Color Sergeant," 17
Columbine, 119
"Commemoration Ode," 17
Comstock, Anthony, 131
Conanicut, 61, 65
Coney Island, 50, 129-132, 140, 142-143
Congress Hall, 34
Connecticut River, 68, 71
"Coon song," 186
Corbett, James J., 138
Corliss engine, 100, 104
Corn-husking, 13
Cosmopolitan, 126-128, 171-176, 197-200
Cotton industry, 76-77, 107, 109
"The County Fair"—SEE ALSO: Agricultural Fair, 78-91
Courland, Prince of, 121
Creole, 106-107, 110
Croquet, 65
Crystal Palace Exhibition, 10, 93-99
Curtis, William Eleroy, 137
Damrosch's band, 127
Dancing, 59, 120
Darby, John, 77

Davis, Charles Belmont, 140
Deer-hunt, 37
DeKoven, 185
Delmonico's, 57
de Melisse, Mlle., 121
Denver, 93
Detroit, 126
"Le Diable à Quatre," 121
"Le Diable Amoureux," 121
Dickens, Charles, 51
Dieppe, 50
Disneyland, 117
"Domestic Tourism," 34-38
Doricourt, 121
Drouette, Melanie, 121
Dunmere, 65
Eagles (baseball team), 11
Eggleston, Edward, 21-23
Electric-cars—SEE ALSO: Streetcars; Trolley-cars, 126
Elia, 152
Ellis, Sophia A., 96
English Derby, 53
Epsom Downs, 53-54
Equestrian circus, 145, 149-150, 152, 154, 174
"Ernani! Ernani!", 120
"Essence of Old Virginny," 180
Faneuil Hall, 17
Farmer, Fanny, 179
Fenelon, Monsieur, 119
Ferrell, Col., 77
Ferris wheel, 93
"Le Fête Champêtre," 121
"Fire and Flames," 132, 139
"First Impressions of America," 10-15
Fitchburg, MA, 127
Fitzpatrick, Miss, 121
"Flatiron" building, 131
"Flying airships," 141
"Foolish House," 131, 136, 141-142
Fortune-tellers, 22, 53, 147
Fourth of July, 22, 39
Franck, Celestine & Victorine, 120, 122
French bathing, 57-58
French gardens, 10
French Mountain, 22
Galveston Flood, 129-131
Gardens, 117-118, 133
Garland, Hamlin, 188

Gay, John, 80
German Restaurant, 104
Germans, 16, 18-19, 124, 181-184
Gilles, Monsieur, 119
Gilmore, Mr., 99, 101
"Giselle," 121
Gissing, George, 137
Gladden, Washington, 24-31
"Godenski," 119
Golf, 65
Gould, Jay, 49
"La Grande Duchesse," 128
Grant, Ulysses S., 49-52, 59, 167
Gravelet, Blondin, 120
"The Great Exhibition and Its Visitors," 94-98
Great Exhibition of London, 17
"The Green Monster," 119
Guerin, Monsieur, 119
Gymnastic appliances, 123
Hall, G. Stanley, 136
Hammerstein's, 185, 188-189
Hampton Roads, 38
Hapgood, Norman, 197-200
Hardy, Letitia, 121
Harlem, 187
Harlequin, 119
Harper's Weekly, 49-77, 123-125, 129-132, 178-184
Harrigan, Ned, 189
Hartt, Rollin Lynde, 133-143
Harvard, 21
Hawkins, Waterhouse, 10
Hazard Castle, 66
Haymarket Theatre, 118
"Head-liner," 195
"Hell Gate," 130, 141
Hemans, Mrs., 15
The History of the Great Rebellion, 167
Hope, Anthony, 137
Horce racing, 10, 58, 72, 81
Horse show, 65-66
Horticultural Hall, 109
Howells, William Dean, 99-105, 189
Huckleberry Finn, 83
Hudibras, 41
Hudson, Mr., 121
Hurlingham, 11
Ice cream, 118
"In and Out of the New Orleans Expositions," 106-111

Indiana, 16, 19
Innes's band, 140
International Hotel, 204
Irish, 16-17, 57, 70, 96
Italian music, 44
Javelli, Madame, 118
"Jeanette and Jeannot," 119
Jefferson, Thomas, 51
Jenkins, Julia, 179-180
Jerome Park, 10
Jerrold, Douglas, 24
Jersey Jockey Club, 53
Jerseymen, 56
"Jocko!", 119-120
Johnson, Dr., 186
Johnstown Flood, 131
Jones (actor), 119
Jones's Woods, 123-125
Joshua's Rock, 22
Kansas, 80-81, 84-85
Kill von Kull, 23
"Kim-Ka," 119
Kingston Road, 65
Knabenshue, Roy, 140
Knaresborough castle, 52
Knickerbocker, 146-154
"Kooch" dancer—SEE ALSO: Little Egypt, 93
Kossuth, Louis, 122
Koster & Bial's, 185
Lago Maggiore, 23
Lake George, 22
Lake Michigan, 115
La Manns, Signor, 119
Latin America, 108
Lavigne, Mlle., 121
Lee, Light Horse Harry, 17
Leeder, Christine, 121
LeGallienne, Mr., 186
Lehman, Adelaide & Flora, 119, 121
Leisure Hour, 10-15
Leonora, Mlle., 179-180
Liberty Bell, 111
"Life at Long Branch," 49-60
"The Life of a Vaudeville Artiste," 197-200
The Life of P. T. Barnum, 167
Lind, Jenny, 94
Lipscomb, A. A., 77
Little Egypt, 78-80, 83, 88
"Living in the Country," 155-156
Lloyd, Nelson, 78-88

Logan, Olive, 49-60
Long Branch, 49-60
Long Island, 15, 62
Longchamps, 53
Longfellow, Henry Wadsworth, 17
Louisiana, 109-110
Louisville, 11, 66, 93
Lottery, 182
Lowell, James Russell, 17
Lowell Lectures, 16
Lubbock, John, Sir, 133
Luna Park, 130, 133
"Ma Ragtime Girl," 186
Macaulay, Thomas, 24-25
Machine Arcade (Hall), 96-97. 100, 103
Madison Square Garden, 81, 175, 185, 189
"Magic Pills," 119
Maine, 68
Manhattan Beach, 129
Manhattan Beach Hotel, 129
"La Manola," 121
Maple-sugaring, 13
Marion, Francis, 17
"Maritana," 128
"Martin Chuzzlewit," 190
Marzetti, Madame & Monsieur, 119-120, 122
Mason-Dixon line, 34
Massachusetts, 68, 127
Matthews, Brander, 61-66
"Mazulme," 119
McChider children, 83, 88
McClintock, Mrs., 97
McClure's Magazine, 157-170
McGonigle, Prof., 83, 88
Mege, Monsieur, 121
Menagerie, 147-148, 155
Merry Jim, 83
Merry-go-round, 127
Metropolitan Hotel, 11
Mexico, 108-109
Midway, 78-80, 90, 93, 134
Midway Plaisance, 93, 114
Mill, John Stuart, 25
"The Milliners," 119
Miniature railway, 127
Minneapolis, 126
"Miranda," 121
"The Miseries of Human Life," 118
Mississippi River, 107, 110

Missouri, 80, 83
Mitchell, Maggie, 52
Modjeska, Mme., 197
"Money," 121
Monmouth County, 51
Monmouth Park, 10, 53, 57-58
"Monsieur Dechalnmeau," 119
Monticello, 51
Montgomery, 76-77
Moore, Thomas, 17
Morse, Prof., 19
Moving-picture machine, 131
Mule-car, 106
Murray, Charles Theodore, 171-176
Music Hall, 17
Naragansett Pier, 61-66
Narrow-gauge railroad, 103-104
Nashville, 108
Navesink, 50
Needlework, 96-97
Negroes and Negro labor—SEE ALSO: Slavery, 109, 127, 148, 150, 152, 180, 186
New Brunswick, 15, 97
New England, 17-18, 66, 75, 127
New Hampshire, 34, 68, 71
New Jersey, 49-60, 62
"The New Narragansett Pier," 61-66
New Orleans, 93, 106-111
New York, 10-12, 15-16, 18-19, 41, 46, 50, 66, 83-88, 95, 98 185-190, 192
New York Clipper, 118-122
New York Herald, 35-36
"New York's New Summer Playground," 129-132
Newport, 12, 36, 49-50, 63, 65, 95
Niagara, 38, 54
Niblo's Garden, 94, 118-122
"Niblo's Seen By a Child," 118-122
North Atlantic Squadron, 63
Ocean Avenue, 49, 55, 57
Ocean Grove, 57-58
Ocean House, 12, 35, 54, 57
Ocean Road, 53-65
Old Abe (bald eagle), 104
Old and New, 16-20
Old Colony House, 105
Old Pleasure Bay House, 58
Old Point, 37-38
Oldfield, Barney, 140

"On the Road with the 'Big Show'," 171-176
"Ondine," 121
Orchestrion, 127
The Origin of Civilization and the Primitive Condition of Man, 133
Outlook, 89-91
Packard, Winston, 140
Palace Hotel, 87
Palace of Liberal Arts, 112
Paris, 12, 36, 53, 60, 104, 112, 121
Paris Exposition, 78, 114
Parkington, Mrs., 41
Paulsen, Charlotte, 96
Pennsylvania railroad, 99, 102
Petersburg, 37
Le Petit Amour, 120
Philadelphia, 10, 12, 66, 93, 99-105, 111, 126-127, 145, 192, 194
Picture gallery, 95
Pierrot & Pippa, 187-189
Pleasure Bay, 57-58
The Pleasures of Life, 133
Poe, Edgar Allan, 96, 130
Point Judith, 61, 64
Point Judith Country Club, 65-66
Polo, 65
Popular amusements, 9-38, 127
Pougand, Leontine, 121
Prince Albert, 93, 98
The Prisoner of Zenda, 137
Prospect Park, 10
Providence, 61
Punch, 49
Puppet shows, 147
Puritans, 25-26
Putnam, Gen., 17
Putnam's Magazine, 39-48, 94-98
Quebec, 95
Quilting bee, 13
Quincy Market, 68
Railroad, 75, 99, 107-108, 127, 162, 172-173
The Railway and Engineering Review, 135
"Railway to the Moon"—SEE ALSO: Roller-coaster, 127
"Raoul," 119
The Ravels: Antoine, François, Gabriel, Jerome, 119-122
Red River, 107, 109
Red-Stockings (baseball team), 11

Reformation, 25
Restaurants, 104
Rhode Island, 65
Rialto, 68
Rice industry, 107, 109
Richards, Signor, 179
Richmond, 37, 66
Ricketts, John Bill, 145
"The Rival," 122
"Robert Macaires," 119
Robinson, Mr., 10
Robinson, Happy Joe, 80-81, 83, 88
Rockaway, 23
The Rocks, 65
Rocky Branch, 39-48
Rod-and-gun clubs, 11
Roller-coaster, 131
Roman games, 24-25
Ronacher's, 188
"The Roof-Gardens of New York," 185-190
Rousset Sisters: Adelaide, Caroline, Clementine, Theresine, 121
Royle, Edwin Milton, 191-196
Saguenay, 95
"Said Pasha," 128
St. George electrical geyser, 133
St. Louis Fair, 78
Salt Pond, 65
Sandy Hook, 50
Saratoga, 10, 12, 34, 36, 49, 95
Saunderstown, 65
Scenic railway, 130, 140
Schwöze, Lizzie & Matilda, 179
Scribner's Magazine, 78-88, 191-196
Sefton, John, 121
"A Sennight of the Centennial," 99-105
Sewing machines, 100
Shakespeare, William, 52
Shooting, 11, 14, 123-124, 182
Show-bills, 155, 157, 165, 167, 170
Sideshow, 166
Singing, 17
Sisters of Mercy, 96
"Sketches of the People Who Oppose Our Sunday Laws," 178-184
Slavery, 36, 109
Sleigh rides, 15
Slocum disaster, 131
Smalley, Eugene V., 106-111
Smoking-cars, 106-107

205

Soto, Señorita, 121
Sousa's band, 127
Southern Literary Messenger, 34-38
Southern Pacific railroad, 108
"The Spectator (at the Fair)," 89-91
Springfield, 75
Stars and Stripes, 111
State buildings, 101
Staten Island Ferry and Railway, 133
Steamboats, 106-107
"Steeplechase Park," 129
Story-telling, 18
Street-cars, 106, 126-127
Street-fairs, 86-88, 134
Sugar industry, 107-110
Sullivan, Mark, 140
Summer resorts & Watering places, 33-66
"A Sunday Evening Sacred Concert," 178-181
"Sunday Evening in a Beer Garden, 181-184
"Sunday in Jones's Wood," 123-125
"Sunday-School" circuit, 194
Swimming—SEE: Bathing
Sydenham, 10
"Sylph of the South," 179-180
"La Sylphide," 121
Taylor, Mary, 122
Tedeschi, Madalina, 97
Tennis, 65
Thackeray, William Makepeace, 36, 51
Theatre (outdoor), 128
Theme parks, 117
Thillon, Anna, 121
Three-ring circus, 173
Tightrope performers, 120, 125, 159
Tilman, Natalie, 122
Tip-cat, 24
Towle, G. M., 13
Trapese artists, 176
The Traveling Circus, 145-176
Trip to the Moon, 130
Trois Frères Provençaux, 104
Trolley-cars, 117, 133

"The Trolley-Park," 126-128
Troubadours, 147
Trouville, 50
Tuskegee Female College, 77
Twain, Mark, 21
United States Building, 103
Ursuline convent, 96
Valley Forge, 17
Van Rensselaer, M. G., 112-116
Vaudeville, 177-200
"The Vaudeville Theatre," 191-196
Vermont, 71
Vienna Bakery, 104
"Volk's Garten," 181-184
Wall Street, 42, 53, 55, 143, 189
Wallach's, 121
Washington, George, 17, 51, 95, 103, 167
Washington, DC, 51
Water tobaggan, 128
"Watering-Place Worries," 39-48
Waters, Theodore, 129-132
Waxworks, 167
Weighing machines, 131
Wells, Henry, 119
West End Hotel, 53
Whalom Theatre, 127-128
Wheatleigh, Charles, 121
White Hills, 34, 95
White Sulphur Springs, 36-38
White-Stockings (baseball team), 11
Wild West shows, 133, 138
Willey, Day Allen, 126-128
Williams, Roger, 64
Willow Grove, 127
Wiman, Erastus, 133-134
Wintergarten, 187-188
Women's Pavilion, 102
Wonderland, 133
Wood, Eugene, 157-170
Wooden horses, 123, 129
Worcester, 75, 127
Worcester railroad, 75
"World's Exhibitions," 93-116
Yachting, 15, 58, 63
Zoo, 128

RAISING THE BIG TOP!

ABOUT WILLIAM L. SLOUT

WILLIAM L. SLOUT recently retired from his position as Professor of Theatre Arts at California State University, San Bernardino. Before embarking on his twenty-four-year academic career, Slout was a working thespian and trouper in circus tent shows, on live television, in commercials, in summer stock theatres across the country, as well as in off-Broadway houses in New York.

Following a stint in the army in World War II, Slout earned a bachelor's degree from Michigan State University in 1949. After completing his master's degree at Utah State University, in 1953 he moved to New York, where he met his wife-to-be, Marte, also an actor, and where he appeared in such notable television series productions as the "Kraft Theatre" and "Playhouse 90."

Slout moved to Los Angeles in the late 1960s and received his Ph.D in theatre history from the University of California, Los Angeles. He began teaching at Cal State San Bernardino in 1968 and, since then, has written and/or edited a variety of books on the history of American theatre. As editor of The Borgo Press series, "Clipper Studies in the Theatre," Slout has edited and compiled such titles as *The Theatrical Rambles of Mr. & Mrs. John Greene* (1987), *Ink from a Circus Press Agent* (forthcoming), *Broadway Below the Sidewalk* (1994), *A Clown's Log* (1993), and *Amphitheatres and Circuses* (1994), all published or distributed by The Borgo Press. His play, *The Trial of Dr. Jekyll*—a "sequel" to the Stevenson classic—was produced by the theatre department at California State University, San Bernardino in 1993 and published by Emeritus Enterprises that same year.

Although now officially "retired" and living in San Bernardino, he and Marte are often seen at a variety of local theatrical productions, both on the Cal State campus and throughout Southern California.

www.ingramcontent.com/pod-product-compliance
Lightning Source LLC
Chambersburg PA
CBHW032112090426
42743CB00007B/327